Economic Failures of
Nehru and Indira Gandhi

Economic Failures of Nehru and Indira Gandhi

A study of 3 decades of deprivation and disillusionment

M L Gujral

VIKAS PUBLISHING HOUSE PVT LTD
VIKAS HOUSE, 20/4 Industrial Area, Sahibabad
Distt. Ghaziabad, U.P. (India)

VIKAS PUBLISHING HOUSE PVT LTD
VIKAS HOUSE, 29/4 Industrial Area, Sahibabad, Distt. Ghaziabad
Branches: Savoy Chambers, 5 Wallace Street, Bombay / 10 First Main Road,
Gandhi Nagar, Bangalore / 8/1-B Chowringhee Lane, Calcutta / 80 Canning
Road, Kanpur/

ISBN 0-7069-0835-X

1V2G5001

Printed at Roopak Printers, Navin Shahdara, Delhi-110032

The national middle class failed when it had the opportunity and instead merely reproduced internally the economic dualism of the international economy as it squeezed agriculture to finance urban industry. What is needed is a complete change of direction. The starting point must be the needs of the bottom two-thirds, and not the demands of the top third. The primary goal of such a strategy would be to provide minimum standards of health, education, food and clothing to the entire population, removing the more obvious forms of human suffering.

STEPHEN HYMER

This book is dedicated to the Harijans, and the exploited, impoverished and oppressed millions that live in the dung-heap villages and the sprawling city slums of Bharat, that is India, and lack adequate food, raiment and shelter, even after thirty years of the country's independence and Congress and Janata misrule.

Foreword

The author of this book, Dr M.L. Gujral, is an old friend and colleague whom I have known since my socialist days, not only as a principled fighter for great causes, but also as a gifted writer.

In this book the author has tried to analyse the causes of India's abysmal poverty and has shown at some length how, as a result of faulty planning under the Nehrus, the country has remained poor and underdeveloped even after thirty years of Swaraj. Nehru had blundered in that he forsook the Gandhian path and followed the western model of development without understanding India's peculiar problems. His daughter made matters worse by her wrong economic policies and authoritarian methods. The result was more unemployment, more poverty, more corruption, more inflation and, therefore, more discontent among the people. All this created an explosive situation which culminated in the mighty upheaval that shook India in 1974-75. Mrs Indira Gandhi saw in it a challenge to her power and she tried to meet it by clamping emergency rule. As a matter of fact, it was a challenge to, and rejection of all the wrong policies and unclean methods adopted by the powers-that-be during the years after independence. This challenge could be met by promising a return to Gandhi which Indira failed to do and was, therefore, overthrown.

The end of Congress misrule followed by the Janata take-over was widely welcomed and the people heaved a sigh of relief. Democracy was restored and with it all the democratic freedoms and liberties of the people. The Janata Party has promised bread with freedom. While freedom has been restored, bread is yet to be provided to the hungry millions. This is the task that lies ahead, and the Janata Party and the Government must fulfil this task before it is too late. They have rightly chosen the pattern of decentralized, agro-industrial, rural-based development which necessitates, as Dr Gujral points out, structural and institutional changes and radical reforms in the land system. This radical Gandhian approach alone can solve the stupendous problems of poverty and unemployment and take the country out of the morass of stagnation in which it continues to find itself.

The performance of the Janata so far has been far from encouraging, specially in the socio-economic fields. True, one or two years, is too short a period to show results. But they must do something to convince the people that they are following the right path, moving in the right direction and choosing right priorities. If the chosen path is that of Gandhi, it must be reflected not only in their preachings but also in their style of functioning. We must seek to follow Gandhi in thought, word and deed. For, as Louis Fischer has put it: 'If man is to survive, if civilization is to survive and flower in freedom, truth and decency, the remainder of the twentieth century and what lies beyond must belong not to Lenin or Trotsky, or to Marx or Mao, or Ho or Che, but to Mahatma Gandhi'.

I hope this book will be read with interest by all students of India's planned development, and even the proud moderner will find in the author's "modified" Gandhian plan an attempt to answer the challenges that face us today.

JAYAPRAKASH NARAYAN

Preface

This book deals primarily with the economic failures of Nehru and Indira Gandhi. Work on it was begun in early 1975, when the country was on the brink of a cataclysm. In July 1975, it had to be abandoned as it was clear that for the time being at least, its publication was completely out of question. With the rout of the Congress party at the hustings in March 1977, the task was resumed. In March 1978, Mr Jayaprakash Narayan penned a foreword for the book. He was satisfied with the restoration of civil liberties by the Janata party but extremely unhappy with its infighting and non-performance. In March 1979 an epilogue on the utter failure of the Janata government became necessary and its leaders were warned of the doom ahead. It has overtaken them and the Morarji government, as predicted has fallen.

In writing this book I have drawn extensively on numerous books, magazines and newspaper articles by economists, journalists, political leaders and others. To all of them I am extremely grateful. I am deeply indebted to Mr Jayaprakash Narayan, for his assent in writing a foreword.

My thanks are also due to Mr J.A. Francis of Encardio-Rite Electronics (P) Limited, Lucknow, for preparing the typescript and to my son Mr Amod Gujral for reading the proofs.

M. L. GUJRAL

Contents

Contents

Introduction

India is a very poor country, one of the poorest in the world. It was systematically exploited and impoverished during the period of the British rule and its arts, crafts and industries wantonly destroyed. The principal factor which led to the decline of the Indian industry during this period was the impact of the Industrial Revolution. Britain's growing economy required raw materials for her industrial development and markets overseas for her industrial goods. Both these objectives were achieved through a disruption of the old Indian economic system and introduction of new economic norms. The khadi produced in the villages was both coarse and expensive as compared with mill-made cloth from Lancashire. The superfine cloth made by urban craftsmen was no doubt artistic and superlative in quality, but could not compete with the mill made cloth in cost. With the gradual disruption of the Indian industry and with the development of railways and communication system in India, vast markets for British manufactured goods opened up in remote and interior regions. India's role became from now on, one of a producer of raw materials and primary goods for the industrial machine of Great Britain. Her industrial development was deliberately stalled. By 1875, Indian handicrafts were almost completely destroyed and the edifice of her cottage industries lay in ruins. The men engaged in these vocations were thrown out of employment. The predatory character of British capitalist interest gave way to free trade which is always advantageous for the richest and the most powerful nation and competitive forces were relied upon to capture Indian and other world markets. India was from this time onward an agrarian appendage of Imperial Britain.

The greatest damage to India and her economy was done, however, by the wanton destruction by the British of the democratic village republics of India. This has been deplored by the Report of the secret Committee of the East India Company, by Sir Charles Trevellyan, by

Sir Charles Matcalf and by R. C. Dutt in his Economic History of India. Metcalf expressed the wish that village constitutions which contributed in a high degree to the 'happiness and to the enjoyment of a great portion of freedom and independence of the people, may never be disturbed'. ..... further added, 'I dread everything that has a tendency to break .   ?ut this was not to be. The concern of the East India Compa.   ~ce its land revenue and the desire to centralize all judicia.   ~cutive powers in its own hands, induced the Company to make direct arrangements with individual cultivators, instead of with the village community as a whole. This led to a deprivation of the powers of the village functionaries and a gradual decay of "village republics". Gandhiji was deeply distressed and moved by this unjustified and immoral act of the East India Company. He was an ardent advocate of self-sufficient, self-governing village republics somewhat like those that flourished in India from times immemorial and survived the break of dynasties and the fall of empires. These had their drawbacks and evils like the caste system and the practice of untouchability but these could be fought and eradicated and the standards of living of the people improved. The plan Gandhiji put forward for the development of the country's economy is based on a number of fundamental principles—simplicity, self-reliance, decentralization, bread labour, full employment, production by masses, swadeshi, prohibition, equality, egalitarianism, humanism, socialism, freedom of the individual, democracy, peace and moral ethical values.

Jawaharlal Nehru considered Gandhian concept of self-reliant village republics a throwback and a regression to primitivism and the past. According to his own statement, he was, as a law student in London vaguely attracted to the Fabians. In 1927 he paid a visit to Soviet Russia and came back greatly impressed. In 1928, as a general secretary of the Congress, he addressed numerous meetings all over the country, spreading "the ideology of socialism". In 1929 he presided over the annual session of the Trade Union Congress at Nagpur and of the Indian National Congress at Lahore. In 1930, at the Karachi session of the Congress, he spoke on the Economic Policy Resolution which advocated Nationalization of key industries and services. Throughout the period of the liberation struggle, he was

[1]J.L. Nehru. 1936. Autobiography, London.
[2]P.A. Samuelson. 1973. Economics, Japan.

building a socialist image for himself. He ridiculed gradualism and reform, commended Soviet achievements and asked for a complete break with the past. His socialist stance undoubtedly made him popular with the peasants, the workers and the poor in general and won him the love and affection of all sections of people. But it appears that it was merely speech day stuff and a facade. In his heart of hearts he knew that he was no socialist. It is clear from his self-characterization in the autobiography, that he was not unaware of the fact that his show of socialism was a mere make-believe and a pretense, and his profession of radicalism nothing more than lip service. He says, 'I myself belong to a class which mixes with these lords of the land and owners of wealth. I am a typical bourgeoisie, brought up in bourgeoisie surroundings, with all the early prejudices that this training has given me. Communists have called me petite bourgeoisie with perfect justification'. P.A. Samuelson, the doyen of the text book writers on economics and now a Noble Laureate, regards Jawaharlal Nehru as a "gradualist reformist" and even brackets him with conservatives and die-hards like Winston Churchill. According to Preman Ady and Ibne Azad, he was a "fake socialist".[3] Professor Joan Robinson refused to grant even a democratic character to Nehru's regime. She writes, 'Nehru's personal prestige made it possible to combine one party rule with trappings of democracy'.[4]

After assumption of power in 1947, it appears Nehru completely forgot his earlier promises. One of the first acts of his government was an assault in 1948 on the Congress Socialist Party. It was made clear to its leader that there was no room for a party within the Congress Party and that if it did not disband itself, it had to quit the Congress. His next onslaught deadlier then the first, sounded the death knell of socialism in India. In the constitution framed for the country in 1950, the Right to Private Property, was included in the Fundamental Rights. For several years after this Jawaharlal continued to harp on socialism but his policies and programmes favoured the class from which he came. At the Avadhi session of the Congress, a socialist pattern for development was announced but three years later by 1958, Jawaharlal had completely strayed away from the socialist path. This is borne out by an article which he wrote

---

[3]Ibne Azad. 1975. In Explosion in a Subcontinent, London.
[4]Joan Robinson. 1974. Selected papers, Trivandrum.

in the AICC Economic Review. In this article he contradicted himself on everything he had said earlier. In his early speeches and writings he had said that there was much in Soviet Russia that he did not like—'its ruthless suppression of all contrary opinion, the wholesale regimentation, the unnecessary violence in carrying out its policies',—and yet 'there was no lack of violence in the capitalist world. . .the very basis of our acquisitive society and property was violence. . .violence was common in both places, but the violence of the capitalist order seemed inherent in it, whilst the violence of Russia bad though it was, aimed at a new order based on peace and cooperation and real freedom for the masses. With all her blunders, Soviet Russia had triumphed over enormous difficulties and taken great strides towards this new order'.[5] In the article under review, he vehemently condemned socialism and Soviet society and wrote in praise of capitalism. He said, 'that capitalism was not the same as it was a generation or two ago and had developed socialist features'.[6]

On the economic front Nehru failed the country in many ways :

His first and foremost mistake was the choice of a wrong paradigm. Like Kuznets, based on the historical growth patterns which operated in Western Europe in the nineteenth century, he equated development with urban industrial growth. He forgot that large-scale migrations and capital transfers which prevailed in the nineteenth century in the developed countries of the West and which made the above transformation possible, did not exist any more. And if these conditions were neither present, nor possible to duplicate, development based on Western model, had hardly any chance of success.[7,8]

Secondly, during his regime, allocation of country's scarce resources, was not well considered. The agricultural sector which accounted for nearly 50 per cent of the country's GNP and on which 80 per cent of the population depended, was starved of funds and what funds were available for agriculture, were cornered by rich farmers and absentee landlords. The country's irrigation potential, which if fully exploited could have made the country free from the vagaries

[5]J.L. Nehru. 1936. Autobiography, London.

[6]J.L. Nehru. 1958. AICC Economic Review, New Delhi.

[7]Simon Kuznets. 1965. Economic Growth and Structure, New York.

[8]Louis Lefeber. 1974. In Economic Theory and Planning, Ed. Asoka Mitra, London.

of weather, was not given the importance it should have been given. The mini land reforms which were introduced, were as Myrdal pointed out, a show and even these were not implemented.

A large amount of available capital was frittered away in setting up large-scale consumer goods industries in the private sector for manufacture of luxury items used by less than 5 per cent of the elites. These industries, highly profit-oriented, led to acquisition of large fortunes by a few big industrial houses but due to the very limited demand of the items they produced, stalled growth and led to stagnation. This would not have happened if the consumer goods industry for production of basic necessaries of life—khadi and handloom cloth, soaps, hair oil, combs, tooth brushes and tooth pastes, mirrors, glass ware, pottery, metal utensils, shoes, cheap and ordinary furniture, small machines etc.—had been decentralized and these essential items produced in village homes and small industries organized on a cooperative basis. As the internal demand for these articles is unlimited, their production would have created vast employment opportunities and raised the standard of living of the village people.

Thirdly, Nehru's Government erred in the import of capital-intensive technology. With a large and growing labour force, it led to rapid and continuous increase of unemployment and underemployment. It led also to penetration of Indian economy by foreign companies through foreign collaborations mostly for the manufacture of non-essential products—tooth pastes, soaps, lipsticks, beauty lotions and creams, brassieres, gin, beer, processed foods, tonics, cough syrups etc.—or for those which could be produced with the help of technology already available in the country.

Fourthly, Jawaharlal Nehru like some other orthodox capitalist economists believed that if there was sufficient growth, it would in the long run 1 generate employment for everybody, and 2 also bring about distributive justice. But in this he was sadly mistaken. As Gunnar Myrdal has pointed out, for this to happen, India would need industrialization on a scale and investments, not possible for her for decades to come. The outcome of growth oriented policy has been massive unemployment and distressing disparity in incomes.

Fifthly, after the British left, the big farmers and the landlords, previously the worst enemies of the Congress, became overnight Congress allies. They, due to their power and influence in the village, became the "Congress Vote Banks". They contested and won seats in the district and state Congress committees and in the houses of legislature. The Congress, to keep itself perpetually in power, entered into a tripartite alliance with the big farmers on the one hand and the city elites both indigenous and foreign, on the other. The power in the states thus passed into the hands of the "Lords of the land" who not only blocked land reform and legislation prejudicial to their interests but also prevented its implementation after legislation.

Sixthly, Nehru who on assumption of power had promised to eradicate illiteracy within a decade, paid little attention to the problem of free and compulsory education of the type which Gandhiji had recommended. The result has been that though the percentage of illiterates fell from 87 per cent in 1947 (population 339 million) to 69.5 per cent in 1974, in absolute numbers, the number of illiterates increased from 295 million individuals in 1947 to 414 million in 1974 (population 600 million), a figure which is higher by 119 million than the figure of 295 million illiterates in 1947, and 73 million more than the total population of the country in that year. If the programme of free and compulsory primary education of seven years duration built round a craft, as recommended by Gandhiji had been vigorously implemented, the problems of unemployment and overpopulation would not have assumed the proportions that they have come to assume.

Seventhly, proper consideration was not paid to, 1 the medical and health care, 2 the women and children's welfare, 3 nutrition, 4 potable water, 5 rural housing and sanitation, and 6 to the socio-economic and political education of the lowest deciles of the rural population, engendering in them superstitious beliefs, evil customs, conformism, servility, total resignation to fate and the lack of will to resist evil.

Lastly, whatever laws were made, Nehru's "soft government", never implemented them. The outcome was rampant corruption, nepotism, hoarding, blackmarketing and profiteering.

Nehru died in May 1964, a sad and a disillusioned man. He failed in solving the problems of growth, distributive justice, unemployment and poverty. But it must be said to his credit that he left behind an infrastructure for development and a force of skilled manpower—engineers, scientists, technologists—that possessed the know-how and the expertise to set up a large number of modern enterprises.

After Jawaharlal Nehru, Lal Bahadur Shastri became India's Prime Minister. He was an unassuming, honest and hardworking though not a brilliant person and before he could find his bearings, was involved in a war with Pakistan. He won the war but lost the peace at Tashkent. The shock of his failure, it is said, killed him.

Indira Gandhi with "low intellectual calibre", and slipshod and perfunctory schooling, was a "shrewd intriguer" and "a crafty woman without depth". Selfish and untrustworthy herself, she had a suspicious mind and could never trust any one. 'Her deep sense of insecurity, right from her days of childhood had warped her mind'.[9] She had been helped into the Prime Minister's berth by the Syndicate bosses who mistakenly considered her to be a dumb doll. To cover her innate inadequacies, she needed advisers but kept on changing them as they became inconvenient or powerful. She used and by turns discarded the Syndicate bosses, the "kitchen cabinet", Raja Dinesh Singh, the Socialist Forum, P.N. Haksar, L.N. Mishra, Uma Shankar Dixit, the ex-communists, the C.P.I. and even the congress with all its veterans. She finally ended up with a caucus of adventurers, goons and sycophants who spelled her doom. During the last days of her regime in 1977, she distrusted everybody and appears to have developed delusions of persecution. In February and March of 1977 she said on many occasions that she had no friends except Sanjay Gandhi and that she was being stabbed from all sides.

The War with Pakistan in 1965 and two years of drought put heavy strains on India's economy soon after she became the Prime Minister. The Fourth Five Year Plan which should have commenced in April 1966, had to be deferred. The country was on a Plan holiday for the next three years. In the third year (1968-69) there was some recovery of industrial production but the production of foodgrains (95 million tons) was three million tons less than in the previous year. In all three years prices had continued to rise.

In September 1967, the Planning Commission was reconstituted with Professor D.R. Gadgil as Deputy Chairman. In view of the precarious state of the economy, the Commission decided to defer the Fourth Plan for another year and start it from 1969-70. The

[9]Janardan Thakur. 1977. All the Prime Ministers's Men, New Delhi.

year 1969 was, however, a most ominous year—the year of the "Great Divde", for the Congress Party. The Syndicate leaders were worsted in the struggle that ensued and people thought that with the elimination of the "right wing", the Congress would travel on a socialist path. The nationalisation of the 14 big commercial banks and the announcement of the 10 point programme of development at the AICC session in Bombay raised the hopes of the common man and were flaunted as socialist measures by the Government and the party in power. But were they really ? The ten point programme was never implemented and the major part of the bank credit as T.A. Pai admitted, continued to be cornered by the big bourgeoisie.

The growth rate of economy between 1964-65 and 1973-74 was harldy 2.5 per cent, about the same as the increase in the population. The populist policies the government pursued after the Congress split, the decline in savings and investment, the large deficit financing with consequent expansion of money supply, the increase in ad hoc current consumption, the way resources were raised for the snap poll of 1971, the massing of 10 million refugees on the Eastern border of the Country, the war with Pakistan in 1971, two years of drought, laxity in industrial licensing policy, exemptions, concessions and subsidies to Indian and foreign companies, the impact of the Third Pay Commission, the cost of subsidising the takeover of foodgrains, the claims of state governments for greater central assistance to bail them out of their near-bankrupt positions, the disregard for plan-budget linkage and the ad hoc special allocations for the educated-unemployed-all contributed to a serious erosion of the real income of the common man and a state of privation which defied solution.

The serious shortages, the spiralling prices, the increasing unemloyment created an economic and a political situation which Indira Gandhi's Government could not control. The net zero aid objective of the Fifth Plan was given the go by and she sought aid from the World Bank and the IMF. They laid down their conditions for "overhauling" the country's economy. These included concessions to the private sector, tax exemptions and subsidies, relaxation of imports, wage and D.A. freeze, compulsory deposit scheme (C.D.S.) and even forcible sterilization. Implementation of this programme aggravated the economic and the political unrest and the 12 May decision against her in the election petition filed against her by Raj

Narain, completely unhinged her mind. She should have resigned but she chose otherwise and to save her Prime Ministership, as well as implement the World Bank-IMF programme, she needed the emergency. The terror which she unleashed during 20 of the darkest months of Indian history and the crimes and corrupt practices for which she is directly or indirectly responsible, form the subject matter of numerous books and newspaper and magazine articles.

At the end of 11 years of her rule, due to a benevolant rain god India's granaries were full and due to remittances by overseas Indians, her foreign exchange reserves ample. Yet saving was of a low order, investment shy and due to massive unemployment and low buying power, people's, stomachs were empty. The country's economy was in a shambles.

In March 1977, when the Janata Party came into power, the people's hopes rose high. It promised much to the people,—freedom and bread. It restored the freedom but as far bread, the less said the better. The people have waited long enough and are now very restive. Their disillusionment with the new Party is well nigh complete.[10]

[10]On 15 July 1979 The Janata Government fell and on 20 August 1979, the Janata (S), Congress (S) coalition led by Charan Singh. On 22 August 1979 a mid-term poll was ordered.

ONE

Irrelevance of Orthodox Economics and Economic Education

Orthodox economics—in common parlance economics—is a "science," which according to the definition proposed by Robbins, 'deals with the allocation of scarce means between alternative uses'.

A large number of competent authorities—Marxian and other have in the past, called into question the scientific nature of classical and neo-classical economics. Their number is on the increase. A science, according to its dictionary meaning is a systematic study of truth. Its generalizations are based on induction from observed instances. It depends on controlled experimentation and its corpus at any moment, as Professor Popper maintains, consists of theories that have not been disproved. Its objectivity is owed not to the impartiality of the individual but to the fact that many individuals are constantly testing each other's theories. It is also value-free.

Orthodox economics—capitalist economy, mixed economy, neo-classical economy or economy of welfare—call it by whichever name you like—however, has little to do with reality or truth. It is not supported by experimental evidence and is based on deductive reasoning. It is a mixture of "untested hypotheses" and "intestable slogans." Professor Joan Robinson has likened the economic behaviour of orthodox economists to that of Thugs—a sect recruited both from Muslims and Hindus who used to strangle way-passers in a particular ritual manner and divide the spoils according to a particular formula. She writes, 'We may admire the discipline, the resolution and the piety of an individual Thug, but we do not approve of Thugee as an economic system.'[1],[2]

---

[1]John Robinson. 1962. Economic Philosophy, London.
[2]Ibid.

The mammoth economic system that the capitalists and the Professors of economics and others have built over a period of two centuries, was conceived by Thugs and self-seekers in their own self-interest. This is clear from the number of principles that were laid down, the doctrines formulated and the Laws discovered by the classical economists. The Law of Perfect Competition and the Laissez-Faire doctrine were the earliest finds. Adam Smith, who may be termed the Founder of the Classical School, in his Wealth of Nations published in 1776 wrote, 'Every individual is continually exerting himself to find out the most advantageous employment for whatever capital he can command. It is his own advantage, indeed, and not of the society, which he has in view. But the study of his own advantage naturally or rather necessarily, leads him to prefer that employment which is most advantageous to the society'.[3]

David Ricardo, one of the foremost economists of all times, was a London Jew and made a large fortune as a stockholder. His book, The Principles of Political Economy and Taxation, is held in high esteem by students of economics all over the world. The great master formulated many doctrines but we shall refer briefly to only two of the "Natural Laws," he discovered. The first is the Iron Law of Wages, which states, 'the natural price of labour . . . depends on the price of the food, necessaries and conveniences required for the support of the labourer and his family. With a rise in the price of food and necessaries, the natural price of labour will rise, with the fall in their price, the natural price of labour will fall'.[4] The second Law he discovered was the Law of Rent, the most famous of Ricardo's doctrines. Rent arises, said Ricardo, because land is not unlimited and is not uniform in fertility.[5]

At the time when the Law of Rent was indited and Ricardo's book appeared, the landowners and the manufacturing class were engaged in a fierce controversy over the Corn Laws—a kind of protective tariff to encourage the cultivation of wheat in England by assuring the farmer a good price for his grain. The high prices for corn brought higher rents to the landowners and put more money in their pockets but hurt the manufacturing class by raising

[3]Adam Smith. 1776. The Wealth of Nations, England.
[4]David Ricardo. 1817. The Principles of Political Economy and Taxation, England.
[5]Ibid.

the wage bill and taking money out of their pockets. The fight, therefore continued, the landowners cried out for protection and the manufacturers clamoured for free trade. Ricardo himself belonged to the class of the rising bourgeoisie and was in the thick of the fray. It is not surprising that the sympathies of the discoverer of the natural laws including the Law of rent, were with the industrialists who wanted the Corn Laws abolished and the era of free trade inaugurated. The Parliament was, however, dominated by the landlords and the Corn Laws remained for a long time before they were repealed in 1846.

Conditions of work in industrial enterprises were far from satisfactory in nineteenth century England; child labour was exploited, wages were low, environmental hygiene poor and hours of work long, often more than twelve hours a day. Efforts to ameliorate these conditions by workers trade unions and social reformers, were ruthlessly resisted by the owners of industry. An eminent economist of the times, N.W. Senior, joined hands with the industrialists and worked out a doctrine which "proved" that hours of work could not be further reduced, because what profit the employer made, came out of the last hour of work.[6] More damaging to the workers than Nassau Senior's "last hour principle," was the "wage fund" doctrine which the employers used, to fight the agitation for higher pay. It was more damaging, as it was believed and taught by most of the economists including John Stuart Mill. In his well known Principles of Political Economy, Mill wrote 'wages not only depend upon the relative amount of capital and population, but cannot under the rule of competition be affected by anything else. Wages . . . cannot rise, but by an increase of the aggregate funds employed in hiring labourers, or a diminution in the number of competitors for hire; nor fall, except either by a diminution of the funds devoted to paying labour, or by an increase in the numbers of labourers to be paid'.[7] The working class challenged the doctrine right from the beginning. They said it was untrue and against their experience. John Stuart Mill whose book had done the most to popularize the doctrine, published a retraction in 1869 and said that the doctrine was without a scientific foundation.

[6]N.W. Senior. 1837. Letters on the Factory Act as it affects the Cotton Manufacturers, London.

[7]J.S. Mill. 1848. Principles of Political Economy, London.

The last nail in its coffin was driven by an American economist Francis Walker in 1876.[8]

The classical economists developed a number of laws which, they said were as true for the social and economic world as were those developed by scientists for the physical world. They were fixed, eternal. But was this really so? Professor J.E. Cairns in his Essays in Political Economy published in 1873, pointed out that 'economics had become a bourgeois-class weapon'. He wrote, when a working man is told that political economy "condemns" strikes . . . looks askance at proposals for limiting the hours of labour but "approves" the accumulation of capital, and "sanctions" the market rate of wages, it seems not an unnatural response that "since Political Economy is against the working man, it behoves the working man to be against Political Economy." It seems not unnatural that this new code should come to be regarded with suspicion, as a system possibly contrived in the interest of employers, which it is the workman's wisdom simply to repudiate and disown'.[9] According to Leo Huberman, Political economy was against the working man. But it was not merely a business man's doctrine. In some respects it was peculiarly English business man's doctrine.

Adam Smith, Ricardo, Sidgwick, Edgeworth and Marshall, were all champions of free trade which before 1914 was in Britain's interest. It is well known that free trade had disastrous consequences for Indian textile industry and her village crafts. It is also well known that free trade is against the interest of all industrially less developed countries. This fact was clearly brought out by the brilliant German economist Fredrich List. In his book National System of Political Economy published in 1841, he attacked free trade and said protection was in the interest of Germany and United States of America.[10] Alexander Hamilton actually instituted a protective tariff on manufactured goods from England. List was in fact one of those who disbelieved in the infallibility of the classical school.

A discipline rooted in selfish behaviour, not much different from Thugee, has been built up by the capitalist society to hoodwink and to exploit mankind. Both theories and economic laws have

[8]Francis A. Walker. 1876. The Wage Question, New York.
[9]J.E. Cairns. 1873. Essays in Political Economy, London.
[10]Fredrich List. 1841. National System of Political Economy, London.

been formulated and propagated to justify the acts and the loot of the marauders, and paraded as science by them and their beneficiaries, the Professors. To prove the system's vicinage to the physical sciences and mathematics, extensive use is made of algebra and calculus, often without need or advantage, to impress and mystify the lay public and the credulous and unthinking majority among graduates of economics employed in government departments and universities, and as advisors to industrial houses.

The teaching of economics in the West and in this country which blindly and without thinking follows their example, is a conditioning and an acculturation process in which students are indoctrinated with notions soaked in prejudices in favour of laissez-faire, free market and free trade. The effort is to turn them into 'efficient mandarins of corporate capitalism.' The textbooks which they are taught suffer from a time lag and are influenced by masters of the nineteenth and the early twentieth centuries. The neo-classical system on which they are fed owes much to tradition and is not a description of the reality which faces them. It deals with theories and concepts which have been seriously challenged, even repudiated—the old equilibrium theory, the law of diminishing returns, the theory of organic composition, the theory of perfect competition, the theory of productivity of capital, Say's Law, consumer sovereignty, Pareto optimality and what not. Important topics like hunger, poverty, unemployment, inflation, business cycles, planning development or distribution, are briefly discussed or completely passed over. Conformity is stressed and thinking is discouraged. All that the students are required to do, is to reproduce what they are taught. If they do so successfully they have saleability in the job markets. If they think, ask inconvenient questions, fail to conform or show interest in Marx or Mao or have visited the socialist countries, the job markets are closed for them.[11]

Neo-classical economics says Galbraith, 'lends itself to endless theoretical refinement. With increasing complexity goes an impression of increasing precision and accuracy. And with resolved perplexity goes an impression of understanding. If the economist is sufficiently "caught up in his data and his techniques," he can overlook social consequences—his attention being elsewhere, he

[11]E.K. Hunt, Schwartz and Jesse. 1972. A Critique of Economic Theory. London.

can even, without damage to conscience, support a system that maltreats large number of people'.[12] He adds, 'It should not be supposed, however, that the present hold of the established or neo-classical system is secure. The link between doctrine and reality cannot be stretched too far. That the comparative development in housing and space travel is a manifestation of consumer sovereignty, will not be believed. Nor does anyone suppose that there is a tendency to equality in wage income as between different sectors of economy. When belief is stretched too far, it snaps; the doctrine is rejected. The same is true of refinement without relevance. It comes sooner or later to seem but a game'.[13] F.H. Hahn, a former president of the American Economic Society quoted by L. Wassily, in his presidential address to the society in 1970 said, '. . .the achievements of the economic theory in the last two decades are both impressive and in many ways beautiful. But it cannot be denied that there is something scandalous in the spectacle of so many people refining the analysis of economic states which they give no reason to suppose will ever, or have ever come about. . . . It is unsatisfactory and slightly dishonest state of affairs'.[14]

The neo-classical economy has a number of built-in drawbacks:

1. It has periodic booms and recessions. The worst recession ever, arrived in 1929 and assumed global proportions. The neo-classical remedy for recession before Keynes arrived on the scene, was to cut down government expenditure and balance the budget. The remedy that Keynes recommended in his "General Theory" published in 1936, was directly opposed to the measures which orthodox economists recommended—deficit budgets and heavy government spending. When economy was slumping, Keynes was not only decrying thrift, he was extolling extravagance. What he was saying, in fact, was that private vices were public benefits. The academic economists were at first puzzled but as they understood the implications of what Keynes was saying they fell in line. Keynes had found a solution for the commercial cycles and for the massive unemployment which resulted during the recessions. There have been minor recessions and some unemployment since the end of

[12]J.K. Galbraith quoted by John G. Gurely. May 1971. The American Economic Review.

[13]J.K. Galbraith. 1971. Economics and the Public Purpose, London.

[14]F.H. Hahn quoted by L. Wassily. 1970. Presidential Address to American Economic Society.

the second world war but never anything like what had happened in 1929 and the early 1930s. Curtailment of unemployment, if not its complete eradication, is now a government policy in all western countries. But whenever anything like full employment was achieved, prices soared and the demon of inflation raised its ugly head. With increased buying power and the rising level of imports the balance of payments difficulty posed a problem. Keynes had found a solution of unemployment but at full employment, stable prices could not be achieved. The precise point at which a balance could be achieved between the employment level, stable prices, adequate growth rate and balance of payments, was most difficult of achievement if not impossible. Even then it can be said that Keynes discovered a partial if not a perfect solution for the commercial business cycle. But again a snag arose. The commercial business cycle, as Kalecki had predicted, was replaced by the political business cycle which has continued to plague British economy during the past two decades. Just before the elections, the economy is given a boost but as soon as the elections are over and the government is secure in the saddle for some years, the boom cannot last and there is a set back to the economy. This stop-go has become a permanent political feature of the English economy and that of many other countries including our own.

2. Neo-classical analysis is largely limited to the activities of firms and not to aggregate concepts. A few such concepts as the well known Say's Law which states that supply creates its own demand, have been found to be superficial and inaccurate.

3. Neo-classical price theory usually limits itself to a static picture without regard to time.

4. Neo-classical economics remains at the level of technical economics concerned with the price and production relationship between commodities, implying only in a hidden and devious manner, a very particular political ideology in defence of status quo.

5. It is silent on the role of government and believes that the economy will work automatically. Yet the immense economic role that the governments have played in the past in aiding the initial development of many industries as well as in the mitigation of the business cycles, is well known. What is not known so well, however, is that the government structure and policy are determined by the nature of economic relations and the technical possibilities open to

the government are in reality drastically limited by the political and economic self-interest of the ruling capitalist class, both at home and in the net work of imperialist relations abroad.

6. Although it does provide an accurate description of price movements, the theory is not useful when applied to the distribution of income between labour and the owners of capital. The fact that the wages equal the "marginal revenue product" of living workers does not prove the lack of exploitation, but is only a truism that holds because capitalists maximize profit by living to the point. The fact that interest equals the marginal cost of borrowing capital, proves that financial capitalists and industrial capitalists are striking a realistic bargain, but does not prove that capital is "productive" or that it "produces" interest.

7. Finally, in the abstruse subject of value the academic economists see only statistics and graphs and not human relations.[15]

The neo-classical system of economics is based on a number of assumptions. First, its acceptance of the socio-economic institutional structure of capitalism which defines the conditions within the bounds of which the task of the economists is clearly delimited; secondly, the premises of social harmony in which apart from a few frictions and difficulties, there are no irreconciliable conflicts of interest between social groups; thirdly, an antiquated and exaggerated individualism; fourthly, the proposition that the state is an impartial arbitrator, not committed to any particular class or group; and finally total lack of historical perspective in which capitalism is accepted for all times—its past evolution from Feudalism is dealt with briefly, and other systems are discussed only to underline the superiority of capitalism.[16]

All these assumptions have been the subject matter of criticism both by those who are inside and outside the camp of the orthodox profession. Among the mainstream insiders are 1 the institutional economists like Richard T. Ely and John R. Commons who advocated a new kind of actual policy-oriented economics that helped to launch in the United States, the unemployment and social security measures of the Roosevelt New Era, 2 Thorstein Veblen, who debunked J.B. Clarks and sided with the institutionalists in

---

[15]Howard J. Sherman. 1972. In a Critique of Economic Theory edited by Hunt, Schwartz and Jesse, London.
[16]E.K. Hunt, Schwartz and G. Jesse. *Op. cit.*

rejecting neo-classical economics, 3 the libertarian apostles of Laissez-Faire—Frank Knight, Henry C. Simmons, Fredrick Hayek and Milton Friedman, 4 the radical economists John J. Gurley and Edward Shaw, 5 the iconoclast J.K. Galbraith and 6 Gunnar Myrdal. Among the others, are the prestigious names of the Cambridge (England) team, whose high priest is paulo Sraffa and leader Joan Robinson. Its other members are Kaldor and Bhaduri, and the Italian economist Pasinetti. They have made an assault on the Solow-Samuelson theory of capital that has shaken its very foundations. The most powerful onslaught, however, has been from Marx, Marxians and leftists of all descriptions—Lenin-Stalin, Mao, Gramschi, Baran, Sweezy, Mandel, Fromm, Goodman and others.

It is amazing that inspite of the battering that the system has received from so many quarters, the Thugs continue to make hay and the system still abides. This can, however, be attributed not to its inherent strength but to the cunning, the force and the wealth behind it, and to its long pedigree. It is my fervent hope that the thinking and the honest economists in the Third World countries and India—and there are any number of these—will not allow themselves to be overwhelmed by the wiles of the Western Capitalist Thugs and the economist sycophants and the Professors in their pay. The papers and the text books produced by them have succeeded in deceiving and blindfolding generations of students of economics and other social sciences in colleges and universities, both in their home countries and their colonial and neo-colonial empires. It is time that the thinking, honest and patriotic economists broke their shackles, gathered courage and exposed the Thugs and their economist agents who teach in our universities and serve in industry and government departments. It is time that they debunked orthodox economics as it is taught. They know too well it is no science. It is Thuggery pure and simple, propogated by Thugs for continuation of the status quo.

TWO

Abject Poverty

The standard of living of an average Indian, is among the poorest in the World. The economic status of a people can be gauged by its spending power. This has been calculated for the Indian people and the average per capita consumption in 1957-58, in 1960-61 prices stood at Rs 254. For the richest 5 per cent it was Rs 767. For the poorest 5 per cent it was only Rs 61 which works out roughly at Rs 5 per month or 17 paise per head per day. Ten years later, in 1967-68, while the consumption level of the top 5 per cent remained more or less the same, that of the lowest 5 per cent rose to Rs 77 or 21 paise per head per day. The consumption level has not risen very much more even today and it is inconceivable how any human being can keep healthy or even alive at a level as low as this.

Judged by Western standards even the top 5 per cent cannot be considered opulent but as our concern is with those who are down and out, and under-privileged, it is necessary to establish a dividing line between the real poor and those who are not-so-poor. This was provided in July 1961 by a working group consisting of Prof D. R. Gadgil, Dr B. N. Ganguli, Dr P. S. Loknathan, Shri Asoka Mehta, Shri Shriman Narayan, Shri Pitambar Pant, Dr V. K. R. V. Rao and Shri Anna Sahib Sahasrabuddhe. They recommended a standard of private consumption at Rs 240 per capita per year at the 1960-61 prices, as the barest minimum. Applying this as a yardstick of minimum subsistence, 58 per cent of the population in 1953-58 and 48 per cent in 1967-68, were found to be below the poverty line. Because of the sharp deterioration of economy and the runaway inflation of 1973-74, Minhas put the proportion of people below the poverty line for June 74 at 66 per cent. This is the current figure given by the Janata Party President Chandra Shekhar.

Let us now consider the per capita availability of cereals and pulses. This fluctuates from year to year, according to the harvest and the import of food. Per capita net availability in 1951 was 333.5 grams for cereals and 60.5 grams for pulses. The highest levels for cereals (418.8 grams) were reached in 1965, following the bumper harvest of 1964-65. The level fell to 360 grams again following the lean harvests of 1965-66 and 1966-67. The net availability figures for cereals and pulses for the First Three Plans are shown below :

TABLE 1

| Period | Per Capita Availability in Grams/Day (Average) | |
	Cereals	Pulses
First Plan	358.4	66.4
Second Plan	379.3	67.7
Third Plan	389.3	56.9

Source: Ministry of Finance, Survey, 1968-69.

The situation with regard to the very poor has been much worse than the average figures show. This is partly due to the fact that the Government sells grain through fair price shops in urban areas to the not-so-poor. A point that needs special emphasis is the declining availability of pulses which constitute the only source of protein for the weaker sections. The low per capita consumption of the poor is related further to the buying power of the poor which in turn depends on the level of employment. With the monthly addition to the population, of one million new lives, the rate of unemployment has been progressively increasing. This is perhaps due to the fact that the Indian Planners have not regarded the reduction of unemployment as a major policy objective in the short run. In the short run they have considered the employment objective as being in conflict with the growth output objective, having equated a high employment strategy with a high consumption/low investment strategy. They considered it important to build up the productive capacity of the economy through a high rate of investment before the problem of unemployment could be tackled seriously. They forgot that an attempt to shove it under the carpet, was likely to render the problem of unemployment more acute. Another factor of great importance which determines low levels of consumption for a large sector of the population, is the great inequality of incomes and wealth between the poor and the rich. It is true both of the agricultural and the industrial sectors. In the agricultural sector the bottom 40 per cent of rural households held 1.25 per cent of total cultivated land, defined as operational holdings in 1954-55. This area was further sub-divided into plots of less than one acre. Similarly, the top 6 per cent of rural house-holds owned or had occupancy rights over 40 per cent of the total cultivated area, held in holdings of 20 acres or more. In the industrial sector as Hazari has shown for the period between 1951 and 1958, there was a significant increase in the concentration of economic power. The four largest groups—Tata, Birla, Martin Burn and Dalmia Sahu Jain increased their part of share capital from 22 to 25 per cent and their share in the net wealth of companies from 17 to 22 per cent. This concentration has further increased during recent years. The continuation of gross poverty in India has been related by Pramit Chaudhary to 1 the inadequate rate of increase in agricultural production in the face of a large, rapidly growing population, 2 the Planning Commission's failure to ameliorate the lot of the very poor through redistribution of income and wealth, 3 the general overall low rate of growth of economy, and 4 the pattern of industrial growth that the Government allowed to develop.

The effects of this unbearable, cruel and crushing poverty, continue to disfigure the face of India's "dung-hill" villages and sprawling slum cities. Visit some for yourself and see how they look.

II

Even after thirty years of the achievement of independence, India is a poor country—a land of abysmal poverty. Four hundred eighty million out of a total population of 650 million people, live in villages untouched by the benefits of modern development. They are hungry, naked and sick. They live in mud houses—dark, dingy, without air and sunlight—and with floors plastered with mud mixed with cow-dung. There is no furniture of any kind—not even a cot, a wooden chair or a wooden table. Men and draught animals commonly share the same room. There is complete absence of sanitation and there are no bathrooms and latrines. Men, women and children shit in the fields and foul the only source of water supply—the village pond, the village well or hand-pump or a running stream—which is used for ablutions, bathing, washing and drinking by both men and domestic animals. The streets are littered with refuse and cow-dung, and both homes and streets are completely unlit. Soon after dark, the whole village goes to sleep and there is not even a burning oil lamp to show from the road the location of the village. Even in good harvest years there is shortage of food, and malnutrition is wide-spread. The population, from shortage of calories, is generally undernourished and the children in particular due to protein deficiency, suffer from marasmus and kwashiorkor. Diarrhoea, dysentery, enteric fever, cholera and helminthic diseases have high incidence due to contamination of food and water supply. Malaria and Kala-azar, after their eradication for some years, are reapearing. Filariasis is still uncontrolled. Tuberculosis, leprosy and venereal diseases are wide-spread. Indiscriminate deforestation and failure to harness the rivers, has made floods more frequent and more destructive. Droughts recur every few years. Famines are frequent although due to improved communications, less devastating than before. Rural industries have not developed, and unemployment and under-employment are rampant. Primary education though free, is not compulsory and most of the adults are still illiterate. The law and order situation is poor and there are daily increasing reports of murders, thefts, larcenies, dacoities and sexual crimes. Armed gangs of hoodlums enter buses and running trains, and rob people at the point of the gun. The weaker sections and the untouchables, still receive "special treatment" at the hands of the toughs. The guardians of law and order are often mixed up in acts of criminality and foul play. The police avoid and even refuse to register complaints against the rich and the powerful. Most cases of sexual crime and murder go untraced due to police complicity and bribery, and involvement of high-ups. Justice is denied to the oppressed and the weak, by the sarpanches and the judicial officers who are either bought or influenced from the seats of power.

This pitiable and horrendous picture of the Indian village, is the outcome of the archaic and the corrupt political and social structure on which rests the "democratic edifice" of the Indian village, that emerged during the Congress rule. The village society in Uttar Pradesh is strictly traditional and caste-ridden and each village has a dominant caste—Brahmins, Bhumiars, Thakurs, Banias or one of

[1]Pramit Chaudhury. 1971. Aspects of Indian Economic Development, London.

the backward castes such as the Ahirs, Yadavas, Jats or Kurmis. The power in the village resides in the dominant caste and is exercised through the Pradhan who is usually a tough and who together with his council—the Village Panchayat—is elected by the village (in fact by the dominant caste); the local politician who may be a member of the House of Legislature and also comes from the dominant caste; the Lekhpal who maintains the land records and has unlimited powers of tampering them in favour of the well-to-do farmers for monetary consideration; and the police head or the Daroga.

The small farmer, the share-cropper and other tenant, the landless, the homeless, the artisan and the Harijan—are all oppressed and exploited by the middle or the rich farmer of the dominant class, many of whose members have marriage and other links with the bureaucracy, the ruling political class and other elites in the city, the state capital or New Delhi. This relationship with the unscrupulous and corrupt Pradhans, Lekhpals, Sarpanches and police on the one hand, and on the other hand with the city elites has not only been responsible for the deprivation, the degradation, the dehumanization and often intense suffering and physical liquidation, of the poorer sections and the Harijans in the village but has also enabled the rich and the powerful sections of the dominant caste in the village to corner all the benefits accuring from power and pelf, and all the money-flow from the centre and the states—irrigation and other facilities, permits, licences, quotas, contracts and jobs—during the five-year plans, for their own benefit. This has not only enriched and strengthened the absentee landlords and the rich village farmers but hampered the economic growth and welfare of the village—rural agriculture, rural industry, rural housing, rural aducation and rural health. What is worse, the flow of both wealth and talent from the village to the city has established a colonial relationship between the urban and the rural areas in the country, analogous to the colonial relationship that exists between the rich and the poor countries.

III

The Indian Cities are sprawling slums. After independence there has been a phenomenal rise in the population of cities—due partly to an influx of refugees from Pakistan at the time of the partition, partly to a normal increase as everywhere else in the country and partly due to a process of urbanization consequent on pressure on agricultural land and resultant unemployment and underemployment, 2 expansion of village education and the exodus of the educated villagers in search of jobs, and 3 movement after the zamindari abolition, of the rich farmers and their families to the cities in search of alternative occupations. This large increase in the population of cities has not been matched by a corresponding increase in the construction industry. This has led to a serious shortage of housing in the urban areas. As a result there have sprung up settlements of jhugees and jhompris[2] and shanty towns in and around all cities and big cities in particular. The population of Delhi increased from half a million in 1941 to more than five million in 1975. More than a million of Delhi's homeless poor construction workers with their wives and children, industrial workers and their families, immigrants from villages in search of scarce jobs, the sick and the maimed, beggars, lepers, pick-pockets, thieves and vagrants live in clusters of rickety shacks made out of bamboos, straw mats and sack cloth without kerosine lamps and water supply or any semblance of sanitation. There they retire after day's toil, there they cook in earthen pots on fire lit out of fire-wood which they have picked up from the streets or pilfered and placed between two low piles of rubble or bricks collected from the neighbourhood, and there they sleep on the floor and mate and multiply. Within yards of where they live they throw their garbage and also shit before daylight or after it is dark. The stench of human excreta which emanates from these dwellings, permeates the atmosphere for hundreds of yards away.

In old Delhi—behind Turkman Gate,[3] Bazar Sita Ram, Chawri Bazar, Khari Bawli, Phatak Habash Khan, Katra Neel, Gandhi Galli[4] and numerous other places—there are streets not more than ten feet wide, with open drains on both sides. The wall-to-wall two or three storey brick houses on either side of these lanes are

[2]Bamboo and Mat tents.

[3]On 14th April 1976, under Sanjay Gandhi's direction, the Delhi Development Authority demolition squad bulldozed a large number of houses in the Turkman Gate area. Poor and wailing men and woman were packed into trucks, carried miles away from the places of their work, and deposited in vacant lots with no amenities whatsoever, not even drinking water.

[4]Name of Streets in Old Delhi.

without sanitary latrines and many without water supply. The rooms are poorly ventilated, do not get any sunlight, and are dark, damp and dingy. Due to extreme shortage of houses, the rents are exorbitant, and there is extreme overcrowding and congestion. Often whole families live in single rooms. The children defaecate in open drains and sometimes in the middle of the streets.

There is not enough of anything for these poor people. There are not enough schools and thousands are turned away at the enrolment time. There are not enough hospital beds and seriously sick patients are put on mattresses on the floor of wards and verandhas. There is not enough public transport and people have to queue up for hours before they are able to secure a place for their destination; many of them stand on the foot-boards and hang on precariously outside. Not enough food, not enough air, not enough water.

There are thousands who do not have even these facilities. They sleep on foot-paths and pavements, in parks and on railway station platforms and third class waiting rooms. On freezing wintry nights they avail of the facilities of a bed on the floor in the Capital's Rahn-Baseras which are leaky, long, filthy dormitories with just sleeping space on the floor. Scores of vagabonds, criminals, beggars, lepers and others throng there to save themselves from freezing to death and for a night's rest which they do not get. The bedding which these "wretched of the earth" get, consists of a torn and tattered blanket below and a similar one for cover—both full of vermin.

Within a few kilometres, often a few furlongs of these infernos, are the air-conditioned villas, palaces and multi-storey marbled flats of the rich and corrupt businessmen, officials and politicians. They live in great style, eat in five-star hotels, smoke foreign cigaretes, drink smuggled whisky, throw expensive parties, travel in imported limousines and send their children to public schools, and English and American universities. Delhi has two fraternities —one of the vulgar, wasteful, dehumanized rich, the other of the deprived, wretched, indigent poor.

Calcutta, a generation ago, writes Mervyn Jones, was already the poorest, the shabbiest and the least modern of Indian cities. It continues to remain so. Delhi, he writes, 'has auto-rickshaws powered by Vespa engines and Bombay has cycle-rickshaws but Calcutta still has rickshaws pulled by trotting feet. Its ten million people—three million in the city and seven million in the Calcutta Metropolitan District, are without proper homes. More than three quarters of the City population lives in overcrowded tenements and bustee (slum) quarters'.[5] According to an official estimate two thirds of the people live in kutcha (unbaked) brick buildings. More than 57 per cent of multi-member families have one room to live in. For more than half of the families cramped into one room quarters, there is only 30 square feet or less of space per family member. One study showed that the indigent of the bustees share a single water tap among 25.6 to 30.1 and a single latrine among 21.2 to 23 persons.[6]

The sight of the Calcutta bustees is blood curdling. A bustee is a connected series of long low buildings with walls of dried mud and roofs of tiles, intersected by narrow lanes where two people cannot pass without touching, and intricately subdivided within. It has only one door leading straight through a corridor along the back, off which the rooms open without doors of their own. Even after the Sun comes up, the light inside is dim. The average room is small and measures about eight feet by six feet and is six feet high. It is home for a husband, a wife and a number of children. The family has no possessions—no furniture, no stove, no lamp, nothing but their rags of clothes and a single pot from which they all eat. So long as the owner of the bustee gets his rent, neither he nor the authorities ask how many souls it contains. The worst and most afflicted of the bustees are largely populated by the poorest people who are sick and have no work. They suffer from malaria, leprosy and phthisis. Some of those who can work, manage to live somehow by running errands, fetching taxis, cleaning cars and selling inexpensive articles on the streets. Others live by begging, stealing or pimping for their real or alleged sisters.

Bombay with its posh residential quarters is outwardly more attractive than Calcutta. But is it really so? 'Seventy per cent of Bombay's ten million share a bath room and 67 per cent share the lavatory. Eight out of ten families live in single-room tenements while only 60 per cent have access to water taps. Two million slum dwellers live in subhuman conditions without any water or sanitary

[5]Mervyn Jones. 1965. In Famine's Shadow, London.
[6]Nirmal Kumar Bose. 1969. In Cities, London.
[7]Ibid.

facilities while for nearly a million, the foot-path is the only home they know'.[8]

Bombay's chawls are the counterparts of bustees in Calcutta, miserable dark holes, overcrowded, sunless, airless. Ten or more people share a windowless room and sleep brings them neither rest nor freshness. The inmates wallow in their own excreta and imbibe its poisons. The food they consume, the air they breathe, the water they drink, is contaminated by it and bowel diseases and worm infestations are common.

The description of Delhi, Calcutta, Bombay applies equally well to other cities. Kanpur, an industrial centre, is the largest city in Uttar Pradesh. It is so filthy and so ugly that it has earned the distinction of being the dirtiest city in India. Lucknow, once the pride of the Nawabs of Oudh and the garden city of India, has numerous slums—on both sides of the Haider Canal, Chowk, Nakhas, Aminabad, Ganeshganj, Daliganj and other areas. Of these slums any city government should be ashamed. In Jaipur, an otherwise beautiful city, run rivers of human excreta in the streets where marble and other images of dieties are carved for installation in temples all over India. In Varansai, the streets in the neighbourhood of the Viswanath temple and abutting on the ghats and the slums on the ghats themselves, present a picture of defilement and squalor that no description can bring to mind and has to be seen to be believed.

[8]Ram K. Vepa. 1975. New Technology. A Gandhian Concept, New Delhi.

THREE

Under Development and its Causes

India is abysmally poor, both in the cities and its hundreds of thousands of villages. More than half its population lives below the poverty line fixed arbitrarily at an extremely low level of Rs 20 per month per person at the 1960-61 prices.

It has been debated by economists whether India should be characterized as a developing country or an underdeveloped country. As the GNP of the rich and the developing countries of the West is rising every year, and they are also developing, it is perhaps best to characterize India, and countries placed like her as underdeveloped. Underdevelopment has been variously defined by Bauer, Kuznets, Lange, Nurkse, Myrdal, Viner and others and a precise definition is difficult. A large number of criteria have been suggested and are considered in some detail under the following heads:

1. Per Capita Income. This is the most widely used measure of the economic progress of a country but it does not provide a true picture of a country's poverty and the data it furnishes are often incomplete, inaccurate, unreliable and misleading. The reasons for this are: (*i*) There is a substantial non-monetized sector in the economy of poor countries which makes an estimation of the national income difficult. A considerable part of the produce is either exchanged for other commodities or is retained for personal use. (*ii*) The farmers build their own huts, and produce articles like milk, ghee and clothes etc., which are not included in the national income. (*iii*) Due to lack of specialization, estimation of national income by distributive shares or industrial origin, is difficult. (*iv*) A large percentage of the farmers are illiterate and keep no accounts. Figures from such sources can only be rough approximations. (*v*) Translating the foreign exchange value of one currency into that of another, gives extremely distorted results. As an example the buying power of a rupee in India, is not one tenth the buying

power of a dollar in New York. (*vi*) The per capita GNP only gives the average, and no indication of the income of the lowest fractiles, which is negligible or near zero.

The World Bank Survery for 1965 divided the countries of the world into four groups in terms of their per capita Gross National Product: Group A, dollars 750 and above; Group B, dollars 300 to 750; Group C, dollars 100 to 300; and Group D below dollars 100. India together with 35 countries in Group D supported nearly half the world population and enjoyed only 8 per cent of the total world GNP. On the other hand 36 countries in Group A with 29 per cent of the world population appropriated and enjoyed 82 per cent of the world GNP. India with a per capita income of 90 dollars ranked 125th in the community of nations and was below China, Ghana, Ceylon, Thailand, Kenya, Pakistan, Uganda and Tanzania. China's GNP was more than two and a half times that of India.[1]

2. Dichotomy of Economy. Almost all underdeveloped countries have a dual economy—a large traditional subsistence sector and a small industrial sector consisting of public, private and foreign subdivisions. The subsistence economy is backward and mainly agriculture-based. The industrial sector is concentrated in enclaves round the big cities and towns. It is modern and produces iron and steel, machine tools, heavy electricals, fine and superfine textiles, television sets, transistors, airconditioners, refrigerators, electrical kitchen equipment, telephones, cosmetics, perfumes, pharmaceutical and other luxury items for use by the elites. The foreign owned part of this sector earns huge profits on equity mainly acquired in the host country and repatriates vast sums home in the shape of profits, dividends, royalties, know-how and patent fees, leading to impoverishment and further underdevelopment of poor countries.

3. Underutilization of Natural Resources. Underdeveloped countries possess natural resources which remain undiscovered as in the case of minerals, metals and oil, or remain unutilized or underutilized. India has about 90 million acres of cultivable wasteland which if brought under the plough, could not only make her self-sufficient in foodgrains but a surplus country in respect of food. She has over 40 million KW of hydro-electric power potential of which only a small part has so far been exploited. Its new finds

[1]M.L. Jhingan. 1976. The Economics of Development and Planning, New Delhi.

of oil in Bombay High, Bassein, Arunachal, Orissa and other areas, promise to make her self-sufficient in oil within the next few years.

4. Agriculture. The number of people engaged in the production of foodgrains and cash crops is very large in underdeveloped countries, sometimes several times as many as the number of people so engaged in advanced countries. In India the number of people engaged in agricultural pursuits is 73 per cent of the total population. In England the member of those engaged in farming is 3 per cent, in West Germany 10 per cent, in France 15.8 per cent and in Italy 22.5 per cent.[2] Some underdeveloped countries have one or two commodity economies, they remain underdeveloped and are at the mercy of the developed nations.

5. Demographic Trends. The rate of growth of population of underdeveloped countries where industrial revolution is slowly coming, is very high. This has been accelerated due to a significant reduction in death rates following the use of modern life-saving drugs and undiminished high birth rates. India has a high growth rate of 2.5 per cent and some African and Latin American countries have growth rates as high as 3 to 3.5 per cent. Such high growth rates neutralize the benefits of all economic growth and although the GNP grows, there is little increase in the per capita income. In India the GNP has increased between 1950 and 1975 at an average rate of 3.5 per cent per year but as the population has also been growing at a rate of 2.5 per cent, the real increase in GNP has been only one per cent.

An important consequence of high birth rates is a large proportion of young age people in the population. In India nearly 40 per cent of the population is made up of children below 15 years of age and while they contribute little to the economy, they do consume. With such large number of dependents, the savings and the investment are affected very adversely.

In underdeveloped countries the expectancy of life and, therefore, duration of productive work is much less. In Western countries with an expectancy of life of over 70 years, the duration of active work is over 50 years; in India where life expectancy is only 56 years, the number of active work years is hardly 30 to 35.

Finally in densely populated countries where the rate of growth of population is high and land suffers from fragmentation of hold-

[2]Source : N.I.E.S.R.

ings, primitive methods of agriculture and lack of inputs like fertilizers, lead to exhaustion of the soil and poor yields, which do not permit economic progress.

6. Unemployment and Hidden Unemployment. There is a great deal of unemployment in underdeveloped countries. This is involuntary as those who are willing to work are unable to find work. As an example five members of a family work on a field on which four can do equally well without loss of output. The fifth person is, therefore, not only not contributing anything, he is actually a burden, adversely affecting the savings or the consumption of the other four. Although it is not easy to measure quantitatively the magnitude of hidden unemployment, most observers agree that withdrawal of 25 to 30 per cent of agricultural workers from the farm labour-force will not adversely affect the level of the agricultural output. The ILO studies of unemployment have so far covered Columbia, Sri Lanka, Iran, Kenya and the Philippines. The Columbia report starts by accepting Arthur Lewis's fundamental premise that underdeveloped countries went wrong in planning for the growth of product rather than the growth of employment, and that they would have been much better off if they had exchanged a lower rate of growth of GNP for a higher rate of growth of employment. The way to economic independence and balanced growth according to him lies not in making television sets and other luxury items for the city elites but to go in a big way for promotion of small scale and cottage industries to provide gainful employment to the millions in the villages who are busy during the sowing and harvesting seasons, but are idle for the rest of the year. It seems that Gandhi's shade is speaking through the voice of Arthur Lewis.

7. Level of Education and Adult Literacy. The role of primary education and adult literacy in raising agricultural production and the level of living is dealt with in considerable detail in the chapter on education. It is sufficient here to say that low levels of education and adult illiteracy are impediments to growth and development.

8. Capital Formation. Lack of capital formation is an important characteristic of underdevelopment. In an underdeveloped country the masses are illiterate and ignorant, and use primitive and outmoded agricultural implements and technology. The productivity and the level of their consumption is already so low, that further restriction and any consequent saving is not possible. It is, therefore,

only the high income groups that are able to save. But they squander their savings in conspicuous consumption, foreign travel, building of luxury villas and flats, and purchase of gold, diamonds and imported durables. The middle groups due to the spread of the "demonstration effect," and in trying to keep up with the Jonese's, emulate the rich. This has a disastrous effect on savings and capital formation.

Capital formation involves an increase in the volume of savings, the existence of credit and financial institutions to mobilize savings into investible funds and their use for acquisition of capital goods. An adequate level of savings should be above 12 per cent of the national income and preferably between 20 and 25 per cent. No underdeveloped country, says Lewis, 'is so poor that it could not save 12 per cent of its national income if it wanted to; poverty has never prevented nations from launching upon wars or from wasting their substance in other ways'.[3]

Saving may be voluntary or forced. Voluntary savings may not be sufficient in amount and therefore, governments have to resort to forced saving through taxation, deficit financing and borrowing from the public. Profits earned by public corporations can also be saved for capital formation and investment. Another avenue of capital formation is to use the savings that accrue from restriction of luxury imports and import of capital goods. According to Nurkse,[4] an important source of capital formation could be the saving potential contained in rural hidden unemployment. Surplus members of the family who do not contribute anything to agricultural produce can be taken away from the family farms and employed in road building, irrigation, railways, housing or other projects not very far from their homes. Their food needs could be met by their relations whose own consumption level should continue to remain, what it was before.

Capital can also come from external sources as aid in the form of grants or loans. Aid, trade and foreign investments, however, have been used in the past, as the present author has explained elsewhere, as instruments of foreign policy and exploitation by the donor countries.[5]

[3]W.A. Lewis. The Economics of Growth.
[4]Ragnar Nurkse. 1952. The American Economic Review, USA.
[5]M.L. Gujral. 1975. U.S. Global Involvement, New Delhi.

No one can question the value of capital accumulation for the process of development but in a country like India where millions of people both highly skilled and unskilled, are without jobs and where a labour-intensive technology could be more useful, is it really that important? The answer is furnished by Joan Robinson, Professor of Economics at Cambridge University.[6]

'The most striking example of development in modern times has taken place in North Korea. The Koreans, with a small amount of help from abroad, in the course of a decade, by a great drive for education, study and learning by doing, mastered the techniques of almost the whole range of modern industry, as well as mechanizing agriculture, and provided themselves with the equipment that it requires, in a country that had been blitzed to the ground. Their engineers read text books or took machines to pieces to see how they were made. The workers were encouraged to put themselves through part-time schools, from primary to university level, side by side with regular education for the young generation.

'By this means with hard work and with initial advantage of good mineral resources, they brought about the greatest economic miracle that has ever been seen, in spite of feeling obliged to build up modern armaments as well. They did not need a class of rentiers to perform the service of waiting, but abstinence was provided by the whole country, in the sense that when a tolerable standard of life had been provided for all, they abstained from consuming luxuries so as to be able to devote a great share of resources to investment.

'The economists in the Third World, on the other hand, under the influence of the neo-classical orthodoxy, believe that what their countries need is "capital" and that to get it, they need capitalists to take the risk of making investment. . .'

9. Foreign Trade. The underdeveloped countries are producers of primary products—oil, minerals, metals, fibers and beverages which they export, and importers of finished goods such as armaments, machine tools and consumer goods. The primary goods are given away at dirt cheap prices but for the manufactured goods and processed foods the prices paid are exorbitant and extortionist. As

---

[6]Joan Robinson. 1974. The Abdication of Neoclassical Economics in Economic Theory and Planning. Ed. Ashok Mitra. Calcutta.

an example the ivory coast[7] pays eleven times as much per gramme of protein imported in the form of canned meat, fish and milk powder, as it earns from proteins exported in the form of peanuts and oilseed cake. To clinch this argument, there is an exhaustive U. N. report which shows that the countries exporting primary products get on an average only a tenth of the final prices that these fetch in the advanced countries. The remaining nine-tenths is made up of processing and distribution charges which progressively enrich the residents of the rich nations. The work of economists like Paul Prebisch, Samir Amin and others has shown that international trade has become the mechanism for a systematic transfer of wealth from the poor nations of the "periphery" of the world economic system to the rich nations of its "core."

The ratio of exports to the total products is usually high and the economy of many of these countries depends on single commodity export. The oil rich countries of the Middle East and Venezuela depend on oil, Chile on copper, Ceylon on tea and rubber, Columbia on coffee, Bangladesh on jute and Honduras on bananas for most of their foreign exchange earnings. Concentration on one or two items in an economy, is harmful to the interest of these countries and exposes them to many risks. First, the development of other sectors of the economy is neglected and the country becomes dependent for most of its needs of consumer goods on developed countries. This raises the import bill of the nation and leads to balance of payments difficulties. Secondly, a depression in the world market, affects the export of the commodity adversely and its price slumps to levels which spell disaster for the economy. Finally, when after a specified number of years, the sources of the raw material dry up or get exhausted, such countries, due to their neglect and failure to develop in other ways, face a bleak future. Many oil rich countries have already realized this fact and have not only slowed the process of extraction, but have also begun earnestly to diversify.

A profound disappointment with the meagre fruits of three decades of planned economic development in the poor countries, has called into question the views widely held and glibly propagated by neo-classical economists—on the interplay of free market forces in trade, the strategy of growth of GNP without any thought

[7]Prem Shankar Jha. 3 June 1975. Times of India, New Delhi.

being given to the composition of its product and the way in which it is produced or distributed, the undue importance attached to certain physical relationships such as the capital-output ratio and the value of capital-intensive technologies for the development of poor countries—and accepted and repeated parrot-like by economists in India and other Third World countries. These views and beliefs have been rightly challenged by a number of economists including Myrdal, Prebisch, Lewis, Singer, Seers, Amin and Myint and it is now obvious even to laymen that these beliefs are wrong, and the strategies of aid, trade and domestic investment based on them are misconceived.

Two recent conferences—the UNCTAD IV in Nairobi and ILO in Geneva—have recently highlighted two closely related problems of underdevelopment. 'While UNCTAD has concerned itself with the international repercussions of the failure of the development strategies of the post-war period, the ILO has been increasingly preoccupied with the domestic implications of this failure, the most obvious symptoms of which are rapidly growing unemployment, uncontrolled urbanization, the growth of slums, and of disease, vice, and crime in the cities. The two big proposals of the UNCTAD IV—to set up a commodities bank to stabilize the price of primary products, and to link the prices of primary products to those of manufactured goods entering international trade, seek only to arrest the further growth of inequalities in exchange. But the tragic part of the UNCTAD IV is that the most innocuous of its five proposals—to set up a fund to stabilize the prices of the raw materials—has failed to receive even token support from the USA, the UK, West Germany and Japan—the four most powerful of the "core" nations. The Times of India correspondent Prem Shanker Jha[8] asks 'whether it would not be better for poor countries to opt out of world trade to the maximum possible extent to check the drain of wealth from them'?

10. Socio-cultural Conditions. Indian society is shockingly stratified and riven by caste and class cleavages, and ethnic, regional and religious distinctions. It is priest ridden from birth to death. The Brahmin Priest is in full command at birth, christening, mundan, thread investiture, marriage, travel, inaugurals of business ventures, house warming, cremation, kriya, pind, tarpan and shradha

[8]Prem Shankar Jha. 6 June 1976. Times of India, New Delhi.

ceremonies. Illiteracy, ignorance, superstition, archaic beliefs, antiquated customs, belief in karma and resignation to poverty, preference for academic education and prejudice against manual work,
stand in the way of development. Joint family system, and kinship
and caste ties, make for corruption, favouritism and maladministra-
tion. The institutional and the structural frame work promotes
social attitudes which encourage hoarding, black marketing, profiteering and tax evasion. The rich farmers, the industrial barons,
merchants and traders who get rich by these practices, invest in
non-productive assets such as real estate, gold, diamonds, jewellery,
luxury goods and imported consumer durables.

According to Peter Donaldson . . . 'the process of transforming
a traditional society requires a fundamental adjustment to human
attitudes and the structures and institutions which it embodies. The
choice may be a painful one. If poor countries want real development, a major upheaval in traditional customs and practices is
often the price which has to be paid'.[9]

The underdevelopment and the stark poverty which plagues
India today, is the direct consequence of the wrong policy decisions,
the wrong planning and the poor implementation of whatever plans
she formulated, during the last three decades. These we shall consider in the succeeding chapters.

[9]Peter Donaldson. 1973. Economics of the Real World, London.

FOUR

Gandhian Economy

Gandhian economics and Gandhian philosophy are built around a number of fundamental principles—simplicity, self reliance, decentralization, bread labour, full employment, production by masses (not mass production), swadeshi, prohibition, equality, egalitarianism, humanism, socialism, freedom of the individual, democracy, peace and moral and ethical values. Gandhiji had not read many books but he was a profound thinker. During his early life he was influenced powerfully by his parents, and Hindu and Jain religious scriptures, and later during the years of South African and Indian struggles by the writings of Ruskin, Tolstoy and Thoreau.

In 1904 during a 24 hour train journey from Johannesburg to Durban, Gandhiji was given by H.S.L. Polak, a book "Un To This Last" by John Ruskin. Once he had begun reading it, he could not lay it aside. He writes, 'I could not sleep that night. I determined to change my life in accordance with the ideals of the book'. He translated the book into Gujarati which was his mother tongue, under the title "Sarvodaya" or the welfare of all. The central ideas he derived from the book were:

1. That the good of the individual is contained in the good of all.

2. That a lawyer's work has the same value as that of the barber, in as much as all have the same right of earning their livelihood from their work.

3. That a life of labour i.e., the life of the tiller of the soil and of the handicrafts-man, is the life most worth living.[1]

Henry David Thoreau provided Gandhiji with the technique of Civil Disobedience which was to be employed by him first in South Africa and later in the struggles he launched in this country. Thoreau, the sage of Concord and the author of "Walden," could

---

[1]M.K. Gandhi. An Autobiography, Ahmedabad.

hardly have imagined that his action in going to gaol for a night in Massachusetts rather than pay an unjust tax, would have provided a "naked fakir" in far off India, a tool to wrest the country's freedom from a most powerful imperialist nation. Later, in Thoreau's own country, Martin Luther King was to use the Gandhian technique for securing equal rights for the American Blacks. Thoreau provided Gandhiji the Raison d'eter for his belief that it was the right of a citizen to disobey an unjust law and that one of the ways of doing so was to cheerfully go to prison rather than obey it.

It was count Tolstoy who gave Gandhiji the conviction that one must practice what one preached. 'It was 40 years back', Gandhiji wrote, 'when I was passing through a severe crisis of scepticism and doubt that I came across Tolstoy's "the Kingdom of God is Within You" and was deeply impressed by it. I was at that time a believer in violence. Reading the book cured me of my scepticism and made me a firm believer in Ahimsa'. Gandhiji corresponded with Tolstoy and sent him a copy of his book "Hind Swaraj." The Russian author wrote back to him complimenting him on leading 'a movement which is one day destined to bring hope to the oppressed millions of mankind'. Tolstoy's idea of "bread labour"—that everyone should labour with his hands for bread and that most of the grinding poverty in the world, was due to failure in this regard particularly appealed to Gandhiji. What had special interest for him, was the fact that Tolstoy dared to practice what he believed in, and that in the 'afternoon of his life, the man who had passed all his days in the soft lap of luxury, took to toil and hard labour'. He took to boot making and farming at which he worked hard for full eight hours a day. Gandhiji derived great benefit from Tolstoy's writings but as the latter himself admitted, he cultivated and developed the method in South Africa to an extent that it looked quite different from 'what Tolstoy had written about and recommended'.

But Gandhiji was no mere eclectic. It appears that in the early period of his life, he had doubts about some of his own ideas and he derived satisfaction from the fact that other thinkers in other lands had also thought on similar lines. It was in this sense that the writings of Ruskin, Thoreau and Tolstoy helped him. But there is no doubt whatever that 'Gandhi would have been much the same even if he had not become familiar with the writings of these persons. He would still have been the unique phenomenon in whom religion and politics mixed to produce a philosophy, a system, a way of life, that was hard to match, much less to beat, by even the most powerful nation on earth at that time. The fact that at many points it touched on the thoughts of others only made it stronger and added to the universal appeal'.[2] Gandhiji according to Vepa 'saw life not in fragments, as most of us do, but an integrated whole. In his mind politics was indistinguishable from religion, and economics from ethics.'

Gandhiji was a practical realist and stood for simplicity—simple living and high thinking. He had a deep insight into the malaise that afflicted modern civilization. He wrote in his book "Hind Swaraj" that modern man laid too much emphasis on material goods and the pursuit of wealth. This had not been the Indian ideal. He wrote, 'the mind is a restless bird; the more it gets the more it wants and still remains unsatisfied. The more we indulge our passions, the more unbridled they become. Our ancestors, therefore, set a limit to our indulgences. They saw that happiness was largely a mental condition. A man is not necessarily happy because he is rich, or unhappy because he is poor. Observing all this, our ancestors dissuaded us from pleasures. . . . It was not that we did not know how to invent machinery but our forefathers knew that if we set our minds after such needs, we will become slaves and lose our moral fibre. They, therefore, after due deliberation, decided that we should only do what we could with our hands and feet'.[3] He further said, 'I whole heartedly detest this mad desire to destroy distance and time, to increase animal appetites and go to the ends of the earth in search of their satisfaction'.[4] Ceaseless pursuit of material goods and wealth has undermined character and human values. It has dehumanized not only the workers but also those who employ them.

The problems posed by unlimited growth such as pollution of the environment by industrial wastes, exhaustion of earth's resources and the population explosion had not assumed in Gandhiji's life time the proportions that they now have, and Gandhiji could not have imagined their impact or import, but he was fully aware of the evils of the mad race for consumer goods by the industrial

[2]Ram K. Vepa. 1975. New Technology, Gandhian, Concept, New Delhi.
[3]M.K. Gandhi. Hind Swaraj, Ahmedabad.
[4]M.K. Gandhi. 17 March 1927. Young India.

society both in Europe and America. He attributed the exploitation of man by man in the West, and the exploitation and subjugation of the countries of Asia, Africa and Latin America to this inordinate greed of the colonial powers. To this also he attributed the violence and the wars that had plagued mankind for milleniums. He had seen several small and two major wars. They ended in great violence, waste and misery both for the vanquished nation and the great majority of the people of the victorious power. They solved no problems. According to Gandhiji the only way to achieve peace was to abjure greed and to curtail wants. Gandhiji said, everyman had an equal right to the necessaries of life. He said, 'if all laboured for their bread and no more, there would be enough food and enough leisure for all'. By bread he meant the necessaries of life.

In 1928, Gandhiji explained, 'According to me the economic constitution of India and for that matter of the world should be such that no one under it should suffer from want of food and clothing. In other words everybody should be able to get sufficient work to enable him to make ends meet. And this ideal can be universally realized only if the means of production of the elementary necessaries of life remain in the control of the masses. These should be freely available to all as God's air and water are, or ought to be. They should not be made a vehicle of traffic for the exploitation of others. Their monopolization by any country, nation or group of persons should be considered unjust. The neglect of this simple principle is the cause of the destruction that we witness today, not only in this unhappy land but in other parts of the world too'.[5]

It must be clearly understood that while Gandhiji enjoined simplicity and curtailment of wants on the people, he never wanted them to take to loin cloth or the life of asceticism. He wanted every single individual to be well fed, well clothed and well housed and with the growth of the economy he wanted their living standards to be improved to enable them to live in freedom and in reasonable comfort.

He was a firm believer in a decentralized consumer goods industry built in and around India's 600,000 villages. An ideal village of Gandhiji's concept was to be 'so constructed as to lend itself to

[5]N.K. Bose. 1957. Selections From Gandhi, Ahmedabad.

perfect sanitation. It will have cottages with sufficient light and ventilation built of a material obtainable within a radius of five miles of it. The cottages will have courtyards enabling householders to plant vegetables for domestic use and to house their cattle. The village lanes and streets will be free of all dust. It will have wells according to its needs and available to all. It will have houses of worship for all, also a common meeting place, a village common for grazing its cattle on a cooperative basis, primary and secondary schools, in which industrial education will be the central fact and it will have panchayats for settling disputes. It will produce grain, vegetables and fruits, and its own khadi'.[6] He said, 'my idea of village swaraj is that it is a complete republic independent of its neighbours for its own vital needs and yet inter-dependent for many things in which dependence is a necessity. Among his vital wants were: balanced and adequate food, suitable and sufficient clothes, proper housing, education, and health and medical care.

Gandhiji's scheme of decentralized industrialization envisaged a network of cottage and small scale industries on a cooperative basis all over the country. From his observation of industrial society in the Europe and elsewhere, he knew of its evils and was uncompromisingly opposed to the introduction of industrialism in India. He wrote, 'my views on national planning differ from the prevailing ones. I do not want it along industrial lines. I want to prevent our villages from catching the infection of industrialism'. He attached great value to self-reliance for everyday consumer necessities. He held manual labour in great esteem. Large scale production, he said, 'could undoubtedly provide more comforts and luxuries to some but was intimately related to economic serfdom. It took away the freedom to be free. Real freedom could not thrive in a centralized industrial society'.[7]

In his scheme cottage industries were to produce the more common requirements—articles of food like gur, milk, eggs, ghee, vegetables and fruit, cloth, soap, simple articles of house-hold furniture like beds, chairs, tables, boxes as well wooden requirements for house construction in the village. Small-scale industries catering for a group of villages, could provide articles for which markets were too small in the individual villages. Small scale industries with

[6]M.K. Gandhi. 1963, Village Swaraj, Ahmedabad.
[7]M.K. Gandhi. The Modern State.

a small capital and local labour could set up small workshops and factories to produce utensils, pottery, sanitary ware, bottled and canned foods, paper, ready made garments, hair oils, combs, mirrors, toys, shoes, leather bags, simple tools and machines, medium quality of furniture and items of construction industry like bricks and lime. Suitable shops for repairs of cycles, sewing machines, motors, pumping sets and diesel engines etc., could also be established for a group of villages.

Decentralization and organization of consumer goods industries in the manner recommended by Gandhiji and modified according to needs as suggested above, would have led to 1 satisfaction of the basic wants of all and eradication of the abject poverty that has plagued this subcontinent for centuries and still stares us in the face after three decades of independence, 2 improvement of the living and educational standards of the people and its impact on population control, 3 full employment for all, 4 a mood of self-confidence and self-reliance which in turn would have saved the country from the burdens imposed by foreign aid and foreign debt, 5 dispersal of industry desirable from the point of view of defence, 6 a great saving in the transport costs as production, distribution and consumption would be localized within a few miles radius and 7 production by masses and establishment of an egalitarian society.

Swadeshi. Gandhiji was a fervent believer in Swadeshi. His doctrine of Swadeshi has been defined by him as 'that spirit in us which restricts us to use the resources and the service of our immediate surroundings to the exclusion of the more remote'.[8] Gandhiji preferred to serve the country through the service of his neighbours by patronizing their goods and establishing socio-economic ties for mutual benefit. Gandhiji rightly believed that the use of imported cloth and other foreign luxury goods by the Indian elites was not merely vulgar ostentation but also extremely harmful for the country's economy. He was of the view that there was no incompatibility between the spirit of swadeshi and universalism, and enjoined on his countrymen to follow the principle of maximum self-sufficiency in the economic sphere but practice the ideal of universal brotherhood in the domain of culture and philosophy.

Machinery. At one time Gandhiji was opposed to the use of all machinery. This attitude arose, it appears, from the knock-out blow

[8]M.K. Gandhi. Khadi Why and How, Ahmedabad.

that Manchester had inflicted on Indian village industry. He wrote, 'it is machine that has impoverished India. It is difficult to measure the harm that Manchester has done to us'.[9] But he later changed his views and was prepared to have all machines that would lighten human labour. He used to cite the example of Singer sewing machine. He was attracted by the sentiments which induced Singer to design and develop a machine to save his wife from avoidable labour. In doing so, he added, 'it not only saved her labour but the labour of every one who could purchase a sewing machine'. In 1924, when asked by an ashram worker Ram Chandran, if he was against all machinery, he replied, 'my answer is emphatically no. But, I am against its indiscriminate multiplication. I refuse to be dazzled by the seeming triumph of machinery. I am uncompromisingly against all destructive machinery. But simple tools and instruments and such machinery as saves individual labour and lightens the burden of millions of cottages, I should welcome. What I object to is the craze for machinery, not machinery as such. The craze is what they call for labour saving-machinery. Men go on saving labour till thousands are without work and thrown on the open streets to die of starvation. I want to save time and labour not for a fraction of mankind but for all; I want the concentration of wealth not in the hands of a few, but in the hands of all. Today machinery helps a few to ride on the backs of millions. The impetus behind it all is not the philanthropy to save labour, but greed. It is against this constitution of things that I am fighting with all my might'.[10,11] Gandhiji was fighting not against machinery as such but against its abuses.

When Gandhiji was asked by Ramchandran where would the sewing machine be made and who would make it, his answer was unequivocal : 'I am socialist enough to say that such factories should be nationalized. They ought only to be working under the most attractive and ideal conditions, not for profit but for the benefit of humanity, love taking the place of greed as the motive. It is an alteration in the conditions of labour that I want. This mad rush for wealth must cease, and the labourer must be assured, not only of a living wage, but a daily task that is not mere drudgery.

[9]M.K. Gandhi. 1908. Hind Swaraj, Ahmedabad.
[10]N K. Bose. 1957. Selections from Gandhi, Ahmedabad.
[11]Ibid.

The machine will, under these conditions, be as much a help to the man working it as to the state, . . . The individual is the one supreme condition. The saving of labour of the individul should be the object, and honest humanitarian considerations and not greed, the motive'. Gandhiji had wanted that the machines to make machines should remain in the public sector. He had intended that all industries—railways, communications, public utilities, heavy industries, basic and key industries—all except the decentralized consumer goods industries, should be nationalized. He was also not against the use of electricity. He wrote, 'if we could have electricity in every village home, I should not mind villager's plying their implements and tools with the help of electricity'.[12]

Socialism and Humanism. He was a socialist and a humanist and believed in non-violence through and through. In his concept of socialism all members of society were equal—none low, none high. He believed that everyone—a lawyer, a physician, a teacher, a businessman, a labourer or a sweeper—should get an equal or a near equal wage. He was opposed to a few fabulously rich people wallowing in wealth side by side with a vast majority living in abject poverty and going without food or raiment. He wrote, 'the contrast between the palaces of Delhi and the miserable hovels of the poor labouring classes cannot last one day in free India in which the poor will enjoy the same power as the richest in the land. A violent and blood revolution is a certaintly one day unless there is voluntary abdication of riches and power that riches give, and sharing them for the common good'. He believed that real socialism had been handed down to the Indian people by their ancestors who taught that all land belonged to Gopal, which in modern language means the State or people. Land and all property, he believed, belonged to those who worked. Unfortunately the workers had been ignorant of that simple fact. Gandhiji was a socialist and his ultimate aim was a human society—a society in which dehumanization ceased, human labour was truly emancipated and man had all the conditions for his self-development.

Gandhi and Marx. Gandhiji believed in the Marxist doctrine, 'from each according to his ability, to each according to his needs but he did not share Marx's interpretation of history, his theories of class war, regimentation of life and labour, the dictatorship of

[12]Ibid.

the proletariat and the withering away of the State. 'The common point between Gandhi and Marx is the extreme concern of both for the suppressed and the oppressed, the resourceless and the ignorant, the dirty and starving sections of humanity. . . Both Gandhi and Marx want to establish an order which would make the masses co-sharers in the gifts of nature and fruits of human labour and genius. But while Gandhi insists upon adherence to truth and nonviolence for achieving this object, Marx does not care about quality of the means provided they appear efficient enough for achieving the end as quickly as possible'.[13]

Gandhi and Mao. Like Mao, Gandhiji believed in a decentralized rural economy and in bridging the three gulfs—between the rural and the urban areas, the poor and the rich, and between the intellectuals and the manual workers. Unlike Mao, however, who believed that power came out of the barrel of a gun, Gandhiji believed in the power of non-violence and satyagraha. For him non-violence was a creed and satyagraha which literally means "insistence on truth" a weapon to eradicate through "collective civil disobedience," the numerous weaknesses in the social and political life. The satyagrahi or the person who practices satyagraha, refuses to cooperate with a social system based upon immorality. At the same time, he tries to build up a different way of life in terms of what he considers to be moral.

Trusteeship. No description of Gandhian economic thought can be complete without reference to his "trusteeship doctrine." The doctrine has been, as he himself admitted, much ridiculed. Yet he stuck to it. His attachment to purity of means was so great that he wanted to bring about even a socialist transformation of society in a nonviolent manner. The doctrine as amended by himself during his long period of incarceration in the Aga Khan palace reads as follows:

1. Trusteeship provides a means of transforming the present capitalist order of society into an egalitarian one. It gives no quarter to capitalism, but gives the present owning class a chance of reforming itself. It is based on the faith that human nature is never beyond redemption.

2. It does not recognize any right of private ownership of pro-

---

[13]K.G. Mashruwala. Gandhi and Marx, Ahmedabad.

perty except so far as it may be permitted by society for its own welfare.

3. It does not exclude legislative regulation of the ownership and use of wealth.

4. Thus under state-regulated trusteeship, an individual will not be free to hold or use his wealth for selfish satisfaction or in disregard of the interest of society.

5. Just as it is proposed to fix a decent minium living wage, even so a limit should be fixed for the maximum income that could be allowed to any person in society. The difference between such minimum and maximum incomes should be reasonable and equitable and variable from time to time so much so that the tendency would be towards obliteration of the difference.

6. Under the Gandhian economic order the character of production will be determined by social necessity and not by personal whims or greed. Gandhiji himself realized how difficult it was to implement and said, 'it is true that it is difficult to reach. But so is non-violence difficult to attain. I think we know the violent way. It has succeeded nowhere'.

Gandhiji was assasinated soon after the achievement of political independence. The Congress Party which held and wielded power, was not interested in building a socialist society. The Constitution that was framed, gave full recognition to the right of ownership of private property. None of Gandhiji's economic ideas—decentralisation, village uplift, basic compulsory education for children between the ages of six and fourteen built round a craft, right to work and full employment etc.—were ever adopted or pursued. Persons who hovered round Gandhiji and who he thought could have qualified as trustees—Birlas and Bajaj's—were the very people who betrayed his trust. The authorities on their part took no legislative action to curb the evil propensities of the tycoons. No minimum living wage or maximum were ever fixed and production was determined not by social necessity but by uncontrolled greed.

Among those who have since Gandhiji has been removed from the scene, acclaimed his methods and spoken and written approvingly of his principles and approach, are such prestigious names as those of Albert Einstein, Aldous Huxley, Arnold Toynbee, Arthur lewis, Bertrand Russel, Chester Bowles, Colin Clark, Ethel Mannin, H.R. Schumacher, Eric From, Gunnar Myrdal, Hiren Mukherji, Ivan Illich, Jai Prakash Narain, J.B. Kripalani, J.K.

Galbraith, John Tinhergen, Harold Laski, Lewis Mumford, Louis Fischer, Martin Luther King, Radha Krishnan, Richard Gregg and others. But it is tragic that those who swore most by Gandhi during his life-time, acted in ways most unGandhian after they climbed into the saddle, and set India on a path of economic development that has spelled disaster for her. Albert Einstein who himself loathed nothing more than war, called Gandhiji, 'the miracle of a man' and said, 'generations to come would scarce believe that such a one as this ever in flesh and blood walked upon this earth'. Louis Fischer his admirer and biographer wrote about him: 'If man is to survive, if civilization is to survive and flower in freedom, truth and decency, the remainder of the twentieth century and what lies beyond must belong not to Lenin or Trotsky, nor to Marx or Mao, or Ho or Che, but to Mahatma Gandhi'.[14]

[14]Louis Fischer. 1970. Journal of Historical Studies, Princeton.

FIVE

Socialist Professions and the Plans

Before India became free, she had a well organized Communist Party, a Congress Socialist Party (CSP), which was a party within the Congress Party itself, a Trade Union Congress (TUC) composed of both right and left wingers and a number of Youth Leagues with a socialist outlook. Jawaharlal Nehru himself was vaguely attracted to "The Fabians," while he was still a law student in England. In the autumn of 1912 he returned to India and attended as delegate the Bankipore session of the Indian National Congress held during the Christmas week. He first met Gandhiji at Lucknow, during the 1916 session of the congress and was closely associated with him and the Congress work ever afterwards. He paid a brief visit to Moscow in November 1927, during the tenth anniversary celebrations of the Soviet. In 1928, as General Secretary of the Congress, he addressed several meetings all over the country. He presided over four provincial conferences—in the Punjab, in Malabar, in Delhi and in the United Provinces. The burden of his address was always much the same. He writes, 'Everywhere I spoke on political independence and social freedom, and made the former a step towards the attainment of the latter. I wanted to spread the ideology of socialism among the congress workers and the intelligentsia, for these people who were the back-bone of the national movement, thought largely in terms of the narrowest nationalism'.[2] He further writes, 'I was by no means a pioneer in the socialist field. Indeed, I was rather backward and I had only advanced painfully, step by step, where many others had gone ahead blazing a trail. The worker's trade union movement was, ideologically definitely socialist, and so were the majority of Youth Leagues. A vague confused socialism was already part of the atmosphere of

[1]Jawaharlal Nehru. 1936. An Autobiography, London.
[2]Ibid.

India when I returned from Europe in December 1927 and even earlier than that there were many individual socialists. Mostly they thought along utopian lines, but Marxian theory was influencing them increasingly.'[3]

In December 1928, a few days before the Calcutta Congress, the All India Trade Union Congress was held at Jharia, and Jawaharlal attended and participated in it for the first two days, before he left to attend the Calcutta session of the Congress. While he was still at Calcutta, he learnt that he was elected President of the TUC for the next year. He states that although his sympathies were with the radical wing, his name was proposed by the moderate wing of the TUC 'probably because they felt that I stood the best chance of defeating the other candidate who was an actual worker (on the railways) and who had been put forward by the radical group'.[4]

In the autumn of 1929 at Gandhiji's instance, Jawaharlal was elected President for the ensuing session of the Indian National Congress at Lahore. As the time of the session was drawing near, events were marching step by step, pushed forward, so it appeared by some motive force of their own. To check this onward march, the British Government took a forward step, and the Viceroy, Lord Irwin, announced a decision about a forth-coming Round Table Conference. A Leader's Conference was hastily called at Delhi and representatives were called from various groups and parties—Gandhiji, Motilal Nehru, Vallabhbhai Patel, and moderates like Sir Tej Bahadur Sapru and others. A joint manifesto accepting the Viceroy's offer subject to some vital conditions which were to be fulfilled, was issued. It was a feat to get a resolution of this kind accepted by all groups, radical and moderate. For the radicals it was, however, a climb down and for them the conditions were vital. But this was not so for the moderates for whom the conditions were not important. As it happened some people were extremely bitter about the joint manifesto; they considered it wrong and dangerous to give up the demand for independence, even in theory and even for a short while. Subhash Chandra Bose definitely refused to sign. Jawaharlal Nehru at first refused to sign but he writes 'as was not unusual with me, I allowed myself to be talked into signing'. He writes further, 'even so I came away in great distress, and the very

[3]Ibid.
[4]Ibid.

next day I thought of withdrawing from the Congress Presidentship, and wrote accordingly to Gandhiji. I do not suppose that I meant this seriously though I was sufficiently upset. A soothing letter from Gandhiji and three days of reflection calmed me'.[5]

The conditions imposed by the Congress were not acceptable to the Viceroy and the year of grace given at Calcutta, was coming to an end. Complete independence was to be declared as the Congress goal and necessary steps taken to carry on the struggle for its achievement.

Before the meeting of the Indian National Congress at Lahore, Jawaharlal had to preside at the Nagpur session of the TUC. He writes, 'It is unusual for the same person to preside over both the National Congress and the TUC within a few weeks of each other. I had hoped that I might be a link between the two and bring them close to each other—the National Congress to become more socialistic, more proletarian, and organised labour to join the national struggle'.[6]

In 1930 at the Karachi session of the Congress, presided over by Sardar Vallabhbhai Patel, Jawaharlal who had accepted the main resolution as it emerged from the Working Committee, found himself in difficulty when he was asked to move it in the open session. He writes, 'I hesitated. It went against the grain, and I refused at first. . . . Almost at the last moment, a few moments before the resolution was taken up in the open Congress, I decided to sponsor it'.[7] He spoke on the other resolutions too, notably on the Bhagat Singh Resolution and the ones on Fundamental rights and economic policy. The Karachi Economic Policy Resolution was a 'step, a very short step, in a socialist direction by advocating nationalising key industries and services, and various other measures to lessen the burden on the poor and increase it on the rich'.[8] The Government of India took a serious view of the resolution and believed that Jawaharlal Nehru moved it under the influence of M.N. Roy who had met him in Allahabad, a few days before he left to attend the Karachi session. But as Jawaharlal says, M.N. Roy had nothing to do with it and 'the idea of getting the Congress

[5]Ibid.
[6]Ibid.
[7]Ibid.
[8]Ibid.

to pass a resolution of this kind was an old one. For some years the U.P. Provincial Congress Committee had been agitating in the matter and trying to get the AICC to accept a socialist resolution. In 1929 it succeeded to some extent in getting the AICC, to accept the principle'.[9]

The years 1930 to 1933 were years of hectic political activity for the Congress—Civil Disobedience, Dandi March, agrarian no-tax compaign in U.P., Gujarat and Karnataka, failure of Round Table Conferences, repression and mass imprisonments. During this period Nehru was in and out of gaol several times and found time to read. He read as many books as he could lay hands on or procure, on socialism and Marxism, on the world situation in the grip of a great depression, and on Indian problems and struggle in the context of the mighty world drama that was being enacted everywhere. His own sympathies, he writes, 'went increasingly with the communist side'. He writes : 'I had long been drawn to socialism and communism and Russia had appealed to me. Much in Soviet Russia I dislike—the ruthless suppression of all contrary opinion, the wholesale regimentation, the unnecessary violence (as I thought) in carrying out various policies. But there was no lack of violence and its expression in the capitalist world, and I realized more and more how the very basis and foundation of our acquisitive society and property was violence. . . . Violence was common in both places, but the violence of the capitalist order seemed inherent in it, whilst the violence of Russia bad, though it was, aimed at a new order based on peace and cooperation and real freedom for the masses. With all her blunders, Soviet Russia had triumphed over enormous difficulties and taken great strides toward this new order. India or any other country could profit by the trimphs as well as the inevitable mistakes of the Bolheviks. . . . Only a revolutionary plan could solve the related problems of the land and industry as well as every other major problem before the country. Russia apart, the theory and philosophy of Marxism lighted many a dark corner of my mind. History came to have a new meaning for me. . . . It was the essential freedom from dogmas, and the scientific outlook of Marxism that appealed to me'.[10],[11]

[9]Ibid.

[10]In 1958 when Jawaharlal wrote for the A.I.C.C. Economic Review, he completely forgot that deprivation and poverty were the worst form of

While Jawaharlal Nehru and the U.P. leaders were pining in Uttar Pradesh gaols, there was a group of young radical intellectuals, incarcerated in another part of India. In 1933, Jaya Prakash Narayan, and some of his friends—Achyut Patwardhan, N.G. Goray, M.R. Masani, K.K. Menon, Asoka Mehta, M.L. Dantwala and others —who were imprisoned in the Nasik Road Central gaol, conferred together and decided to set up a socialist party within the Indian National Congress. After their release from gaol they communed with some friends in Banaras and in May 1934, on behalf of the Socialist Party of Bihar Jaya Prakash Narayan, issued an invitation to such members of the Congress Party who believed in the objectives of socialism, to meet in Patna. On a personal request from him U.P.'s veteran socialist leader, Acharya Narendra Dev agreed to be the Chairmam of the Patna Conference in which a formal decision was reached to set up a Congress Socialist Party (CSP) within the Indian National Congress. In October of the same year, the party was actually launched in Bombay under the chairmanship of Sampurnanand. For many years after its formation, its principal leaders—Acharya Narendra Dev, Jaya Prakash Narayan, Ram Manohar Lohia, Achyut Patwardhan, Asoka Mehta and Yusuf Meher Ali—remained very close together in their espousal of the socialist cause. Strangely enough, Jawaharlal Nehru whose relations with all these leaders were extremely cordial, and who also professed socialist views kept aloof from the group.

The Congress in 1934 was, as it is today, a platform and not a party. In view of the approaching elections to the legislatures, it was looking more and more to the right and trying to win over the moderate and conservative elements in the country. In May 1934, soon after the formation of the CSP, the Congress Working Committee passed a resolution in which it was stated that the Karachi Resolution 'neither contemplates confiscation of private property

---

violence that capitalist society inflicted.

[11]Ibid.

All his admiration of the triumphs of Soviet Russia and the great strides she made while the rest of the world was in the grip of a great depression, his view on gradualism, his idea of a revolutionary plan that alone could solve the two related questions of land and industry for India, his complete break with the existing order, his love of the theory and philosophy of Marxism, the Marxist interpretation of history and the scientific outlook of Marxism, vanished into thin air after he came to power.

without just cause or compensation, nor advocacy of class war. The Working Committee is further of the opinion that confiscation and class war are contrary to the Congress creed of non-violence'. As Jawaharlal Nehru was one of those who had spoken in favour of the Economic Resolution at the Karachi session, he was deeply pained by the Congress Working Committee Resolution which 'made it clear that the Congress Executive were not going to be moved from their new path by this nibbling from the left. If the left did not behave it would be sat upon and eliminated from the Congress'.[12] The first shot on the CSP was fired soon after the party came into existence. One wonders whether it was this resolution which dissuaded Jawaharlal Nehru to associate himself with this new party of the Left. He did not want to be sat upon and eliminated from the Congress.

A deep attachment had grown between Nehru and Gandhiji and no two leaders were more closely associated with each other than these two during the freedom struggle. Yet there was a distance between them and temperamentally they were poles apart. Gandhiji stood for simple living, decentralized rural economy on cooperative basis, swadeshi, village autarchy, non-violence, compulsory and free primary education built round a craft, adult literacy, labour intensive technology and use of simple machines which could be run by hand or power and freely used in and around every village home to fulfill the consumer needs of the people, 80 per cent of whom lived in the rural areas. The basic and the key industries, he said, were to be in the public sector. Non-violence and purity of means were for him a creed and he would not allow violence even for the achievement of socialism. He was not against higher standards of living provided they could be made available to all. His concept of Sarvodaya which has been reduced to a farce by some of his most devoted disciples, was welfare for all. He was totally against glaring inequalities and said that they could not last for one day in a free India.

Jawaharlal Nehru's goal was a good life and an affluent society and his prescription for building it, was through large-scale industrialisation. He considered Gandhiji's decentralized economy and village autarchy as retrograde measures and as a regression to primitiveness and the past. He was not against swadeshi but he

[12]Ibid.

said, 'we are tied up, with the rest of the world, and it seems to me quite impossible for us to cut adrift. We must think, there-fore, in terms of the world, and in these terms a narrow autarchy is out of question. Personally I consider it undesirable from every point of view. Inevitably we are led to the only possible solution—the establishment of a socialist order, first within the national bounda-ries, and eventually in the world as a whole, with a controlled pro-duction and distribution of wealth for public good. How this is to be brought about is another matter, but it is clear that the good of a nation or of mankind must not be held up because some people who profit by the existing order object to the change. If political or social institutions stand in the way of such a change, they have to be removed'.[13] The main drive in future, he further wrote, 'will have to be a complete overhauling of the agrarian system and the growth of industry. No tinkering with the land . . . . will do the slightest good. The land system which we have is collapsing before our eyes, and it is a hinderance to production, distribution and any rational and large-scale operations. Only a radical change in it, put-ting an end to the little holdings and introducing organised collec-tive and cooperative enterprises, and thus increasing the yield greatly with much less effort, will meet modern conditions. The land will not and cannot absorb all our people, and large-scale operations will (as Gandhiji fears) lessen the workers on the land. The others must turn, partly it may be to small-scale industry, but in the main to large-scale socialized industries and social service'.[14] Jawaharlal Nehru believed that democracy and capitalism which grew together in the nineteenth century were not mutually com-patible. 'There was a basic contradiction between them, for demo-cracy laid stress on the powers of the many, while capitalism gave real power to the few'.[15] He was during this period a Marxist and though he hated violence, he was definitely not committed to Gandhian non-violence. He believed that although the means cannot be ignored, the final emphasis must necessarily be on the end and goal in view.

[13]Ibid.

[14]Ibid. Tinkering with the land problem has still not ended, and foreign and Indian large-scale enterprises continue to exploit the poor man.

[15]Ibid.

II

Between the mid 1930s and the late 1940s, many important events took place—Stalinist purges in Soviet Russia, the World War II, the development and use of atomic weapons, the disintegration of colonial powers, the emergence of newly liberated countries and the Kalecki-Keynesian Revolution in economic thought which transformed the capitalist system and gave it a new lease of life. These events and particularly the Stalinist excesses, the atom-bombing of Hiroshima and Nagasaki, and the rapid economic growth under capitalism, must have made a profound influence on the mind of Jawaharlal Nehru. By 1947 when India became free and Jawaharlal Nehru her first Prime Minister, it appears, he had already lost a good deal of his enthusiasm for Marxism and socialism. The complete break with the past[16] and the radical solution of the land problem[17] about which he earlier wrote, were both things of the past. Even during the years of liberation struggle, under pressure from the Liberals, the moderate groups within the Congress and Gandhiji himself, he had been known to shift his stand and climb down from the radical position he had erstwhile taken. Such shifts from extreme and leftist positions to those of moderation and even reactionism are not unknown in the history of political or economic struggles. Instances of shifts from revolutionary to pro-imperialist, from leftist to centrist or from socialist to capitalist positions, have been frequent in the past and will continue in the future. Professor J.K. Galbraith makes a very interesting observation in respect of the West European socialists. He writes, 'an Englishman, Frenchman or German can be an ardent socialist. But, howsoever ardent, he is also practical. So he will not seriously propose that banks, insurance companies, automobile plants, chemical works or, with exceptions steel mills be taken into public ownership. And certainly if elected to public office he will not press legislation to such end. However, much he favours such action in principle, he will not be for it in practice'.[19] Jawaharlal Nehru like the European socialists of whom Galbraith

[16]Ibid.
[17]Ibid.
[18]Ibid.
[19]J.K. Galbraith. 1975. Economics and the Public Purpose, England.

speaks, favoured socialist action only in principles. P.A. Samuelson, the doyen of the text book writers on economics and now a Nobel Laureate, regards Jawaharlal Nehru as a gradualist reformist and even brackets him with conservatives and die hards like Winston Churchill.[20] From Jawaharlal Nehru's self characterization in the Autobiography, it is amply clear that he was not unaware of the fact that his show of socialism was a mere make-believe, a pretence, and his profession of radicalism nothing more than lip-service. He wrote, 'I myself belong to a class which mixes with these lords of the land and owners of wealth. I am a typical bourgeoisie, brought up in bourgeosie surroundings, with all the early prejudices that this training has given me. Communists have called me a petty bourgeoisie with perfect justification'.[21] According to Premen Addy and Ibne Azad, 'Jawaharlal Nehru was a fake socialist'.[22] Professor Joan Robinson refuses to grant even a democratic character to Nehru's regime. She writes, 'Nehru's personal prestige made it possible to combine one-party rule with trappings of democracy'.[23]

I have described Nehru's assessment of himself and by others, not to minimize his achievements. He dominated Indian and International politics for a decade and a half after 1947. He suffered much in the cause of his country's freedom. His achievements in building a great infrastructure for Indian economy cannot be lightly ignored. He is the author of non-alignment which is playing and will continue to play a big role in the relations between the under-developed and the developed countries. But inspite of his socialist professions and pronouncements, he failed the country in one very important respect, viz. to pull it out of the boa-constrictor grip of the neo-colonial and capitalist powers.

His failure in this respect may be traced to the very development of his personality. The only son of a rich father, his early education was under English governesses and tutors. At the age of 15, he went to school at Harrow. Among his fellow students were sons of Maharajas of Baroda and Kapurthala. While still at Harrow, he developed an interest in politics. News from home—Lajpat Rai's

[20]P.A. Samuelson. 1973. Economics, Japan.
[51]Jawaharlal Nehru. 1936. An Autobiography, London.
[22]Premen Addy and Ibne Azad. 1975. In Explosion in a Subcontinent, Ed. Blackburn, Robin. England.
[23]Joan Robinson. 1974. Selected papers. Trivandrum.

and Ajit Singh's deportation, B.G. Tilaks' struggle for Home Rule, Swadeshi, Boycott of foreign goods—began to attract and agitate him. In 1907 at the age of 17, he joined Trinity College Cambridge where he studied for three years and took his Natural Science Tripos with second class honours. His subjects were chemistry, botany and geology but his interests were much wider. Among his contemporaries at Cambridge, were J.M. Sengupta, Saifuddin Kitchlew, Syed Mahmud, J.A., Sherwani and S.M. Suleman. Among those who visited Cambridge during his time were Bipin Chandra Pal, Lajpat Rai and G.K. Gokhale. After leaving Cambridge in 1910, he hovered round London for two years. His law studies did not take much time and he did a lot of general reading. He was 'vaguely attracted to the Fabians and socialistic ideas, and interested in the political movements of the day'. In 1912 he returned to India and plunged headlong into the fight for national freedom. His highly sensitive and impetuous make-up often drove him into radical and extreme postures in politics and economics but the countervailing influences of his high birth, early education by English governesses and tutors, student years at Harrow and Cambridge, love of finery and life in a society of "the Lords of the land and owners of wealth," pushed him in the opposite direction. When he came into power, he found himself in a situation in which many others before found themselves. Jawaharlal Nehru's conversion was in fact in no way different from that of many another eminent person in his own walk of life. A case in point but not of one in politics, is that of the great English economist, Alfred Marshall. Joan Robinson quotes Marshall to show how he cured himself of his socialist leanings. Marshall says, 'I developed a tendency to socialism, which was fortified later on by Mill's essay in the Fortnightly Review in 1879. Thus for more than a decade, I remained under the conviction that the suggestions, which are associated with the word, "socialism," were the most important subject of study, if not in the world, yet at all events for me. But the writings of socialists repelled me, almost as much as they attracted me; because they seemed far out of touch with realities; and partly for that reason, I decided to say little on the matter, till I thought much longer. Now, when old age indicates that my time for thought and speech is nearly ended, I see on all sides marvellous developments of working class faculty; and, partly in consequence, a broader and firmer foundation for socialist schemes than existed when Mill wrote. But no socialist scheme yet advanced, seems to make adequate provision for the maintenance of high enterprise and individual strength of character; nor to promise a sufficiently rapid increase in the business, plant and other material implements of production to enable the real incomes of the manual labour classes to continue to increase as fast as they have done in the recent past, even if the total income of the country be shared equally by all'.[24]

Another instance related once again by Joan Robinson is that of John Maynard Keynes whose mood often swung from left to right. 'Capitalism was in some ways,' writes Joan Robinson, 'repugnant to him but Stalinism was much worse. In his last years, certainly, the right predominated. When I teased him about accepting a peerage, he replied 'that after 60, one had to become respectable.'[25] One wonders whether Nehru like Alfred Marshall was influenced by immense growth within the capitalist system or was he like Keynes trying to be respectable? Whatever be the answer to these questions, the fact remains that Nehru was no longer the Left-winger of the 1920s and 30s—a progressive member and President of the TUC and one who had moved the economic resolution at the Karachi session of the Indian National Congress. He was gradually swerving more and more to the right.

III

The Congress Party was a conglomeration of many heterogeneous groups and parties. It drew its membership from the landed aristocracy, urban propertied classes, business interests, industrial magnates, and parties of the right, centre and left. Such a party could hardly be expected to be an instrument of socialist transformation, and its first assault on the CSP came within a year of the achievement of independence. Sardar Vallabhbhai Patel, the Deputy Prime Minister of India and a most powerful member both of the Congress Party and the Congress Government, made it plain beyond the shadow of a doubt, that there was no room for a separate party within the Congress Party. The CSP must either disband itself, he said, or quit the Congress. The CSP left the Congress in 1948 and the Socialist Party of India was formed.

[24]Alfred Marshall. Trade & Industry. Quoted by Joan Robinson in England.
[25]Joan Robinson. 1973. Selected Economic Writings, Trivandrum.

Mention must be made at this stage of two significant features of the Indian Constitution of 1950. The first relates to the inclusion of the Right to Property in the Fundamental Rights. This was a direct blow and an outright rejection of the policy of socialism. The second was the adoption of universal adult franchise which unexceptionable by itself, conferred a new political role on the rural power-holders, the landlords who dominated factional alignments in the villages.

'The Congress leadership, in the context of electoral contest forged new links with these local-level power-holders, that reversed the earlier antagonistic relationships. For the latter too, close links with the successor regime were no less valuable than their earlier links with the colonial regime. The role and the influence of these local-level power-holders in India, is widely recognized. One liberal academic anthropologist, refers to them as "vote banks."[26]

In post-independent India, a tripartite alliance came into being between the imperial bourgeoisie, the indigenous bourgeoisie and the landed aristocracy. To prevent the introduction of land reforms legislation, the land-lords and the big farmers, joined the Congress in big numbers. They contested on the Congress Party tickets for the Houses of Legislature and after election captured the main body of the Congress machine. Their influence with the State Governments has not only stalled the passage of progressive land legislation but has also stood in the way of its implementation even after its passage. At the central level strategic decisions have been greatly influenced by the alliance between the imperial and the national bourgeoisie. As producers of the marketable surplus of. raw materials, there is a close link between the landlords and the big farmers on the one hand and the twin bourgeoisie—the national and the imperial on the other. The enhanced income of the landlords and the big farmers, due to a rise in prices of the agricultural produce, also gives them a considerable weight in the total consumption of imported and manufactured goods, giving further strength to the link between the three dominant classes.

[26]Hamza Alvi. 1975. Socialist Register, London.

IV

Planned economy within the framework of capitalism, is an exercise in futility. No third-world country trying to develop within the framework of the capitalist system has made a success of it. Yet this is, on what Jawaharlal Nehru embarked when the First Five Year Plan was launched in 1951. The Plan was a modest one, prepared in great hurry and as a means to integrate post-war reconstruction projects undertaken by the Union and the State Governments to repair the damage done to the economy by the Second World War and the partition of the country. The Plan envisaged an outlay of Rs 2,029 crore for the public sector which was revised to Rs 2,378 crore, but the actual amount spent was only Rs 1,960 crore. Total investment both in the public and the private sector amounted to Rs 3,360 crore, 94 per cent of which came from domestic and 6 per cent from foreign sources.

National income during the Plan period increased by 18 per cent, per capita income by 11 per cent and per capita consumption by about 8 per cent. It was essentially an agricultural Plan and in the agricultural field the production of food rose by 20 per cent, that of cotton by 45 per cent and of oil seeds by 8 per cent. Industrial production rose by 38 per cent. The overall installed power capacity rose from 2.3 to 3.4 million kilowatts. Irrigation facilities were extended to 10 million acres of land. During the Plan period, work was accelerated on a number of mult-purpose river projects such as the Bhakra-Nangal, Damodar Valley, and Hirakud, while many new major projects were started on the Chambal, Rihand, Koyna and Kosi. A significant step was the launching of the Community Development and National Extension Services Programme on 2 October 1952. Over the Plan period money supply increased by a little over 10 per cent and the price level came down by 13 per cent in 1955-56 as compared with 1950-51. The cost of living index registered a decline.

The Plan, however, made no attempts to have annual breakdowns of the various targets of development and in the absence of annual control figures, it became extremely difficult to assess the pace of development during the Plan period. It did not solve the problem of unemployment which assumed serious proportions by 1953. A most serious drawback was the utter neglect of the industrial sector—chiefly the heavy and basic industries.

The Second Five Year Plan, launched on 1 April 1956 was much bigger and more ambitious than the First Five Year Plan. Its broad objective was to establish—as had been decided at the Avadhi session of the Indian National Congress in 1954—a socialist pattern of society in a welfare state. Keeping in view this broad aim, the Second Plan laid down the objectives of a sizable increase in 1 national income so as to raise the standard of living of the people, 2 rapid industrialization with particular emphasis on the development of basic and heavy industries, 3 a large expansion of employment opportunities, and 4 reduction of inequalities in income and wealth and a more equal distribution of economic power.[2]

The implementation of the Plan needed Rs 7,200 crore for the entire Plan period. Of this 72 per cent was available from domestic sources and the balance of 28 per cent had to come from abroad as aid. 'After the depletion of India's sterling balances, towards the close of the First Plan, India applied to the World Bank for a loan. The World Bank stipulated the condition that the public sector should be reduced. The Indian Government refused the loan. But after Nehru's visit to the United States, he became less radical and his criticism of the U.S. policies less sharp. The 1957 balance of Payments crisis took India back to the United States and the World Bank and she accepted both the loan of 600 million dollars and the conditions. India dropped the rule that in joint enterprises 51 per cent control should be in Indian hands, and the most profitable areas of economy previously reserved for the public sector were thrown open to private firms—notably aluminium, drugs, heavy electricals and engineering, fertilizers and synthetic rubber. A series of tax concessions were given to foreign firms. An Indo-U.S. currency convertibility was provided for. As a result the whole course of Indian development was swung completely away from its goal of "socialism" and towards free enterprise'.[27]

V

In 1958, Jawaharlal Nehru had already strayed away from the socialist highway. He was meandering in the byways of mixed economy, socialist pattern or planned economy within a capitalist framework. His break (not with the existing order about which he

[27]M.L. Gujral. 1975. U.S. Global Involvement, New Delhi.

earlier spoke) but with scientific socialism, was well nigh complete. This is clear from two articles which appeared in the AICC Economic Review on 1 August 1958.[28],[29] The first article was written by Sampurnanand, the Congress Chief Minister of Uttar Pradesh and the second "The Basic Approach" by Jawaharlal Nehru who wrote his article after a perusal of Sampurnanand's article.

The distance that Jawaharlal Nehru had travelled from his cherished dream of socialism of the late 1920s and the mid 1930s, may be surmised from a comparison of the quotes from his Autobiography given in the earlier part of the chapter with the opinions he expresses in his 1958 article from which a few excerpts are presented. In the first excerpt one discerns a religious and metaphysical turn in Jawaharlal Nehru's thinking. It says, 'There is much talk in communism of the contradictions of capitalist society and there is truth in that analysis. But we see the growing contradictions within the rigid framework of communism itself. Its suppression of individual freedom brings about powerful reactions. Its contempt for what might be called the moral and spiritual side of life, not only ignores something that is basic in man, but also deprives human behaviour of standards of value. Its unfortunate association with violence encourages a certain evil tendency in human beings'.[30] In the second quote, Jawaharlal Nehru speaks of violence in the two systems. Whereas earlier he had talked about a purpose behind communist violence and the meaninglessness of capitalist violence, the assault is now on the former. He writes in the article under review : 'Communism charges the capitalist structure of society with being based on violence and class conflict. I think this is essentially correct, though that capitalist structure itself has undergone and is continuously undergoing a change because of democratic and other struggles and inequality. The question is how to get rid of this and have a classless society with equal opportunities for all. Can this be achieved through methods of violence or can it be possible to bring about those changes through peaceful methods? Communism has definitely allied itself to the approach of violence. Even if it does not indulge nor-

---

[28]Dr Sampurnanand. 1 August 1958. AICC Economic Review.
[29]Jawaharlal Nehru. 15 August 1958. AICC Economic Review.
[30]The early militant Nehru had overlooked the 'contempt' for moral and spiritual values in communism. After his metamorphosis he highlights them.

mally in physical violence, its language is of violence, its thought is violent, and it does not seek to change by persuasion or peaceful democratic processes, but by coercion and indeed by destruction and extermination'.[31] The next excerpt is a panegyric of mixed economy, welfare state or capitalism. He writes, 'Capitalism in a few countries at least, has achieved this common welfare to a great extent. . . . Democracy allied to capitalism has undoubtedly toned down many of its evils and in fact is different from what it was a generation or two ago. In Industrially advanced countries there has been a continuous and steady upward trend. Even the terrible losses of World Wars have not prevented this trend in so far as these highly developed countries are concerned. Further this economic development has spread though in varying degrees to all classes. . . . Capitalism itself has, therefore developed some socialistic features even though its major aspects remain'. The last excerpt is on means and ends : 'The basic thing, I believe, is that wrong means will not lead to right results'.[32] Mark the difference from his earlier belief 'that although the means cannot be ignored, the final emphasis must necessarily be on the end and goal in view'.

VI

India's First Five Year Plan was a small one. The monsoons were good and though there were shortfalls, it went well. Trouble, however, started early during the Second Plan period. Inspite of impressive gains in the industrial sector—building of steel plants at Durgapur, Bhillai and Rourkela, machine-tool industry, heavy electrical equipment, tractors, automobiles, sewing machines, electrical appliances, newsprint, antibiotics, pesticides, dyestuffs etc.—there were serious shortfalls both in the agricultural and industrial sectors. The Plan had to face the adverse facts of bad weather, closure of the Suez Canal, the balance of payments crisis, the conditions imposed by the United States and the World Bank in respect of aid and the rising prices. The Second Five Year Plan failed to achieve its targets in

[31]This is the conventional language of the leaders of the ruling class who want to maintain the status quo. For those who want a social change, the language is different and Nehru himself talked in that language during the British period.

[32]Balraj Mehta. 1974. Failure of Indian Economy, New Delhi.

many fields. The National Income was less by 5.5 per cent from the target figure and the number of unemployed persons rose to 9.5 million.

Food and agricultural production in the Third Plan period was poor largely because of poor weather conditions. Shortages of raw materials for industry caused shortfalls in industrial production. The failure of growth rate of the National Income to reach the target level of 5 per cent and of the rate of population growth to fall, kept the per capita income at the end of the Plan period at about the same level at which it was at the beginning of the Plan. The Plan failed to check the continuous rise in the price level. This trend started with the Second Five Year Plan, received an upward thrust during and after the War with China, and has since been on the increase. Upto 1962-63 the rise was moderate but after this it became sharper. In 1965-66 the general index of the wholesale prices was 32 per cent higher than 1960-61. In respect of foodgrains it was 48.4 per cent higher.

Too much emphasis put on meeting the financial outlay of the Plan, led to the largest amount ever of deficit financing—Rs 2,133 crore and sluggish agricultural output, led to inflationary pressures on the economy. A rise in the level of imports to Rs 1,335.3 crore in the final year of the Plan, and fall of exports to a level of Rs 781.8 crore, gave rise to a serious balance of payments crisis. The pressure of foreign powers and international agencies forced the Indian Government to devalue the rupee. It was expected that this step would improve the level of exports but this did not happen, and the economy deteriorated further. The Planning Commission summing up the position at the end of the Third Plan period, attributed the poor performance to 'unfavourable weather conditions which gave a serious setback to agricultural production, failure to take preparatory action, delays in finalizing schemes, time taken in negotiating foreign assistance and obtaining equipment, hangover of certain shortfalls in the Second Plan, aggression on our borders and the long gestation period and phasing for most of the projects and programmes'.

The year 1967, was a year of great political turmoil. There were dissensions and factional quarrels in the Congress Party in all states. Due to defections from it, an anti-Congress combine of the opposition parties, the Congress Governments fell in several states. The

Communists came into power in West Bengal. The DMK was
firmly established in Tamil Nadu. With the rise to power of SVD
Governments in Punjab, Haryana, Uttar Pradesh, Bihar, Orissa and
Madhya Pradesh, the prestige of the Congress was at its lowest
and the power of the Central Government where Congress had a
precarious majority, had dwindled like that of Bahadur Shah under
the Moguls. All the powers—financial and others—that the Central
Government enjoyed were needed and deployed during the ensuing
years to topple the non-Congress Governments in the States. They
were used with deftness and cunning, and the proverbial carrot and
stick approach was made use of, to bundle the non-Congress Governments out of power, without any regard to the purity or otherwise
of the means employed. The Central Government had during this
period, little or no time to spare for the economic development of
the country.

The Third Five Year Plan ended on 31 March 1966 only three
months after Indira Gandhi became Prime Minister and the
Fourth Plan should have commenced on 1 April 1966. A draft out-
line was in fact prepared and brought out in August 1966, but its
finalization was deferred due to political instability, a bad drought,
and severe strains in the economy. The country was put on a Plan
Holiday. In the first of the 'Annual Plan' years, the weather conditions were bad, the foodgrain production only 76 million tons and
the increase in income only 1.1 per cent. In the second year, the
foodgrain production due to a good monsoon, was 98 million tons.
Both during the first and the second years, there was a serious
deceleration of industrial production. In the third year (1968-69)
there was some recovery of industrial production but the production of foodgrains was 3 million tons less than in the previous year.
In all three years the prices continued to rise, though there was
some respite in the closing months of 1968-69. During 1966-67,
wholesale prices rose by 16 per cent and prices of foodgrains by 18 per
cent, and the consumer price index rose from 169 in 1965-66 to 191
in 1966-67. During 1967-68 wholesale price index rose further by
11 per cent and of foodgrains by 21 per cent. The consumer index
rose to 213 per cent as compared with 191 for 1966-67. In September
1967, the Planning Commission was reconstituted with Prof. D.R.
Gadgil as the Deputy Chairman. In view of the precarious state of
the economy, the Commission decided to defer the Fourth Plan for
another year and start it from 1969-70. The year 1969 was, however,

a most eventful year—the year of the "Great Divide," for the Congress Party. The Syndicate leaders were worsted in the fight and two Congresses—the Congress R and the Congress O came into being. The Presidential Candidate of the Congress was Sanjivya Reddy, whose name was incidentally proposed by the Prime Minister herself, who later decided not to back him. He lost to V.V. Giri who contested as an independent. People thought that the elimination of the Right wing from the Congress would set the Congress on a socialist path and lead to an adoption of a radical programme, and amelioration of the lot of the weaker sections. The nationalization of the 14 big commercial banks and the announcement of a 10 point programme of development at the Bombay session of the AICC, raised the hopes of the common man and were flaunted as socialist measures by the Government and the party in power. But were they really? The 10 point programme was never implemented and the major part of the bank credit continued to be cornered by the big bourgeoisie.

The broad objectives of the Fourth Plan were "growth with stability" and "the progressive achievement of self-reliance". These were proposed to be achieved through accelerating the tempo of economic development and economic stability by stabilising foodgrain prices, reducing dependence of foreign aid, preventing concentration of economic power and regional imbalances, and promoting social justice and equality of employment opportunities. The targets set were modest—an annual rate of growth of 5.7 per cent per annum, an annual increase of agricultural production by 5 per cent, industrial production by 8-10 per cent and exports by 7 per cent.

The set-back to the economy since the mid-sixties can be assessed from the fact that the aggregate real national income in 1968-69, the last year of the "plan holiday" was less than that envisaged for 1965-66 or the rate of the growth postulated in the Third Plan. The Fourth Plan, when it was launched, therefore, had to make a start from a very feeble base.

According to Balraj Mehta, the trend for productive investment which had been continuously rising during the First Three Plans, was interrupted for the first time in 1966-67. The investment for this year was less than that in 1963-64. 'Domestic savings as percentage of net domestic product (at market prices) which increased from 8.6 per cent in 1961-62 and 12 per cent in 1965-66, showed a sharp decline in the subsequent years and could recover only to 11 per cent by 1970-71. The ratio of net investment to net domestic product, which reached a level of 14.7 per cent in 1965-66, declined to 10.8 per cent in 1969-70 and had picked up only to 12 per cent in 1971-72. Development expenditure which, in 1965-66 formed 59.4 per cent of the total expenditure of the Central Government, declined to 57.1 per cent during the three years, 1966-69, and further to 46.6 per cent in 1971-72, and to just 46 per cent in 1973-74. The share of capital formation expenditure in the total which stood at 47 per cent in the Third Plan came down to 3 per cent in 1973-74. The rate of growth of industrial production also reached its peak in 1966, averaging 9.3 per cent a year during the six years, 1960-66. During this period a modest rise in prices was experienced. But it was also the period when industrial workers saw their real wages moving upwards. The average rate of annual growth in industrial production in the next six years, however, slumped to 4.5 per cent. The cumulative effect of slow development, lower investment and poor capital formation, was the emergence of all round shortages and severe inflationary conditions.[33] The drastic price rise and the acute shortages that resulted between 1972-74 were the indirect outcome of reckless spending of the resources in current consumption and unproductive development by the government, and of the use of resources including bank credits for building inventories, hoarding and speculating in commodities in short supply by the private sector. The consequent imbalances and distortions in the economy gave rise to an unparalleled increase of more than 50 per cent in the wholesale price index during the two years under consideration.

The growth rate of economy between 1964-65 and 1973-74 was hardly 2.5 per cent, about the same as the growth rate in the population. But during the same period the amount of money supply increased by nearly 10.4 per cent per annum. During the three years 1971-72 to 1973-74, national income rose by 7 per cent but the money supply increased by 54 per cent. Monetary expansion of this magnitude had no relation whatever to development expenditure or production requirements of the economy in the public or the private sectors.

Even for the reduced levels of development the government depended on additional taxation and deficit financing which reached a peak level of Rs 1,147 crore in 1972-73. If the extra resources

[33]Ibid.

raised by the government had been invested and used for productive purposes and if the resources placed at the disposal of the private sector had not been frittered away in building inventories, hoarding and speculation, but used instead for expanding production, the economy would have picked up but this was not done. It was 'a losing struggle all along the line in savings, investment and development for nearly a whole decade'.[34]

The populist governmental policy following the Congress split and the series of subsequent concessions to influential groups which directly encouraged current consumption at the cost of capital formation, two years of drought, the influx of 10 million refugees on the eastern border, the Indo-Pakistan War, the large deficit financing with the consequent expansion of money supply, the persistence of price rise in the midst of growing unemployment, the impact of the Third Pay Commission, the cost of subsidising the take-over of foodgrains, the claims of the State Governments for greater Central assistance to bail them out of their near bankrupt position, the disregard for plan-budget linkage and ad hoc special allocations for the educated-unemployed for advance action on the Fifth Plan— all contributed to a serious erosion of the real income of the common man and a state of privation which defied solution.

The mid-term appraisal of the Fourth Plan showed grave shortfalls in its implementation. Instead of these being rectified as was hoped for, the Plan ended with even bigger shortfalls. This was the first occasion that a Five Year Plan closed with a cut in the development budget in its final year. 'The budget for the last year of the Plan and its structure, was a reflection of the dead end that had been reached'.[35]

The miserable plight of the Indian economy towards the close of the Fourth Plan period, was spotlighted by the resignation of Dr B.S. Minhas from the Planning Commission. The impression that was sought to be created was, that Minhas did not favour the projected 5.5 per cent growth rate for the Fifth Plan and wanted the Plan to aim at a lower growth rate. This was, however, not the issue as Minhas made clear in the note on the Draft Fifth Plan he submitted prior to this resignation.[36] He said that the choice was

[34]Ibid.
[35]Ibid.
[36]The Note was laid on the Table of the Lok Sabha on 27 February 1974.

not between 'a big plan and a small plan', and that he was 'in favour of having as big a plan as would seem feasible and consistent with our immediate as well as long-run socio-economic objectives'. He said that the Fifth Plan in its present form was unrealistic, unfeasible and not capable of being implemented. The arguments he gave in favour of his assertion, were irrefutable:

1. In the Approach Document, the total resources availability, he said, was Rs 51,165 crore split into Rs 35,595 crore for the public and Rs 15,570 crore for the private sector, on the basis of 1972-73 tax rates and 1971-72 prices. In the Draft Document, the estimated resources were raised to Rs 53,411 crore consisting of Rs 37,250 crore for public and Rs 16,161 crore for the private sector on the basis of 1973-74 tax rates and 1972-73 prices when the rupee had lost 30 per cent of its value between the two periods. Minhas asked, how was this possible?

2. The Draft Plan assumed the availability of foreign assistance to be larger by Rs 1,008 crore, commercial credits by 200 crore and fresh resource mobilization by Rs 235 crore. Minhas did not consider these increases realistic.

3. In the Draft Plan the household savings were shown as Rs 35,579 crore as compared with Rs 24,069 crore in the Approach Document. The manner in which the objective circumstances in the country had changed in the past one year were likely to be prejudicial to the growth of savings rather than add to them.

4. It was desired to achieve a growth rate of 5.5 per cent with an investment of Rs 51,165 crore at 1971-72 prices. How was it possible he asked, to achieve the same result with the same amount of investment a year later when the rupee was 30 per cent less than its previous value?

5. The balance of payments situation was alarming and the trade gap estimated at Rs 378 crore in 1974-75, he said, would in fact amount to Rs 488 crore.

6. The estimates of the foreign exchange requirements for 1974-75 were in his opinion a gross understatement due to the rise in the prices of crude and nitrogen.

7. There was a gross overestimate in respect of the availability of foreign aid of upward of Rs 1,000 crore in 1974-75. He asked, even if this aid was available, was it consistent with "the neat objective of zero net aid by 1978-79"? And would it not deplete the foreign exchange reserves within the very first year of the Fifth

Plan and also force the government into further dependence on aid givers?

Minhas did not stand for a lower growth rate or for lowering the sights. All that he was saying was that the Draft Plan was unrealistic, that the targets it laid down were impossible of achievement, and that shortfalls in achieving the targets, would totally destroy the credibility of planning in the country. In fact this is precisely what happened. Minhas' predictions were proven to the hilt and the planners were for a second time on a plan holiday.

In 1973-74 the country was facing a very serious crisis. A quarter of a century of tinkering with land reforms and problems of agricultural development on the one hand, and mismanagement of industry on the other, had brought the country to the brink of ruin. War with Pakistan and care of 10 million refugees from what is now Bangladesh, had put heavy strains on the exchequer. Displeasure of the weather God and failure of two successive monsoons shattered the economy further and led to acute scarcity and shortages of foodgrains and other essential consumer goods. The situation was exploited by anti-social elements—rich farmers, traders, merchants, industrialists, hoarders, black-marketers, smugglers and corrupt officials and politicians including senior Cabinet Ministers. The prices soared and hyper-inflation became insufferable. There were lay-offs and strikes and the level of general and educated unemployment rose high. Price hiks and loss of buying power aggravated the misery of the common man. There were food riots, gheraos and frequent bandhs. The country was rocked by Nagarwala, Maruti, Tulmohan Ram, Gulabi Chana, Bajra, Rice-seed and other scandals —each one of them bigger than the Watergate scandal that pushed Nixon out of the White house. The non-fulfilment of the Congress promises of the "Garibi Hatao" days had replaced the Indira wave by an Indira Hatao wave. She came to be regarded as the "Gangotri of corruption" and people's fingers were pointed at Bansilal, Sanjay and herself as the trio responsible for the economic ills in which the country was engulfed. Fierce attacks were daily mounted on them in the Parliament, State Legislatures and the press.

In 1973 the State of Gujarat had one of the worst monsoon failures and passed through a severe drought. There were numerous starvation deaths and thousands of cattle perished for want of fodder. The State Government, which should have arranged supplies for the stricken people, failed to discharge its duties and came down with a heavy hand on those who clamoured for food. Food riots were quelled with lathi charges and bullets. The people, especially the students and youth became restive. The Nav Nirman Samity gave a call for the dissolution of the State Assembly and the resignation of the State Ministry. Jaya Prakash Narayan, Morarji Desai, L.K. Advani and other leaders joined their powerful voices to those of the people of Gujarat. On 10 January 1974, life in Ahmedabad was paralysed by a bandh in protest against shortages of food and other essential goods, price hikes and corruption. Morarji Desai had to resort to a fast unto death to compel the Centre to advice the Chief Minister to resign. President's rule was imposed on Gujarat on 8 February 1974.

The Jan Sangh President, L.K. Advani, in his Presidential address at the Jan Sangh session in April 1974, said 'The Gujarat happenings were the result of inflation, corruption and youth frustration. It was the explosion of the people's anger, not so much against a situation as against a system under which the collusion of corrupt politicians and hoarders was starving them of food. . . . And such collusion and allied practices were by no means confined to Gujarat'.

From Gujarat trouble travelled to other States in the country. In Bihar the turmoil started first over student disabilities. Their main grievances were favouritism in admissions, nepotism in appointment of teachers, lack of recreational, library and hostel facilities, rising cost of education and paucity of jobs after completion of education. As the authorities failed to provide any redress, the trouble readily spread to the general public. Student's Action Committee and Jan Sangharsh Samities were formed and a Statewide movement for educational reform, eradication of corruption and electoral reforms was launched under the guidance of Jaya Prakash Narayan. There were peaceful demonstrations and strikes by the students, and statewide meetings, processions, gheraos and bandhs by the public, asking for recall of elected representatives who had failed in their duty, dissolution of the State Assembly, and resignation of the Council of Ministers. The Bihar Government's reply to the popular outburst was abrogation of civil rights and repression. Public meetings and processions were broken up by use of tear gas, lathi charges and even police firings. Many people including students lost their lives. A 5-member Citizen's Committee was set up by J.P. Narayan to inquire into police firing in Gaya on 12 April 1974.

Another 7-member Committee of Enquiry of eminent Indians including Minoo Masani and A.G. Noorani, was set up by him on 20 April 1974, to inquire into police firings, damage to property and violations of civil liberties in the wake of student's agitation on 18 March 1974. On 31 July a no-tax campaign was launched in Bihar. This marked the beginning of a new phase in a 5-month old agitation for dissolution of Bihar Assembly and in protest against rising prices, high-level corruption and mounting unemployment. Student's action committees and Jan Sangharsh Samitis offered dharnas before wine shops, and Satyagraha and dharnas were offered before all places from where government got licence fees and taxes.

As the economic situation in the country deteriorated, drastic measures to crub inflationary pressures were enforced through two Ordinances promulgated by President V.V. Giri on 6 July 1974. The measures included strict credit squeeze, wage and D.A. freeze, restrictions on issue of bonuses, CDS, and ceilings on dividends. On 17 September 1974, a MISA Ordinance against smugglers came into force. Numerous smugglers who had amassed millions like Haji Mastan, Bakhia and Yusuf Patel, were held. In an interview with Shamim Ahmed Shamim in the Illustrated weekly of India, Haji Mastan made no secret of his link up with high police, customs and other officials, and politicians including ministers. The Minister of State for Finance, K.R. Ganesh who was entrusted with the task of liquidating them, probably took his job more seriously than Indira Gandhi wanted. He was soon shifted from the post of the Minister of State for Finance to the Ministry of Petro-chemicals where he became a thorn in the side of foreign International giants engaged in the pharmaceutical industry in the country. The fervour with which he carried out his new duty, soon deprived him of this new ministerial post. The present author who was associated with him as the Chairman of the National Convention for Independence and Perspectives of Drug Industry, had warned him, months before he was eased out. As T.A. Pai, Union Minister of Industries in Indira Gandhi's Cabinet—in a blistering attack he made on the mother and son—revealed, the black money circulating in the country, was the inevitable outcome of the policies the Government pursued.[37]

The movement which began in Gujarat and gathered great strength in Bihar, spread all over India and especially in Uttar

[37]T.A. Pai. 5 and 6 May 1977, A.I.C.C. Session, New Delhi.

Pradesh, Delhi, Punjab and Haryana. The Government used brutal repression to stem it. The date for J.P's historic Peace March on Patna was fixed for 4 November 1974. More than a million people were expected to participate. The Central and the State Governments became panicky and besides the Bihar Police, large contingents of Border Security Force and the Central Reserve Police went into action and prevented entry into Patna by bus, rail or air. The route of the processionists was barricaded at various points and hundreds of thousands of marchers who joined the rally, were tear gassed and lathi charged by the Central Reserve Police. Attempt was made on the life of Jaya Prakash Narayan and a CRP man nearly killed him. The lathi blow aimed at him was averted by a conscientious Bihar policeman and Nanaji Deshmukh. The Lok Naik received some lathi injuries on his shoulder but the attempt to murder him was foiled. Indira Gandhi denied the charge of assault in the Parliament but the Statesman photograph by Raghurai, gave the lie to her statement.

On 26 November 1974, leaders of opposition parties met in New Delhi to take stock of the situation and to plan future strategy. As a result of the deliberations, the opposition moved closer to each other and extended the movement to other States.

On 2 January 1974, L.N. Mishra, the Railway Minister—a close confident of Indira Gandhi—who had ruthlessly put down the Railway strike, was killed mysteriously in a bomb explosion at Samastipur in Bihar. His death is still shrouded in mystery.[38]

A number of Congressmen high-up in the Government or the Organization—men like Mohan Dharia, Chandra Shekhar or Krishna Kant—men who saw the justice of J.P's demands and not only wished to avoid a Government-J.P. confrontation but act as bridges between the two, incurred the leader's displeasure. Mohon Dharia had to resign from the Central Cabinet on 2 March 1975, following an intimation from her that she was dropping him. Chandrashekhar was expelled from the Congress Working Committee. On 18 March, Indira Gandhi appeared in the Allahabad High Court to defend the election petition filed against her. On 12 June 1975, for her the heavens fell. Justice Jagmohanlal Sinha found her guilty of corrupt practices.

[38]Mathew Report on the death of L.N. Mishra was submitted after Janata Party came into power but not satisfied with its findings. Mrs L.N. Mishra, her son and others are pressing for a new enquiry.

The judgement set aside her election to the Lok Sabha and debarred her from holding any elective office for six years.

Of the two counts on which she was held guilty, one was that she used the services of Yash Pal Kapoor, Officer on Special duty in her Secretariat, while he was still in Government Service. The judgement also found her guilty of obtaining assistance of State Government officials—the District Magistrate, the Superintendent of Police and the PWD engineer from hydel, for constructing a rostrum and other arrangements for the election meetings in Rae Bareli during the campaign.

Massive rallies were held and processions taken out from all parts of the country asking Indira Gandhi to resign. She should have gracefully accepted the verdict of the Court and stepped down, at least for the time being, till her appeal before the Supreme Court was decided. Many of her senior Cabinet colleagues advised her to do so. But Sanjay Gandhi, Bansilal and a few others advised her to stick on.

On 16 June, a deputation of 15 non-CPI opposition leaders waited on the President, Mr Fakhruddin Ali Ahmed who gave a sympathetic hearing to their plea for issuing a Presidential directive to Mrs Indira Gandhi 'to relinquish the office of the Prime Minister with immediate effect'. A 1,000 word memorandum presented to the President, reiterated the point that Mrs Gandhi 'had forfeited her moral and legal right' to continue as Prime Minister after the Allahabad High Court judgement which unseated her as member of the Lok Sabha and debarred her from contesting any election in the next six years on grounds of corrupt practices.

The memorandum charged her with mobilizing the support of Council of Ministers and the officials of the Central Government to keep up a campaign for her continuance in office and in the process encouraging demonstrations denigrating Mr Justice Jagmohanlal Sinha who pronounced the judgement against her. The massive rally of one million people led by Jai Prakash Narayan on 25 June in New Delhi demanding her resignation decided her to take a step which was to spell her disaster.

On 26 June 1975, a State of emergency was declared. The Sarvodaya Leader Jaya Prakash Narayan and the leaders of non-CPI opposition parties were whisked away to jails and all effective protest and dissent shut. The press was completely gagged and demoralized. High Court judges were superseded and transferred.

The powers of the courts were drastically curtailed. Recourse to legal remedies was denied. Legislatures were hamstrung in their functions with their presiding officers tamed into abject compliance. The Constitution was amended and subverted to pander to the needs of the Dictator. A different set of laws was enacted for the Prime Minister who could not be punished or challenged for anything she said or did in any court of law. Lawless laws worse than the Rowlatt Act were legislated. Dissent from any quarter was dealt by recourse to MISA. People were taken to police stations, tortured and beaten to death. Some like Rajan from Kerala never came back.[39] People were confined in solitary cells and subjected to all manner of torture. Lawrence, brother of George Fernandes, was birched and drubbed so cruelly in police custody and jail, that he became a ghost of his previous self. Jaya Prakash Narayan himself was kept in solitary confinement, denied all privacy and had to go through mental anguish far exceeding any inflicted on him during the British period.

As T.A. Pai in this speech at the AICC session said, Sanjay Gandhi was the virtual ruler of the country throughout the period of the emergency. The Cabinet Ministers, the State Ministers, the big officials both civil and military, and the industrial tycoons, shined his shoes and did his behest. Chief Ministers were pulled down and new ones installed in their places. High ranking officials in ministries, the Reserve Bank of India, airlines and other places were superseded, demoted or transferred, if they refused to further his financial interests. Newly built housing colonies, and shanty towns and slums were bulldozed and demolished at his pleasure. If people resisted they were taken care of under MISA. Some of them were shot down like dogs. In furtherance of his family planning drive programme, unthinkable atrocities were committed. In Uttar Pradesh, Punjab and Haryana, Harijans, landless labourers, poor peasants, construction workers, rickshaw pullers and others were forcibly taken to camps and sterilized. Many young people ran away from their homes and hid themselves in fields or forests, or went to

---

[39]Rajan was an engineering student, who was arrested, taken to a concentration camp and beaten to death. Karurakaran who was Home Minister in Achuta Menon's Ministry and later became the Chief Minister had to step down due to his inability to produce Rajan in court after the withdrawal of the emergency.

other states where forcible methods were not in evidence, to save themselves from the seizing parties. In Pipli, Haryana and in Sultanpur and Muzzaffarnagar, Uttar Pradesh, where people re-volted against forcible sterilisation, police resorted to firing and many lives were lost. In Muzaffarnagar a mini jallianwala Bagh was enacted. Houses and business premises of people who criticized Sanjay, Indira Gandhi or their hirelings, were raided, their properties seized and if they opened their lips in protest, their personal safety or freedom imperiled. Film stars and playback singers were harassed and punished if they failed to appear or entertain audiences at cultural shows organized in their honour. The police terror stalked the land. The rule of law was in a shambles. A thick pall of silence descended on the people.

In October 1974, three months after promulgation of two ordi-nances by President Giri to curb inflationary pressures, prices started coming down. The down-ward trend persisted for a period of 18 months when they again began to rise. This shows that neither the emergency nor Indira Gandhi's 20-point programme had any-thing to do with the arrest of inflation and the fall of prices. If this were so, the prices would have continued to fall for the full period the emergency lasted. But this did not happen.

The public sector enterprises which had previously always re-mained in the red, for the first time earned profits in 1972-73. Following "efficient professional management" and industrial peace during the emergency, the public sector performances improved. In 1976-77 the World Bank in a discreetly worded report gave faint praise to "strong financial stabilization of efforts" initiated by the Government. It gave India credit for scoring "a major success" in controlling inflation. The Bank's report stated that the success was attributable to a good monsoon, increased foreign financial sup-port and conservation of energy through the use of substitute fuels. The report was quick to add that 'while India seems to have weath-ered its short-term problems, it continues to face major long-term challanges'. The report made note of particular emphasis placed on "agriculture, energy and a large family planning programme" in the country. Continuing in its negative strain, however, it added that "few gains have reached the poor" and that improvement in the industrial sector had not matched success in the agricultural field.[40]

[40]M.V. Kamath. 22 September 1976. Times of India, New Delhi.

With the stabilisation of the prices, the National Development Council which was in a state of hibernation during all this period, met after three years on 24 September 1976, to finalize the Fifth Plan. The last meeting of the NDC was held on 8 and 9 December 1973, when the Draft Fifth Plan was approved. Addressing the meeting of the Council which was to approve the Plan on the following day, Mrs Gandhi said, 'our difficulties are by no means over, and that it was essential to exercise the strictest discipline in spending. No doubt the huge food buffer stock and foreign exchange situation looked well for the immediate future. But the long-term problem of raising the rate of domestic savings and investment remains as intractable as ever'.

Mr P. N. Haksar disclosed at a press conference that the Fifth Plan outlay of Rs 69,300 crore which was expected to generate an annual growth rate of 4.3 per cent was much larger in monetary terms than the outlay of Rs 53,250 crore in the Draft Plan, but in real terms it was somewhat smaller than the outlay of Rs 53,250 crore in the Draft Plan, owing to the price rise since the formulation of the Draft Plan.

Dr S. Chakravarty, Member of the Planning Commission, said that the Draft Plan goal of self-reliance and reducing net foreign aid to zero had been given up. This was because of a 'very sharp deterioration in the country's terms of trade by almost 50 per cent since 1972-73. This deterioration had eroded the real value of net aid. Even though in monetary terms net aid expected in the Fifth Plan was put at Rs 5,400 crore against Rs 2,200 crore in the Draft Plan, it had less value in terms of balance of payments support. So zero net aid was "non feasible".

The Planners were forced to lower their sights from an annual rate of growth of 5.5 per cent to 4.3 per cent. The outlay of the Plan had been raised from Rs 53,250 crore to Rs 69,300 crore. The objective of net zero aid had been given the go-by. And the target of raising the consumption levels of the lowest three deciles of population by 60 per cent during the Fifth Plan period, had been thrown to the winds. Could Minhas have been more right in his criticism of the Draft Plan?

A 1976 review of the economy,[41] despite the apparently pleasing economic scenerio-record foodgrain stocks with the government agencies, an expected growth rate of 11.5 of industrial production,

[41]D.P. Sharma. 21 October 1976. Times of India, New Delhi.

the excellent foreign exchange position with over Rs 2,000 crore of reserves, an appreciable increase in the rate of domestic saving and investment and a break through on the oil front—was not without a number of disturbing aspects which in fact were of a more fundamental nature. These included the lack of disposable incomes available to the masses, the unlikely improvement over the past years' record agricultural produce, the industrial landscape with mismanagement in a sick private sector, the upsurge in prices during the past half year and were all matters of serious concern requiring more than ordinary measures to energise the economy during the remaining period of the Fifth and any subsequent plans.

VII

Dr B. S. Minhas has drawn a beautiful caricature of Congress socialism in practice: 'Socialistic intentions of independent India were pitted against outmoded attitudes of strongly feudal, and caste and status-conscious society, which was unwilling to accept a rigorous code of private as well as public behaviour implied in the concept of socialism. Indian socialism in practical terms turned out to be a pernicious programme for the administration of public largesse to the not-so-poor. The case for this characterisation of Indian socialism is based on pervasive evidence'.[42] The instances of public largesse to the richer sections that Minhas enumerates include examples from the construction and operation of public sector enterprises, construction of infrastructure facilities in the field of irrigation, power, transport etc., operation of a licensing system for control of investments and imports, or the distribution of food and fertilizers. He states that industries are overcapitalized and elaborate townships are provided and included in capital costs but the rents charged are uneconomic, that the pricing policies for the produce of public industries are not sound, that big dams, and irrigation and power projects are built at public cost and collection of development levies and proper irrigation and power rates forgotten, that food and fertilizers are distributed at prices far below costs, and that there is a big spurt in construction of big and luxurious houses in cities but no attempt to improve living conditions in the sprawling slums. Minhas makes an important point when he

[42]B.S. Minhas. 1974. *Planning and Poor*, New Delhi.

states that in India the Government for all practical purposes has always meant something alien to the society it governs. The people, therefore, consider themselves free to cheat the Government, to steal material from Government works, to dodge taxation, to avoid responsibility and to make use of public office for private ends. This he rightly attributes to the glaring failure of the process of political and social education. He states that the society is riddled with ossified, regressive social attitudes and to seek evidence for the inegalitarian attitudes, one does not have to go far. Right inside the Yojana Bhavan, where programmes for social democracy are formulated, one can see evidences of glaring inequality. Luxurious, air conditioned comfort is reserved for high civil servants and their bosses, while in the adjacent rooms, the clerical staff bang their cold fingers on type-writers in winter and smudge sheets of paper during the summer. Clean water and non-smelling urinals, he says, are welcome alike to the poor clerk and the big officer, but as one moves vertically upwards from the second floor to the third, fourth and fifth, the standards of sanitation deteriorate. This is true of all Bhavans in New Delhi. Car parks and toilettes bear signs such as 'For Officers Only'.

To drive his point home, Minhas relates an interesting story. He draws attention to an office order issued for the observance of two minute silence on Martyr's Day in the Transport Bhavan in 1969. It said that all officers with the rank of under-secretary or above, were to meet in the Secretary's room, all other officers in a second room and the rest in a hall. Instances of this type are common and can be multiplied ad infinitum.

Professor V.M. Dandekar in his Presidential Address to the Fifty-sixth All India Economic Conference held in December 1973, spoke scathingly of socialism having been "reduced to a slogan and a joke". He went on to warn that the main roadblock 'on the socialist path is the democratic power structure as it has emerged during the past 25 years'. For further progress towards socialism in his view, this power structure must be attacked at its source, demolished and removed from the way.

Delivering his S. Nijalingappa Endowment Lecture on 'Planning and Prices in India', early in 1974, Dr K.N. Raj made a pointed reference to the inherent snags in the present socio-economic system which impede progress. He expressed the deeply pessimistic view that 'equivocations and evasions of responsibility at almost all levels offers no hope of a reasonably smooth transition to a more civilised economic social system'. He went on to suggest that in today's conditions economists might well take a back seat for some time to their own and other's advantage. Most economic problems, he said had ceased to be amenable to the advice or intervention of experts. Their solution needed the support of forces that could emerge only through social and political processes.

The results of Indira Gandhi's 20-point economic programme that came into operation in the wake of the emergency were watched with great interest. To serious socialist thinkers, however, the programme was only peripheral in its scope and the central point— radical change in property relations—was completely overlooked. The programme was moreover never intended to be seriously implemented. The mere introduction of the word "socialism" in the preamble of the constitution did not delude the people into believing that socialism had come.

In a conversation reported in the press, Mr Zacharia, a minister in the Maharashtra State Government, while travelling in the same plane with Indira Gandhi humorously told her, 'Madame you have put all men in their proper places'. Judging from the behaviour of her cabinet colleagues and senior Congressmen in Delhi and the States, seasoned journalists, intellectuals and others, it appears she really had. At any rate she herself genuinely believed in their total depersonalization.

Early in 1977 Indira Gandhi decided to go to polls. The reasons that impelled her to do so were:

First, she thought that she had effectively crushed all opposition and she hoped she would be returned to the Parliament with an even bigger majority than she already had. Secondly, she could never believe that the non-CPI opposition parties like the Jan Sangh, the BLD and the Socialists with their disparate ideologies could even get together. Thirdly, she was wanting to repair and refurbish her international image which had suffered a severe set back. Fourthly, the prices had again begun to rise and in a period of nine months since March 1976, there was a price rise of 11.5 per cent. The food position was comfortable and the foreign exchange reserves large but the long term prospects of the economy were most unsatisfactory. Fifthly, Carter had hinted that unless the democratic processes were restored, the US Congress was sure to block aid by the world agencies. And lastly, emergency had lasted a long time and people were getting used to it.

But she had miscalculated. She had not gauged the mood of the people, and the resentment and anger that was building against her son, her close associates, her administration and herself. As soon as the elections were announced and the emergency relaxed, the pent up storm of anger and hatred burst all bounds and "Indira Gandhi that was India," lost even her own Rae Bareli seat.

T.A. Pai who was Minister of Industries in Indira Gandhi's Cabinet made a very interesting observation on her socialist professions. Speaking at a meeting of the AICC in New Delhi, he said, 'Indira Gandhi's socialism consisted in distributing of largesse to 20 per cent of the people in upper brackets'. A much harsher indictment of both the father and the daughter is made by James Cameron. He writes, 'the tragedy of the Nehrus has been on an almost classic pattern: They proclaimed and believed in principles of social democracy, and sustained and promoted their Party through the nastiest aspects of unbridled and dishonest capitalism. . . . Congress has been sustained by corruption for ever by the black money from the business houses who, as quid per quo, have been tacitly allowed to run their own parallel economy for their personal enrichment and the growing impoverishment of the people. This was the case even in Pandit Nehru's days. It was no secret that this honest man in his final weariness was well aware of the sycophancy and corruption that flourished but he was too vain to acknowledge it and too weak to fight it'.[43]

The Janata Party Government was installed in New Delhi in the last week of March 1977. In its election manifesto the Party promised to develop the country on Gandhian lines and to eradicate unemployment and poverty within a period of ten years. After a phenomenal success at the hustings, the Party leaders took a pledge at Gandhiji's Samadhi to work for a decentralized village economy and rural development.

Mr H.M. Patel's first budget introduced within a month of the take over, gave no indication of any such intention on the part of the government. It was no different from any of the previous Congress budgets and evoked criticism from all quarters. The Finance Minister was apologetic and said he had little time for the formula-

[43]James Cameron. 1977. Quoted by Janardan Thakur in All The Prime Minister's Men, Delhi.

tion of the budget proposals and moreover he could not terminate halfway many of the projects which had been launched by the previous government.

The Fifth Five year Plan (1974-79) was terminated, a year before its completion. The Draft of the Sixth Five Year Plan,—a rolling Plan was placed before the Parliament and a little later before the National Development Council. It has a total outlay of Rs 1,16,240 crore out of which Rs 69,380 crore are to be in the public sector. The Plan has been given a rural bias, and the outlay on agriculture and rural development is of the order of 43.1 per cent of the total outlay. The production of foodgrains is expected to increase from 121 to 141 million tons, oilseeds from 9.2 to 11.2 million tons and cotton from 64.30 lakh bales to 81.50 lakh bales. The annual growth stipulated for agriculture is 3.98 per cent, for industry and minerals 6.92 per cent, for electricity 10.80 per cent, for construction 10.55 per cent, for transport 6.24 per cent and for other services 6.01 per cent. The overall target for rate of growth is 4.7 per cent and it is expected that a potential of 5.5 per cent growth, will be built up by the end of the period. These objectives, however, have not been advanced by a single step even though the Party has been in power for two years.

People who expected much from H.M. Patel's second budget in March 1978, were sadly disappointed once again. It levied more indirect taxes which hurt the poor and showered numerous exemptions and concessions on the rich. It was a rich man's budget and brought no succor to the suffering indigent.

During the year that has elapsed since H.M. Patel's budget proposals were announced, no dent has been made on the unemployment situation, the rate of growth of population has shown no decline and the prices of essential items of food like the pulses and manufactured goods are spiralling upwards. In the countryside no relief has been afforded to the poorest sections of the people, and the atrocities on the Harijans and tribals have increased. In the urban areas there is an unprecedented increase of vice and crime, and a spate of protests, demonstrations, bandhs and strikes.[44]

Due to non-performance and poor performance of the Janata Government, the promised goal of humanist socialism remains as distant today as it was in Nehru's or Indira Gandhi's days.

[44]The third Janata budget by Charah Singh is a Kulak and richman's budget and hurts both rural and urban poor and middle classes.

SIX

Population

I

DEMOGRAPHIC EXPLOSIONS

The increase in numbers of Man over a period of millenniums and its relationship to the increase in the means of subsistence, has been described in three periods:

1. The period of Hunting and Food Gathering Man.
2. The period Following Agricultural Revolution.
3. The period Following Industrial Revolution.

For thousands and thousands of years the hunting and food gathering man, the predatory man, lived by hunting, fishing and gathering wild roots and fruits. He slept in caves and drank from streams. The population density during this period was extremely low, sometimes as low as one per square kilometer or two per square mile. The total population of the planet before Agricultural Revolution which occurred in the Near East sometime after the tenth millennium BC, has been placed between five and ten million people.[1] The small size of paleolithic societies has been attributed to a high death rate and a short span of life. Since, however, the species survived, the conclusion is reasonable, that early man had also a high fertility rate. From a study of the fossil remains Weidenreich concluded that death in most cases was the result of violence.[2] The conclusion is confirmed by Krzywicki in respect of Paleolithic man of historic time. He observes that the most frequent causes of death were infanticide, war and head hunting.[3] Illness and starvation were

[1]J. Huxley. 1957. New Bottle for New Wine, New York.
[2]F. Weidenreich. 1949. The Duration of Life of Fossil Man in China, New York.
[3]L. Krzywicki. 1934. Primitive Society and its Vital Statistics, London.

among the other causes that took a heavy toll of life. The sparse bands of hunters wandering over limited territories were immune to the ravages of contagious diseases and epidemics.

With the development of agriculture and the domestication of animals and as the Agricultural Revolution spread to different regions and continents, the population began to grow. The demographic growth that followed the Agricultural Revolution, usually found expression in—at least in the earlier period—an increase in number of settlements rather than in the increase in size of the individual units. In the course of time as technology improved and standards of living rose, population densities increased appreciably and large villages and towns appeared.

Agricultural societies before the Industrial Revolution were characterized by high birth rates which varied from 35 to 50 per 1,000 and also high death rates ranging generally between 30 and 40 per 1,000. The population of an agricultural society increased by a rate of growth between 0.5 and 1 per cent per year. The population increases did not attain the dimensions they would otherwise have, due to recurrent and catastrophic peaks of death rates caused by epidemics, famine and war. A high periodic catastrophic death rate in addition to a high death rate in normal times, is an index of a lack of adequate control over the environment and whenever agrarian populations grew at a rate out of proportion to the produce of the soil, the probability increased of sudden catastrophes. In normal times the high death rate was accounted for by high infant mortality (of 1,000 new born infants, 200-500 usually died within a year) and low expectancy at birth averaging between 20 and 35 years.

In agricultural societies of the past, man's total effort was needed to satisfy his most elementary needs—food, clothes and shelter. A very small minority of people engaged themselves in trade and centers where trade grew and flourished, developed into big and prosperous towns and cities. After the discovery of sea routes to India and America, maritime nations of Europe—Spain, Portugal, England, France and Holland—developed trade relations with countries of America, Asia and Africa and in course of time subjugated the people of the colonial countries. The wealth they plundered from these countries provided them the capital needed for transition from agricultural to industrial economies. The time during which English traders and Englishmen in general made large fortunes abroad coincided with the time the Industrial Revolution was set on foot.

Industrial societies differ from agricultural societies in a number of ways: 1 the per capita real income is higher, 2 there is more and better food for the mass of people, 3 the absolute amount spent on food is more but decreases as a percentage of the total amount expended by a person, 4 there is a general decline in the relative importance of the agricultural sector and other productive sectors tend to lose their dependence on agriculture, for instance the building industry substitutes cement and steel for timber and textile industry artificial fibers like rayon, dacron and terene etc. for natural ones, 5 there is decline both in the percentage of people employed in agriculture and the income derived from agricultural sector while expansion takes place in chemical, mechanical and metallurgical sectors, 6 population increases but production rises noticeably faster than population, 7 due to acquisition of new scientific knowledge and progress in medicine and sanitation, there is prevention of famines and epidemics, and almost total disappearance of the recurrent and catastrophic peaks of death-rate, 8 advances in medicine and sanitation, higher standards of living and better nutrition, help to eliminate many diseases and reduce the incidence of others, and the normal death-rate is also pushed down to around 15 per 1000, the most important component in the decline being a drastic reduction in infant mortality, 9 the average span of life is longer and the expectation at birth is 60 or over and 10 the birth rate too, eventually follows a downward trend but it adjusts to the fall of the death-rate with a time lag.

In each of the three types of societies—The hunting and food-gathering, the agricultural and the industrial—there exists at least potentially an equilibrium mechanism that controls population growth.[4] For the hunting, food-gathering societies, with allowance made for some taboo contraceptive practices and infanticide, the equilibrium consists of a high death-rate matching a high birth-rate. For the agricultural societies the mechanism generally consists of a high and highly fluctuating death-rate that checks a high but more stable birth-rate. The death-rate is normally lower and the population tends to increase but eventually catastrophic peaks of death-rate level the population size. For industrial societies, the mechanism is a loose, equilibrating adjustment of birth-rate to a very low death-

[4]Carlo M. Cipolla. 1965. The Economic History of World Population. England.

rate. There is, according to Cipolla, long-run incompatibility of noticeably divergent fertility rates and death-rates. It should be borne in mind, however, that the equilibrating mechanisms are never altogether rigid and both birth and death-rates have a range of possible variation.

The demographic explosions that accompanied both the Agricultural and Industrial Revolutions, were different, in many respects. In agricultural societies the starting point was a high birth-rate of 35-55 per 1,000 and a high normal death-rate of 30-40 per 1,000 combined with a highly fluctuating (150-300-500 per 1,000) death-rate. With the Industrial Revolution the high, recurrent death peaks tended to disappear. Due to the impact of improved standards of living, and more balanced and nutritious diets the 'normal death-rates' also declined. The birth-rate too showed an eventual, equilibrating downward trend but it adjusted to the death-rate with a time lag. The extent, however, of this time lag was considerable and during this period a demographic explosion was bound to occur. With improvements in educational and living standards, the age of marriage was deferred, contraceptive practices found favour with the masses and the birth-rate was brought down. An equilibrium was established but at a higher absolute level.

This is precisely what happened in England and Europe where the Industrial Revolution started. Despite migration from the parent country, England's population grew at a rapid pace from 10.5 million in 1801 to 37 million in 1901. After 1875, the rate of growth began to decline and with this the increase in population also began to fall. By the end of the nineteenth century, due to introduction of the Factory and the Education Acts, children under the age of 14, were no longer a source of income. Other factors that decided people to opt for small families were, 1 the insecurity of industrial life with the accompanying risks of unemployment and sickness at a time when there was no social insurance, 2 the desire for better standards of life, 3 the emancipation of women of better educated classes looking for careers, and 4 the desire and the pride to belong, as small families became fashionable. During the economic slump of the 1930s when unemployment was at its height due to late marriages and widespread use of contraceptives, it looked that England's population would undergo rapid decline but the fears were unfounded and after World War II, the population picked up again.

The first "demographic explosion" of the Industrial Revolution abated toward the end of the nineteenth century. It abated as the reduction of birth-rates is in some way related to a substantial improvement in the standard of living and also because the people of Europe where the explosion occurred, had the "empty" and the "underdeveloped" continents to colonize.

With the liberation after World War II of the colonized and subject peoples of the world, a second—a more violent and more widespread population explosion—is now ongoing. This explosion differs from the European explosion in many important respects: 1 it operates from a very large base. The existing population of the world is at present 4 billion, 2 the annual growth-rate in densely populated areas of the world is from 2.5 to over 3 per cent, 3 rates of growth are quite high in U.S.A., U.S.S.R. and several other developed countries, 4 there are no new countries or continents to which people from over-populated, lands can migrate, 5 living and educational standards in over-populated, underdeveloped countries are low and militate against lowering of birth rate or accumulation of capital and improvement of the standards of living. If the capital-output ratio is set at 3, then with a population growth of 2 per cent per annum, 6 per cent of the net income has to be invested only to maintain the previous level of living for the increased population. If the rate of population growth is 3 per cent per annum, 9 per cent of the national income has to be invested to reach the same result. The higher the rate of population growth, the more difficult it becomes to improve the living standards. A vicious cycle comes into operation. Because of high rates of population growth, industrialization, is difficult to obtain. Because there is no industrialization, the birth-rate and the rate of population growth remain high, 6 many of these countries have "agricultural" birth rates and "industrial" death-rates with the result that the "demographic explosion" is bound to assume alarming proportions.

About the year 10,000 BC, the total world population was between 5-10 million. After the Agricultural Revolution and its diffusion and spread, the world population rose, and in the year 1750 AD it was between 650 and 850 million. When the Industrial Revolution set in, the first demographic explosion pushed the population to 1200 to 1300 million in 1850 and to a much higher figure by the end of the century. With the spread of industrial revolution, however, a second and more serious population explosion has been now set into motion.

The world population touched the 4 billion figure in 1975 and the projected figure for the year 2,000 AD is 6.5 billion.

II

THE GROWTH OF POPULATION IN INDIA

(*a*) *The size and the Rate of Growth.* In Akbar's reign (1600 AD), India's population is said to have been about 100 million. During the subsequent three centuries, due to the presence of positive checks—epidemics, famines, wars, infanticide and absence of widow remarriage and consequent high death' rates, the population grew only very slowly. In 1921, the population of undivided India was only 250 million, in 1931 it was 279 million and in 1941, 319 million. In 1951 divided India's population was 361 millon. In 1961 it rose to 431 million and at the next census in 1971, it was as high as 548 million. This shows that the population more than doubled itself between the early 1920s and 1971. At the present time the population figure is around 620 million and if it continues to grow at this rate, it will be around 920 million in the year 2000 AD. In 1971 the rate of increase of population growth was 2.48 and today it is higher still.

(*b*) *Death-rate.* The death-rate in India has rapidly declined after 1931,due mainly to advances in medicine and the development and use of new and effective drugs in the treatment of infective diseases which previously took a heavy toll of life. The decline in mortality as Gunnar Myrdal[6] points out,has been particularly pronounced for infants. He considers that the fall is largely "autonomous" and unrelated to 'any preceding or concomitant rise in incomes and levels of living'. Death-rates of over 40 per 1,000 declined by 1961 to 22.8 per 1,000 and to 18.1 per 1,000 by 1971. The expectation of life at birth has increased from 32 to 56 but is still much less than that in the developed countries.

(*c*) *Birth-rate.* With the decline of the death-rate to 18 per 1,000 and the continuance of the old birth-rate, India is passing through a depressing and a calamitous "population explosion". Efforts to reverse the birth-rate, in spite of some expenditure and a campaign for family planning by the Indian Government, have so far met with small success. During the First Five Year Plan (1951-56), an amount

[5]A.J. Carlson. 1955. Journal of the American Medical Association.
[6]Gunnar Myrdal. 1970. The Challenge of World Poverty, London.

of Rs 60 lacs was spent on the Family Planning Programme. During the second and the third plan periods the expenditure was stepped up to Rs 3 crore and Rs 27 crore respectively. But by 1970 the reduction in birth-rate from 41.4 to 39.9 per 1,000, was only marginal. In keeping with the objective of reducting the birth-rate to 32 per 1,000 by 1974, the outlay on family planning was increased to Rs 315 crore in the Fourth Five Year Plan. The Planning Commission target, however, could not be achieved and the birth-rate was reduced only to 35.5 per 1,000 at the end of the Fourth Plan Period. The outlay provided in the Fifth Plan was of the magnitude of Rs 516 crore and the birth rate target 25 per 1,000.

We shall now consider briefly, those parameters which have an influence on the birth-rate. These are: (*i*) the death-rates, (*ii*) the age of marriage, (*iii*) urbanization, and (*iv*) standard of living.

(*i*) *The Death-rates.* According to Robert Cassen[7] in under-developed countries there is 'continuation of high death rates and no social security, or, to put it in another way, the desire of parents is to ensure that some at least of their children will survive as long as they themselves do'. The same view is expressed by Walter Elkan[8] who states, 'in low income countries children are an insurance for old age'. He asks, 'in the absence of governmental system of social insurance who else other than today's children will look after the old'? 'A high child mortality rate', says Myrdal,[9] 'is generally assumed to be one of the factors upholding fertility. If more children were to survive, parents would be less eager to give birth to additional children'.

(*ii*) *The age of Marriage.* Postponement of the age of marriage of girls from 16 to 20 or more and of the men from 22 to 25 or more, can make an effective reduction in the birth-rate. This was observed in England in the 1930s when during the worst ever economic crisis and high level of unemployment couples opted for late marriage and in Japan after the War where marriage age of 22 among girls, coupled with other measures (legalized abortion) brought down the rate of population increase to 1 per cent.

(*iii*) *Urbanization.* Marital fertility and birth-rates are somewhat

[7]Robert Cassen, in Aspects of Indian Economic Development. Ed. Chaudhury Pramit, 1971. London.
[8]Walter Elkan. 1973. An Introduction to Development, London.
[9]Ibid.

higher in rural areas than in urban but the rural urban population distribution in India has remained essentially unchanged from 1951 onwards. According to the 1961 census, 18 per cent of the total population of India belonged to the urban group. By 1971 this figure increased to 20 per cent—an increase of only 2 per cent in ten years. Urbanisation of this magnitude can hardly make any dent on the birth-rate and the size of the population.

(*iv*) *Standard of Living.* Where there are no food shortages and diets are adequate and balanced, where sanitation and medical facilities are good, where people are not illiterate and ignorant and have a high level of education, where women are emancipated and engaged in business, service or professions and do not wish to be burdened with bearing and rearing large families, where people are desirous of a better standard of life for themselves and their children, married couples favour the use of contraceptive practices and opt for small families. Under such circumstances the birth-rates decline. Where on the other hand, people are steeped in ignorance and poverty, where the food is insufficient in calories and poor in quality, where per capita incomes are small and the standard of living low, families are large and no saving or capital accumulation is possible, to break the vicious cycle of poverty leading to high birth-rates and high birth-rates aggravating poverty.

Having considered the effects of lack of social security, age of marriage and living standards on the birth-rate, let us now discuss briefly how in under-developed countries like India birth-rates influence employment, dependence and economic growth.

1. Employment. In a country like India plagued with a high level of unemployment and under-employment, a high birth-rate compels large numbers to join the growing army of the unwilling unemployed. At the beginning of the First Five Year Plan, India had a considerable back log of the unemployed and the under-employed, both in the rural and urban sectors. As a result of high birth-rates, this back log, in spite of the developments in agricultural, industrial and other sectors, has not only, not been reduced but has actually become much larger at the end of each plan period. In the agricultural sector, with the growth of population, the land-man ratio has declined and there is considerable pressure on land. This gives rise to disguised unemployment and a reduced per capita productivity. The increased consumption of food by a larger rural population eliminates the saving which could have

accrued if there were less mouths to feed. There is little or no capital formation to invest and no improvements can be made to permit higher yields. The economy gets bogged down.

With free primary education in the village, many who finish school and consider themselves surplus for the small holding of land that the family owns, or expect to get a higher wage outside, migrate for jobs to the towns. Expansion of education in the urban areas turns out a fairly large number of people from the schools, polytechnics, colleges and universities every year. The numbers that pass out each year are much larger than the number of jobs in industry, or private or government departments. The number of unemployed and under-employed goes on increasing.

2. Dependence Growth. With high birth-rates the age structure of the population takes up the shape of a broad based pyramid with more than 40 per cent of the population under the age of fifteen.[10] This age group is idle and non-productive, as are people over the age of 59 and unemployed people between the ages of 15 and 59. According to the 1961 census, these three groups together add up to 57 per cent of the total population of India and are non-productive, and dependent, on 43 per cent of the active people between the ages of 15 and 59 years. This is too high a percentage of dependents on the working population and has many adverse effects on the economy. Ansley J. Coale and Edger M. Hoover[11] draw attention to the time profile of benefits that accrue from a population control policy after the onset of decline in fertility in a population in which the dependency ratio is high. They do so by comparing the changes in per capita income level in two countries which are equal to begin with. One country then continues with the initial high fertility rate, whereas the other reduces the fertility rate gradually and halves it within a period of 25 years. As soon as the birth-rate falls, the age structure of the population begins to alter; the population in the active group begins to increase relatively to the dependent group. If the productivity per head in the active group does not decline, the per capita income will rise, firstly, because there are fewer people to share the income, and secondly, because the total output

[10]Not all children under the age of 15 are inactive in India, though many are.
[11]Ansley J. Coale and Hoover, Edgar M 1958. *Population Growth and Economic Development in Low Income Countries*, London.

has been raised by the relative increase in the size of the active population.

Moreover the decline in the number of children will immediately begin.to release some resources and the savings and investments will increase. The precise level will depend on public policy and parsimony. More capital accumulation and investment will provide work for a larger labour force and further increase output per head.

When depleted children groups grow up to adult age, there would be a decline in the relative number of people in the reproductive age group and the favourable composition of the population would be stabilized.

III

SOLUTION

India has made some progress in the development of both her agricultural and industrial sectors but the progress has not been enough. Secondly, whatever progress has been made, has been annulled by a corresponding or greater increase of population. The GNP has increased but the per capita income has not shown any significant gain. Moreover, the per capita income is only an average and does not indicate the abject poverty and deprivation of the lowliest and the lost. The rich have grown richer and the poor have become poorer.

To solve India's population problem both the economic growth and the demographic measures need to be stepped up at a much faster rate than has hitherto been possible.

The Economic Solution. The economic solution lies in increasing the means of subsistence at a higher rate than the rate of growth of the population.

Most experts and all knowledgeable persons believe that this solution is central to all others and an improvement in the standard of living is an essential condition for the limitaion of births or at least a very favourable factor.[12]

India's population is growing at a rapid rate of 2.5 per cent. If the capital output ratio is 3.1, approximately 8 per cent of the annual income must be saved and invested to maintain the present rate of growth. If the standard of living has to be raised, the saving

[12]Ibid.

should be of the magnitude of 16 to 20 per cent of the annual income and must be rightly invested—the right kind of investment implies that its urban bias must be ended and the economy oriented to meet the needs of 80 per cent of the country's population that lives in the countryside. The per capita income in India is distressingly small (Rs 341 at 1960-61 prices) and is no indication of the abject poverty of the lowest deciles. The number of people, however, with small purchasing power, is enormous. This vast market is of people who can buy simple and cheap, manufactured goods. The standard of living of these masses will rise only if our economy is diverted from its present production of luxury goods for 1 per cent of its elite to the manufacture of simple and cheap articles which 99 per cent of our people with their very small and limited incomes can buy. With the rise in the standard of their living, the birth-rates are bound to fall as they have done elsewhere.

The Demographic Solution. On the basis of the estimates for the cost per prevented birth and the returns on conventional investment Enke[13] has made an astounding deduction.

'If economic sources of given value were devoted to retarding population growth rather than accelerating production growth, the former resources could be 100 or so time more effective in raising per capita income in many less developed countries'.[13]

Cassen[14] using a different approach, estimates the effects of a programme which would effectively reduce the 1975 population of India by 40 million over a period of ten years and compares the alternatives of 630 million and 590 million people. The net gain of per capita income when the population is 630 million, is Rs 1.5, whereas the net gain per capita income from birth control (Population 590 million), is Rs 30 representing a return of more than 15 times.

Ohlin too is deeply impressed with the low economic costs of the family planning programmes and states that 'population control might bring the dawn of sustained economic growth within sight of the developing countries'.[15]

Difficulties of Family Planning in India. The subject has been extensively discussed by Gunnar Myrdal[16] in "The Challenge of

[13]S. Enke. 1966. The Economic Aspect of Slowing Population Growth, Economic Journal.
[14]Ibid.
[15]G. Ohlin. Population Control and Economic Development, Paris, 1967.
[16]Ibid.

World Poverty." The principal difficulties that may be encountered in the implementation of a family planning programme are:

1. The populations which have the greatest need to practice birth control—the illiterate and ignorant, the tradition bound and the poor villager—are the ones among whom no one has ever seen it practiced before.

2. The population problem is controversial. The Catholic church is opposed to it. The Communists take the line that birth control is not necessary if a determined development policy is carried out. The Muslims[17] in India are interested in increasing their numbers relative to the majority community and have recently expressed their views against the practice of birth control. The Buddhists and the Jains equate birth control with destruction of life and like Catholics, regard the practice sinful. The Hindus, like the other religious communities in India, believe in prarabdha Karma and have solicitude about a practice that offers to free people from their appointed destiny. Also a son by the Hindus, is considered essential for the continuation of the line and the performance of the death rites. Many parents who have a number of daughters and hope and desire to have a son, keep on getting more children.

The other side of the picture must, however, be also stated. The Catholic and the Communist opposition has been recently weakening and birth control is at the time being practiced in China. The masses of the Hindu community have come to appreciate the benefits accruing from it and are freely participating in the programme. The viewpoint of the educated Muslims is embodied in what Justice M.C. Chagla said, 'If population is not checked our progress would be writing on sand, with waves of population growth washing away all that we have written'.

3. In a society in which there is no old age security, male children are desired by parents to look after them in their old age.

4. Inspite of the progress already made in this field, there is need for a safe, simple, effective and acceptable method of contraception well within the means of the poorer sections of the community.

5. The administration of the programme particularly at the lower

---

[17]In reply to the Chief Minister of Maharashtra, they said in March 1976 that application of intended legislation for compulsory sterilization after two pregnancies, to the Muslim Community, would be interference in their Personal Law.

level is not an easy task. Lack of an adequate number of doctors and other trained personnel is a serious bottle-neck.

6. Anxiety is being expressed just now in the Western press[18] about falling of population in some developed countries such as France. This creates a suspicion in undeveloped countries about the double standards of the advanced countries—increasing the birth rate in their own countries and advocating birth control for the under-developed countries.

The problems created by the rapid depletion of the known resources and pollution, call for a reduction in the population of all countries alike. Advocacy of one set of standards for themselves and a different one for the poor countries smacks of duplicity and hypocrisy on the part of the developed countries and will seriously undermine the efforts by undeveloped countries in attempting the difficult task of making 'millions of individual couples change their most intimate sexual behaviours'.

Family Planning Methods and Preferences. Which is the most popular method of Family Planning: Coitus interruptus, rythm method, condom, diaphrgam, the pill, intrauterine device, sterilization or abortion? According to a recent report by Bruce Stokes, the answer is sterilization. It has truly become the contraceptive of choice in the 1970s. In 1950 only four million couples in the world made use of the method to limit the size of the family. Twenty-five years from that date, in 1975, four million sterilisations were performed in Europe alone and around 70 million couples around the world now use it as the preferred method of birth control. The method is popular in Europe, the United States of America and a number of Asian countries. In Puerto Rico 33 per cent of all married couples using contraception choose sterilisation, in the United States 25 per cent and in South Korea 19 per cent. In Singapore, voluntary sterilisation was legalised in 1975 for consenting married persons over the age of 21 years. In 1976, in contrast, Sweden removed all obstacles to sterilisation for persons 25 years of age and older.

Sterilisation by consent was gradually becoming the most favoured method of contraception in use in India, when unfortunately the IMF—World Bank and the Aid India consortium countries urged India to embark on a programme of forced sterilisation. P.N. Dhar, Hanumantha Rao and many others close to Indira Gandhi were op-

[18]Times of India, New Delhi, March 1976.

posed to the proposal but the dictator's fool-hardy son approved. The Western powers approved also and on 23 March 1976, Britain announced a £ 3 million grant in support of India's forced sterilisation family planning development.

Don Quixote and his Sancho Panzas were on the march. Sterilization targets were set both for the Union territories and the states, and instructions sent to Chief Ministers to see that the targets were achieved. The states of Punjab and Maharashtra enacted legislation for sterilization of couples having two or more children. S.B. Chavan, Chief Minister of Maharashtra, speaking at a rally of agricultural labourers in Akola, said, 'the government will no longer tolerate a situation where the people had the liberty to increase the population'. While cash awards ranging between Rs 100 and Rs 150 were given to those who submitted to the operation, couples with two or more children that refused were subjected to all types of harassment. Salaries were withheld, cheap and subsidised rations from government shops and housing accomodation denied and housing sites and surplus land to the landless in rural areas refused. Government and municipal employees, school teachers, nurses and health visitors and gaon and block workers were all asked to motivate at least two cases to sterilization. If they failed their salaries were not paid and they were punished in other ways. The worst brunt of the attack was borne by Harijans and the poorer sections of the people. Beggars, pavement and slum dwellers, rickshaw pullers, labourers and poor peasants were rounded up by sterilization and police-squads, shoved into lorries, taken in lakhs to camps and forcibly sterilized. They included 'the old and the young, the newly married and the long widowed, those with children and the childless, and many who had been sterilized already'.[20] Achieving high targets meant a bonanza for the officials who were paid a cut on each operation. No wonder they strained every nerve to clock in as many vasectomies and tubectomies as possible. A pretty admirer of Sanjay Gandhi, Rukhsana Sultana made over 80,000 rupees for her motivations to sterilization and Mr Radha Raman the Chief Executive Councillor of Delhi netted a neat amount of about Rs 15,000. In the market town of Bassi, 45 kilometres north-

[19]Bruce Stokes. 19 June 1977. Reported by Kamath, M.V., *Times of India*, New Delhi.
[20]David Selbourne. 1977. *An Eye to India*, England.

west of Sholapur in Maharashtra, 1,000 poor villagers who came to
town between 25 January and 3 February, were packed by force
into prowling garbage municipal trucks and taken to camps for
a quick sterilization. On 19 April 1976, sterilization squads that
followed the demolition squads at Turkman Gate, New Delhi, came
into conflict with an angry mob that resisted forcible sterilization. In
the encounter which ensued, the police opened fire and dozens of
people were said to have been killed and many wounded. The
official report said that only six had died. On 17 October 1976 eight
persons died at Sultanpur while police opened fire on a mob attac-
king family planning officials. Reports of resistance and tussles
came from many other places—Basti and Gorakhpur in Uttar
Pradesh, and from Punjab, Haryana, Madhya Pradesh, Bihar
and West Bengal. The worst clash occurred on 18 October
1976 in Muzaffarnagar in Uttar Pradesh where more than forty persons were killed. Chaudhary Charan Singh compared the brutal
killings in Muzaffarnagar to the Jallianwala Bagh massacre at
Amritsar. The savage and the inhuman approach to population
control was an important reason for the rout of Indira Gandhi and
the Congress Party at the hustings in March 1977. While few except
her minions are sorry for the fate that has overtaken her and the
Congress Party, there are many who are extremely unhappy at the
serious harm caused to the vital programme of family planning in
the country. A preferred tool of population control has suffered
debasement from which it may not recover for a long time.

The pill closely trails sterilization as a preferred contraceptive
and 55 million couples around the world employ it at the present
time. It is reported to be extremely popular and its use seems to
be on the increase on all continents. In countries just developing
family planning programmes, according to Stokes, it is often the
standard bearer of the new contraceptive revolution. The "pills"
are formulations containing aestrogenic agents or combinations of
aestrogenic and progesteronic agents. They are expensive and beyond the means of poor and common people. They must be taken
regularly and are not without side effects. Fear has been expressed
that their use may result in psychological disturbances or even
cause malignancy. It is yet too early, however, to say anything with
precision. Long or sustained action pills and injections have also
been developed and more are in the process of development.
A safe, cheap and reliable long acting formulation whether for oral

use or injected and implanted under the skin, would be a useful addition to the family planning kit.

In the United States of America, well educated women apparently prefer the diaphragm and it has been noted that one year after the test began, only one woman out of five women given the diaphragm, gave up its use. In Japan, the most highly industrialised country in Asia, the popular method seems to be the use of the condom, the oldest and the simplest means of contraception. Condoms as 'Nirodh' are available in India and sold at a subsidised price of 25 paise for three but even this low priced device is beyond the reach of the poorer sections in this country as an estimated 300 to 475 are required for a prevented birth. To be of any use at all, Nirodh must be available gratis to all who need it.

Both in Japan and China widespread legal abortion has helped greatly in reducing the birth-rates. Laws regarding abortion were liberalised in this country in 1972 and any woman can now attend a hospital and ask for the operation without any names being entered or questions asked. Abortion has the advantage over sterilization, that if due to any cause one or both children are lost, parents still have the possibility of having a child. As sterilization has fallen into disrepute in the country, at least for the time being, abortion facilities should be rapidly expanded and extended into remote villages through the use of abortion vans.

Coitus interruptus as a method of contraception has been used from very early days. It was the method most commonly employed successfully all over Europe to reduce the size of the family and is widely used even today. It is not foolproof and the failure rate is high.

The rythm method depends upon the knowledge of the safe period and is permitted by the Catholic church. But as the safe period varies from woman to woman and its precise period is difficult to determine, the method has not been found to be much use in actual practice.

From his worldwide study of contraceptive practices, Stokes concludes, first, that as there is no one best contraceptive, there is no single way to fill the family gap and that each country must find its own path, designing programmes that are 'sensitive to the cultural, political and economic realities it faces'. Obviously in a large country like India, a method that seems right for one part may not be so for another. Secondly, that the most successful family planning programmes have been like the Chinese programme, the most decentralised ones. According to Stokes they win over more people to contraceptive continuation rates and are less expensive.

A simple rule-of-thumb for determining the relationship between falling birth-rates and the availability of family planning services has been given by Bernard Berelson. He states that countries with 30 per cent of their population using birth control methods have a birth-rate close to 30 per 1,000. The rule is that for every difference of two points in the percentage using contraception, the birth-rate usually changes by about one point. Thus South Korea's 34 per cent rate of contraceptive practice corresponds roughly to its birth rate of 28 per thousand. Hong Kong has a 61 per cent, Singapore 77.7 per cent and even Thailand a 32 per cent rate of contraceptive use; the present level of contraceptive use in this country is extremely low—a mere 16.9 per cent. For making a perceptible dent on the birth-rate, the per cent rate of contraceptive use must be rapidly accelerated.

After the failure of the programme during the first three Plan periods and the annual plans following the Third Plan, a large budget of 315 crore was provided in 1970 for expenditure on family planning during the period of the Fourth Five Year Plan. The net target was an exposure of 50 per cent of the 90 million couples in the reproductive age group between the ages of 15-45 years, to sterilization or one of the conventional contraceptive methods mentioned earlier and bring down the birth-rate to 32 per 1,000. Unfortunately even this modest target could not be achieved. In the Fifth Five Year Plan, an even larger budget of Rs 516 crore was approved. If the average cost of preventing a birth is accepted as Rs 100, an amuount of Rs 516 crore should have helped prevent fifty-one and a half million births and reduced the birth-rate appreciably by the end of the Fifth Plan period. But without adequate organisational and administrative measures this could not be done; the hope has been blasted by the brutal use of the sterilizer's knife and the family planning programme so essential to the health of our economy, now lies in ruins. It will need a great deal of wisdom and skill both on the part of the rulers and the people to resuscitate, reorganize and revivify it.

IV

Conclusion

Besides the birth control measures considered in the last section, the following additional measures are necessary and recommended for simultaneous implementation:

1. Raising the age of marriage by legislation both for men and women. This has yielded high dividends both in China and Japan and is bound to do so in this country if the enacted legislation is also enforced. The enforcement of such laws cannot be regarded as a drastic measure by any stretch of imagination. In China, late marriages are the rule and while marriage for girls at the age of 18 is apparently legal, waiting until the combined age of the bride and the groom equal at least 50 years, is rapidly becoming obligatory.

2. All births and all marriages must be compulsorily registered.

3. Provision of old age pensions on a scale which will assure a reasonable level of living. Although it has been recognised that married couples want children to look after them in their old age, the suggestion has not been made that old age pensions or social security must be provided forthwith to old people to weaken or eliminate the reason for their wanting to have more children.

4. Eradication of illiteracy and ignorance, promotion of adult education and bringing home to people by social, economic and political education that larger sizes of population and economic well being do not go together.

5. Rapid economic development of the country with bias toward rural development.

6. Emancipation of women and provision of more jobs for them. The more women find employment, the smaller families they would wish to have. Women's employment like old age pensions, should form an important plank in the campaign for family planning. Unfortunately both economists and demographers have never considered these measures in the light in which the author wishes them to be considered.

7. Mother's clubs should be organised all over the country both in cities and the rural areas. Every village should have its own mother's club where women meet 'more out of a sense of participation than out of a feeling of not wanting to be left out. Meetings should be held once or twice a month and mother's and child

health problems discussed. Monthly supplies of pills or condoms should be distributed from the clubs free of cost to member's families. All mother's clubs should be supplied contraceptive agents free of cost by the State. Such clubs (apzaris) are being successfully run in Indonesia. In South Korea mother's clubs have in addition to their primary work of promotion of family planning, ventured into other fields. They have established credit unions, initiated representation projects, developed new rice lands, bought livestock herds and opened cooperative grocery stores.

8. Education and Factory Acts should be passed and enforced as was done in England a long time back.

9. Use should be made of enlightened leaders of different communities to create an atmosphere favourable to the promotion of birth control measures among their followers.

SEVEN

Education

I

In 1947 only 13 per cent Indians were literate. In absolute terms, out of a population of 339 million people, 44 million were literate and 295 million illiterate. There has been since then a rapid expansion of primary, secondary and tertiary education in the country and in 1974 the level of literacy rose to 29.5 per cent. In absolute terms the number of literate people rose from 44 million in 1947 to 186 million in 1974. Very impressive increase indeed. But if one considers that India's population in 1974, was around 600 million, the picture changes its character and the mood of optimism gives way to one of gloom. The absolute number of illiterates in 1974, amounts to 414 million people—a figure which is higher by 119 million than the figure of 295 million illiterates in 1947, and 73 million more than the total population of the country in that year.

The overall percentage of literacy in 1974 was 29.5 per cent; for males it was 39.5 per cent and for females 18.7 per cent.

According to official figures, in 1947, 14,100,000 children between the ages of 6 and 11 years attended primary schools. Their number rose to 66,200,000 in 1974, the increase being 350 per cent. The number of children between the ages of 11 and 13 years that attended classes 6 to 8 or junior high school in 1947 was 2,000,000. In 1974 the figure rose to 15,300,000 and the percentage rise was 654. The number attending high schools or classes 9 to 11 was 85,000 in 1947, and it rose to 7,400,000 in 1974, the increase being of the order of 900 per cent. In respect of college and university education, the number for 1947 and 1974 were 256,000 and 2,612,000 respectively with a percentage of 900 again.

These are very telling increments if only the percentage gains are trotted down, but they hide much, and this is brought out when absolute numbers and the size of the population in the years under review, is also taken into account.

The leaders of the nation had held out a promise at the time of independence that illiteracy would be eradicated by the end of the first decade and at most within two decades. It is painful to know that not only the promise remains unfulfilled but 32 years after the attainment of independence, the absolute number of illiterates in the country exceeds the total population of the country in 1947, by no less a figure than 73 million.

II

OBJECTIVES

The objectives of a progressive education may be summarized as follows:

1. In the words of John Dewey[1] 'to take every one out of his class and into one common humanity'.

2. To promote democratic, cultural and human value such as:
    (a) Truth and non-violence.
    (b) Equality and social justice.
    (c) Brotherhood of man.
    (d) International peace.

3. To,
    (a) Encourage learning rather than teaching.
    (b) Encourage curiosity, independent thinking and initiative.
    (c) Encourage scientific approach, honesty and hard work.
    (d) Encourage practical learning by doing.
    (e) Offer help and cooperation to the weak, the backward and the handicapped.

4. To relate teaching to work in the farm, factory, office or elsewhere.

5. To,
    (a) Eradicate Illiteracy.
    (b) Ensure education, through teaching a craft that would secure the basic needs of every individual for food, clothes, shelter and medical and health measures.
    (c) Secure a life of reasonable comfort.

6. To :
    (a) reject bank-deposit education and replace it by pro-

[1]John Dewey. Philosophy, Modern Library, New York.

blem-posing education.

(*b*) Reject cramming.

(*c*) Reject competition.

(*d*) Reject grading and examinations.

(*e*) Reject failure and wastage.

(*f*) Reject compulsory attendance.

It is necessary to dilate a little on some of these objectives:

1. Progressive Education. Dewey's philosophy of education was formulated during the period following the Civil War when America's industrial economy was developing at a fast rate. The country and the people were confronted by problems posed by concentration of wealth within a minority, exploitation and poverty of the working classes, and problems posed by immigration, over-crowding and sprawling slums, and lack of equality and social justice generally. His concept of a progressive school combined, practical learning of science and technology, a democratic community, a spontaneity of feeling liberated by artistic appreciation, freedom of phantasy and animal expression freed from the pontiff's self-denial and the school master's rod. His line of thinking on education was related to that of Louis Sullivan and Frank Lloyd Wright on architecture trying to invent an urbanism and an aesthetic, suited to production of machines and yet human, and the engineering orientation of the economic and moral thought of the author[2] of "The Theory of The Leisured Class". These pundits were trying to train people to realities of industrial and technical life working practically with machines and learning by doing. According to Dewey good teaching is that which leads the student to learn something more.

2. Democratic and Cultural Values. A reference has already been made to the promotion of democratic and cultural values. These must be emphasized right from the start and throughout the school years. Indolence, lying, dishonesty, selfishness, waste, greed, stealing, arrogance and quarrelsomeness are vices that children and students should be taught to eschew both by precept and by example. Austerity, simple living, fearlessness, respect for life, hard work, service of others, selflessness, cooperation, honesty, social justice, love, truth and non-violence in thought, word and deed, are virtues that need to be inculcated among children and all others at all times. In India the gospel of truth and non-violence was taught and propagated by Gautam Buddha and Lord Mahavira earlier and by

[2]Thorstein Vehlen. The Theory of the Leisured Class, New York.

Gandhiji in our own days. It has special significance both for the rulers and the ruled in this country where every thing un-Gandhian has been and is being done in the name of the Gandhian principles and his philosophy reduced so soon after his death to utter mockery. Gandhiji stood for democratic ideals of equity and social justice; and liquidation of illiteracy and degrading, dehumanizing poverty. He fought against untouchability and for a casteless society. He preached respect for life and love of man irrespective of religion, race, and the colour of the skin. His non-violence was the non-violence of the brave. He equated Truth with God, abhorred war and stood for peace among nations. His ideas and his concept of Basic Education have great relevance for all and particularly for his own countrymen. Let this country in this hour of crisis, listen to the voice of this great compeer of Buddha and Christ, and encourage children, students and others to learn from his example.

3.   Curiosity to Learn. A child has his interests and whether he is at home, in the school or elsewhere, he is curious to learn. He is attracted by other children, his parents, brothers and sisters; other adults; toys, books, pictures and articles of household use; coloured objects, shops, stores, cinema houses, theatres and museums; radio, television, mechanical contrivances and machines; flowers, leaves, plants and trees; insects, birds, fishes and animals; ponds, streams, lakes and mountains; stars, moon and sun, and other objects. These and many more are his teachers. He wants to and is curious to learn about them and from them. As parents and adults we need patience to understand them, discover their interest and arouse their curiosity for learning. But do we? On the other hand, to be rid of them and to prevent them from coming in our way, we send them to baby-sitting institutions—nurseries, kindergartens and children's schools. The teachers understand them less than the parents, shut them up for a few hours daily in the class room, suppress their animality and self-expression and order them to keep quiet. They are exposed to lessons which are dull, and fail to hold their attention. They are asked to learn their assignments and achieve certain levels of performance. If they move from their seats, talk to their friends in the class, or fail to achieve the levels demanded by the teacher, they are punished.

Education by learning and learning by doing, are of much greater value than education by the traditional methods of teaching. Gandhiji's Basic Education—which like everything Gandhian has been relegated in this country to the limbo of oblivion—is an approach that promotes learning by doing. Its wide-spread application at the present time is a priority of the highest order both in the rural and the urban areas.

4. General versus Craft Education. The teaching in our schools and colleges is far too academic and has little or no relevance to the tasks that the individual has to perform in the business of living. The education imparted in the primary schools in the village does not make a better farmer out of the child nor does it help him to learn a craft and set up a cottage or rural enterprise and help solve the problems of rural unemployment, under-employment or hidden unemployment.

What applies to the primary schools, is true of the secondary schools, the polytechnics, the colleges and universities and even the professional colleges and institutes. From many of these institutions, hundreds of thousands of unemployable young men and women are turned out every year and have to be trained on the job for several months and sometimes a year or two, before they are able to acquire the necessary skill and efficiency that is demanded from them.

5. Eradication of Illiteracy and Adult Education. Before the assumption of power and during the period of the British rule, Jawaharlal Nehru and other Indian leaders held out promises that soon after achievement of independence, illiteracy would be liquidated. After the British left, the promises were re-iterated time and again but very little was done to fulfil them. W.S. Wyotinsky[3] who visited India in the 1950s relates the practice of revolutionary students who during the latter decades of the Tsarist rule went into the countryside to teach the 3 Rs to the peasants. After they took over power, the Communists made it their official policy. In his book[4] on India, he recalls the experience of his youth and ruminates: 'We noticed nothing similar to that crusade in India. We heard complaints about mass unemployment among young graduates of the universities, but we could get no answer to the question, why cannot a million of them be mobilized for rural teaching'? Such a mobilization would be possible if Indian intellectuals felt the urgency of primary education for the villages as keenly as did the Russian intellectuals in the days of my youth'. But the Indian Intellectuals

[3]W.S. Wyotinsky. 1957, India. The Awakening Giant, New York.
[4]Ibid, 1957.

have never felt this urgency, first, because of the lack of their iden-
tification with the poor, and secondly, because of the rigid elite-class
structure in which they have been brought up.

Commenting on the deplorable situation J.P. Naik, Member-
Secretary of the Education Commission wrote in 1965, 'The liquidation of adult illiteracy is the most important programme of national
development and on it depend several other programmes such as
agricultural production, family planning etc. This sector has been
criminally neglected and it is extremely desirable to undertake a
large scale programme in this sector and to liquidate mass illiteracy
in a few years—five or ten at the most'.

Had illiteracy been eradicated during the first few years after the
achievement of independence, it is probable that the population
problem would not have assumed the seriousness that it at present
has, the gains of economic growth would not have been neutralized
and the standard of living and per capita income would have been
higher than it is at the moment.

The liquidation of adult illiteracy is important for many
reasons:

(*a*) It is needed for acquiring higher skills in agriculture, manufacturing industry as well as trade. Agricultural productivity in areas
with high levels of adult literacy has been shown to be greater than
other areas where the level of literacy is low.

(*b*) The enrolment in primary schools is higher in the case of
literate parents. The number of drop outs is also much smaller.

(*c*) It helps appreciation of one's economic situation—the factors which lead to exploitation of one country by the other and of
the rich by the poor in the same country. This realization is a pre-
requisite of any remedial action. It helps to make people politically
aware—awareness being important for participation in the democratic process both for right exercise of franchise and for organizing
resistance against unjust laws or repressive measures.

(*d*) It helps one to fight superstitions, evil and harmful customs,
and class and caste prejudices.

In a socialist system (Congress leaders were never tired of bran-
dishing socialism at the people) with efficient organization and proper utilization of resources, proper education should prepare all for
work to ensure for them at least the basic necessities of life. These
are 1 sufficient and nutritious food, 2 clean raiment for both summer
and winter, 3 a neat even though small house simply furnished and

provided with a toilet and bath, supply of piped water and electricity, and 4 proper medical and health care. With the growth of the economy it should be possible to raise the living standard of the people within another couple of decades and to provide a life of reasonable comfort for all the inhabitants of the country without exception.

Side by side with efforts aimed at raising the standard of living, education should tend towards improving the cultural level of the people. Dull, drab, dreary, repetitious work is killing and not compatible with high levels of productivity. Hard work should be interspersed with periods of rest and relaxation, holidays, enjoyment of leisure, hobbies, and graphic and performing arts.

6. Bank-deposit versus Problem-posing Education. The current academic education in most countries and in India has fundamentally a "narrative" character. It is a transfer—a "communique"—from a narrating subject to 'patient, listening objects, the students'. Paulo Freire[5] is a bitter critic of the universally applied, narrative method of education and has christened it as the bank-deposit approach. This approach leads the students to memorize mechanically the narrated content and worse still, it turns them into "containers" or "receptacles" to be filled by the teachers. The more completely he fills the receptacles, the better teacher he is. The more meekly the receptacles permit themselves to be filled, the better students they are.

In this concept, the teacher is the necessary opposite of the taught and the process of education is a teacher-student contradiction. The teacher is a depositor and the students are the depositories, he teaches and the students are taught; he knows everything and the students know nothing; he talks and the students meekly listen; he chooses the programme content and the students who are not consulted, adopt themselves to it; he is the subject of the learning process and the students are mere objects—things. The concept is similar to Jean Paul Sartre's "digestive" or "nutritive" concept of education in which knowledge is "fed" by the teacher to the student "to fill them out." It is anti-dialogical and an instrument of domination by the elite. It thrives on myths indispensable to the preservation of the status quo—the myth that the oppressive order is a free society; the myth that all men are equal, when the question—

[5]Paulo Freire. 1972. The Pedagogy of the Oppressed, London.

do you know who you are talking to?—is so frequently asked; the myth that private property is fundamental to personal human development; the myth that rebellion is a sin against God; the myth that the dominant elites promote the welfare of the people, so that the people in a gesture of gratitude should accept their words or conform to them; the myth of industriousness, generosity and honesty of the ruling class, and of the laziness and dishonesty of the oppressed. The fundamental characters of narrative education are conquest, manipulation, cultural invasion and divisiveness. It makes use of these and many other tools to preserve for the oppressors their riches, their power and their way of life and maintain the status quo. It helps them to divide the people and keep them divided to avert a threat to their own rule.

The model of education recommended by Paulo Freire is the problem-posing model which resembles in many ways the type of education recommended by John Dewey and is referred to earlier in this chapter. It resembles also though not wholly the models recommended by Paul Goodman,[6] John Holt,[7] Erich Fromm,[8] Ivan Illich[9] and Mahatma Gandhi.[10] It is the opposite in all respects to the bank-deposit or the narrative model. It is the method of discovery; it arouses curiousity, encourages independent thinking and develops initiative. It is dialogical and begins with the resolution of the teacher-student contradiction by reconciling the poles of the contradiction so that both are simultaneously teachers and taught. It promotes cooperation and the unity of the people among themselves, and with their leader's help organizes them for their liberation from the elites.

III

LEGACY OF BRITISH RULE

The structural framework of the educational system in India is a legacy of the British rule. During the British period, as it is now,

---

[6]Paul Goodman. 1971. Compulsory Miseducation, England.
[7]John Holt. 1971. The Underachieving School, England.
[8]Erich Fromm. 1966. The Heart of Man, England.
[9]Evan Illich. 1973. Deschooling Society, England.
[10]M.K. Gandhi. 1962. Village Swaraj, Ahmedabad, India.

the unit of administration in India, was a district. The head of the district was the district magistrate or the deputy commissioner who was invariably a white Englishman belonging to the Indian Civil Service. Associated with him and under his administrative control were a number of departmental heads, all of them whitemen and members of the All India Services—police, revenue, educational, engineering, medical, forest, railway and others. Senior military officers above the rank of a captain and judicial officers such as high court, and district and sessions judges were also whitemen. To help and assist these people in running the administration at all levels both in the centre and in the states, a large number of clerks and subordinate officials were needed.

It was to fulfil the need for clerks and deskmen that secondary schools with preparatory primary schools were set up in the towns and cities. The education imparted in these schools as well as in colleges for training subordinate officials, was of a general and literary character. There was little or no teaching of science and technical subjects as it was not the intention of India's foreign rulers to encourage growth or development or help build a manufacturing industry in the country.

The motive for establishing the schools, both secondary and tertiary, was not the education of the masses of the Indian people. Moreover, most of the schools and colleges were started and run not by the government but by the religious or denominational bodies and were financed through fees collected from the pupils, public donations and some token yearly government grants. They were not free schools in the sense they are in independent Western countries. As schools were run not for the benefit of the people, there were no schools whatever in the rural areas and countryside over large stretches of territory.

The pupils that attended these schools belonged mainly to the middle and upper class families—from among those who were eager to avail themselves of the opportunities of financial gain that service of the masters provided.

A small number of engineering and medical schools and a few training institutes that were established, suffered from the same disadvantages that afflicted the secondary schools and colleges. The teaching was mainly theoretical and the academic standards were poor, designed to train assistants and understudies to the white experts made in England.

There were some other types of schools too—public schools for the children of Indian chiefs and rulers, big zamindars and taluqdars, some European and Anglo-Indian schools for Indian born Europeans and for mulattoes; and convents for the daughters of the well-to-do. The result was a thorough stratification with "Homo Britannica" at the apex of the pyramid. The whitemen in India whether civil or military officers or belonging to the English or other European houses, were a closed community. They lived in cantonments and separate enclosures, wore clothes and shoes made in England, smoked English cigarettes, drank Scotch whisky and belonged to clubs to which no Indians were admitted. They had a large number of low-paid and fawning servants—ayahs, peons, cooks, bearers, barmen, gardeners and sweepers—to help them and their mem-sahibs in their household chores. Next to them came the Indian elites—the landed aristocracy, Rajahs and Nawabs, Khan Bahadurs and Rai Bahadurs, deputy collectors, sub-judges, munsifs, eminent doctors and lawyers, inspectors of police, rich merchants and owners of big stores, big traders and contractors, principals of colleges and headmasters etc. They were mostly ji-hazoors[12] who sought favours from their white masters and cringed before them. They together with their women folk and children emulated the 'English way of life', had their own compliment of servants and were large consumers of textiles, woolens, cosmetics, pharmaceuticals, liquors and other articles manufactured in England. They read English classics, played bridge, and talked and wrote letters to each other in the language of their masters. Third in the order of hierarchy were a large number of minor officials and clerks whose education stopped at the middle or high school level. Occupations involving manual labour, doing things by hands, or even soiling one's hands had, in the elite and the educated circles, an opprobrious connotation. All educated persons wanted white collar jobs and the entry to these was through secondary school, diplomas and college degrees. The teaching was narrative in character. The teachers taught, the students listened, crammed, stored and reproduced. The emphasis was not on learning for the sake of learning or self-employment through a craft but on passing of examinations and the acquisition of a degree or a diploma as a passport for a white collar job.

[11]A munsif is a minor judicial officer.
[12]A ji-hazoor is a sycophant.

Complete neglect of free and compulsory primary education as imparted in the West, coupled with adult illiteracy on the one hand, and the use of the English medium on the other, raised an insurmountable wall between the educated elite and poverty-stricken ignorant masses. This served the purpose of the colonial rulers and was also in the interest of the Indian elites.

During the British period very little attention was paid to the problem of national education. A number of schools by religious or denominational bodies were set up but the pattern of education except for religious instruction, did not deviate from those in schools and colleges established by the government. Among the few Indians who gave some thought to education were Sir Syed Ahmed Khan, M.M. Malaviya, Bhagwan Das, Lajpat Rai, Swami Shradhanand and Rabindranath Tagore. The university established by Sir Syed at Aligarh provided higher education for Muslims from all parts of the country but the pattern of education except for an Islamic bias conformed to the one in institutions of higher learning elsewhere in India. In Banaras Hindu University too the teaching in the faculties of arts, science, commerce and law, was on conventional lines but the university provided a much higher level of training in engineering and technology than that obtained elsewhere. Gurukul Kangri founded by Shradhanand at Hardwar in Uttar Pradesh laid emphasis on the knowledge contained in ancient Indian scriptures—Vedas, Bhagwad Gita, Brahmsutras, Arthshastra and Ayurveda etc. It enjoined austerity, celibacy and respect for the gurus in the tradition of the ashrams of old. Its graduates who were called sanātaks were austere and disciplined pastors, put were failures in the business of living. Their training did not prepare them for self-employment and their degree was not recognized by the government for jobs. Bhagwan Das was the founder of the Kashi Vidyapeeth where famous men like Bhagwan Das himself, Acharya Narendra Dev and Sampurnanand taught. India's second Prime Minister Lal Bahadur Shastri and many other prominent Indians were the products of this institution. Lala Lajpat Rai wrote a volume on national education and founded an institution in Lahore which awarded the degree of B.A. (National), which again had no value in the service market. Rabindranath Tagore's Shantiniketan at Bolpur in Bengal, had sylvan setting and was the outcome of a poet's dream. It attracted many talented pupils from all over the country and trained them in crafts, and in graphic and performing arts. None of these ventures, however, had any bearing on the overall problem of national education.

It was, however, Gandhiji's prudence and foresight that enabled him to comprehend the problem in its totality and offer a feasible and practical solution which if it had been implemented, would have changed the face of the country.

Writing on 18 September 1937, Gandhiji[13] deplored, 'We have up-to now concentrated on stuffing children's minds with all kinds of information (it has the ring of Freire's bank-deposit education), without ever thinking of stimulating and developing them. Let us now cry a halt and concentrate on educating the child properly through manual work, not as a side activity, but as the prime means of intellectual training'. Three weeks later,[14] he wrote, 'I am a firm believer in the principle of free and compulsory primary education for India. I also hold that we should realize this only by teaching the children a useful vocation and utilizing it as a means for cultivating their mental, physical and spiritual faculties'. The course of primary education that he recommended was to last for at least seven years (7-14 years) and included general education gained up to matriculation standard less English, but plus a substantial vocation.

Gandhiji deprecated the idea of adding a handicraft to the ordinary curriculum of education followed in the schools which signified that the craft was to be taken in hand wholly separately from education. He called it a fatal mistake. According to him the craft teacher was to correlate his knowledge to the craft, so that he could impart all knowledge to the pupil through the medium of the craft he chose. He gave the instance of spinning and said, 'Unless I know arithmetic I cannot report how many yards of yarn I have produced on the takli or how many standard rounds it will make or what is the count of the yarn I have spun. I must learn figures to be able to do so, and I must learn addition, subtraction, multiplication and division. In dealing with complicated sums I shall have to use symbols and so get my algebra'.

Gandhiji said he could teach children the geometry of the circle through the disc of the takli without mentioning the name of Euclid. He could, he said, teach children history and geography while teaching them the art of spinning. This would involve des-

[13]Harijan. 18 September 1937.
[14]Ibid. 9 October 1937.

cribing to them the conditions under which the cotton plant grew, the places where it grew and their history and geography, for instance how the merchants of the East India Company destroyed India's handicrafts and particularly her cotton industry and thereby built their own in Manchester, and how those who came to trade ended by becoming India's rulers. All education, Gandhiji said, should be imparted through the medium of the provincial language. He advocated the political verbal education of adults side by side with teaching them the three Rs.[15] He wanted all education to be self-supporting and said that primary education should equip boys and girls to earn their bread by the state guaranteeing employment in the vocations learnt or by buying their manufactures at prices fixed by the State.[16] He further said he would revolutionize college education and relate it to national necessities. 'There would be degrees for mechanical and other engineers. They would be attached to different industries which should pay for the training of the graduates they need. He warned against indiscriminate expansion of college and university education.[17] He stood for compulsory co-education upto the age of 14 years and if possible upto the age of 16. His views on education were progressive and egalitarian and his "new education" and "basic education" were concepts related to life.

Before the achievement of independence, Nehru and other Indian leaders were wont to delivering long harangues in favour of free and compulsory primary education, adult literacy and other educational reforms. But after taking power they made no effort in this direction. Was it due to complacency and a policy of drift, or was it to satisfy the elites and maintain the status quo? It is difficult to say. But the fact remains that the old inegalitarain, divisive, exploitative, academic, colonial model, was permitted to continue. Only it was much expanded.

The bane of the urban secondary school education during British days was the existence of two types of schools. This has been greatly aggravated during the past thirty years. The public schools[18] for the childern of the elites have extensive campuses running at times into hundreds of acres, palatial buildings, large play grounds,

[15]M.K. Gandhi. 1961. Constructive Programme, Ahmedabad, India.
[16]Harijan. 2 October 1937.
[17]Harijan. 2 November 1947.
[18]The public schools in India are no more public than Eton and Harrow are in England. The nomenclature is misleading.

well equipped libraries and laboratories, audio-visual devices, and well trained often foreign qualified staff. The other type—the government run and the denominational schools for the children of the common people, are poorly housed, poorly equipped and poorly staffed. The first type of schools cater to the needs of the rulers— the daddy's boys who corner all the fat jobs in the state govern- ments, the central government, the army, the railways, the inter- national agencies and the large business houses both foreign and Indian. The second and the cheaper type look after the education of the children of the common people, the poor, in Plato's language the "slaves." The existence of two types of schools in the country is a denial of the equal opportunity that constitution provides. It is designed to perpetuate the affluence of the well-to-do and the poverty of the paupers. The well-to-do have developed a vested interest in the continuance of two types, for in this way they ensure both fat salaries and positions of power for their children and themselves. The continued poor standards of education in the com- mon schools are advantageous to the children of the elites. More- over, it is the elites who make policy decisions and hold the purse strings; they will not do anything to improve the condition of the poor man's schools. The rich have a vested interest in the status quo which helps them reserve all the fat jobs for their children, and they will not move their little finger for the improvement of the poor man's school. The public schools, the central schools, the sainik schools and the convents need to be closed immediately, if education as a whole has to improve. The need of the country is one type of school—the neighbourhood school which the UGC[19] has also recommended, and in which all the children—the rich and the poor—will receive one type of education. When this happens and when the "daddy's boys" suffer, their education suffers, will the rich and powerful wake up and devise ways and means for improving the level of education in the neighbourhood common schools.

IV

DRAWBACKS OF THE PRESENT DAY SYSTEM

The education as it prevails today suffers from a large number of serious drawbacks :

[19]University Grant's Commission.

1. The formal education system in India is a gigantic enterprise with about 700,000 institutions, 3.5 million teachers, 100 million students and an annual expenditure of Rs 2,500 crore. Yet it benefits mainly the upper and the middle classes for whom it was originally designed. It accords very low priority to programmes of free and compulsory primary education, adult education and non-formal education which would benefit the masses. About 70 per cent of the people are still outside its ambit. It has been truly said about it that the system is designed for "not educating the people." Its primary objective is not to spread education among the people, but to function 'as an efficient and merciless mechanism to select individuals who should continue to remain in the privileged sector or enter it afresh. It does not discharge, even this task impartially. . .'[20]

2. The method of instruction is much too programmed and the programmes are drawn up by the educationists and teachers without consulting those who are taught. The programmes are also irrelevant to the needs of the society in which the students have to live. The students are taught many things which they do not need and not taught those which they need. Far too much time is devoted to academic teaching and they are left with little or no time to browse freely in the library or for learning outside the schools. The method encourages cramming of much useless stuff. The students are over-burdened with homework for which parent's help is needed or private and expensive tutors have to be engaged. It is forgotten that the method of discovery is far superior to the bank-deposit method. Less or no homework gives students time for out-of-the-class learning. The method of discovery develops initiative and independent thinking.

3. The competitive method which is used, implies frequent tests, grading and examinations. A few students secure positions; the great majority are condemned to positions of mediocrity and backwardness. The remark card handed out to the student after the performance tests, condemns a large majority to inferior jobs and positions for life. The preferred method is one of cooperation in which the mediocre and the slow performers are helped by the teachers and the better students to a higher level of achievement.

[20]Education for our People. 1978. Citizens for Democracy, New Delhi.

If the school does not do this it is no school. It is like the hospital[21] which treats the healthy and throws out the sick.

4. Out of millions of students that take high school and intermediate examinations every year, half or more than half fail and repeat. Such a high rate of failure is a national waste that no country should tolerate. If emphasis was on learning and not on passing examinations, this waste could be avoided. If weak students were helped to learn and not failed, it would save money for the state and the parents, teaching time (another year) for the teacher, and time and effort for the pupil. If teachers were paid as workers are often paid for piece work only for students that pass, they would take pains to see that students learn and are not failed. The weak students in their turn would shed their inferiority complex, be saved from the humiliation of repeating and achieve higher performance in life. Adverse remarks on cards and reports, lower students in their own estimation and leave wounds which hurt throughout life—much more so than even corporal punishment which is soon forgotten. They are uncalled for and do incalculable harm.[21]

5. The narrative method of teaching is far too "general" and literary. It militates against learning by doing. It promotes a psychology and attitudes that induce a preference for white collar jobs which are getting harder and harder to come by, and a dislike for learning by doing which is the essence of education and the acquisition of a craft or a vocation that would ensure lucrative self-employment. Half at least of the time and half the money spent on education should be spent on practical learning which has relevance to life. In China, Cuba, North Korea and North Vietnam, half the teaching time is spent in academic learning and the other half in learning crafts, farming, work in mines, factories, offices, shops and other places. The progress in all these countries has been phenomenal.

6. The present system teaches conformism. It encourages flattery and sycophancy of the establishment to get to the top. It takes away independence and the capacity to resist injustice and oppression and makes of men not "ubermenchs" in the Nietschean sense but "untermenchs," of a servile variety.

[21]School of Barbiana. 1973. Letter to a Teacher, England.

V

REORGANISATION

The reorganisation proper of the system of education in India is proposed to be considered under the following heads:

1. Adult education
2. Child-care centres
3. Primary schools
4. Secondary schools
5. Vocational education
5. University and higher education
7. Out-of-the.school education

But before I do so, I shall briefly consider the relationship of education to ideology, ethics and morality, and to home and the family.

Education and Ideology. The method of education in a society is related intimately to the method of production and the political organisation of the society. Our educational system from the primary to the university level is geared to the mode of capitalist production. Our leaders are, however, never tired of repeating that they are building a socialist society. If they were serious about it they would have tried to give a socialist direction to our educational system which continues to remain discriminatory, socially divisive and profoundly inegalitarian. One wonders how people—students, government officials, legislators, political leaders—who have learnt their history from Rostows, their political science from Morgenthaus, their economics from Marshall, Pigou, Keynes, Hanson and Samuelson, can bring about a socialist transformation. The very fact that there has been no change in the capitalist orientation of education in this country appears to be a clear indication of the fact that the powers that be, have no intention of building a socialist society, however much they may gabble about it.

Moral and Ethical Education. In a country like India when people professing different religions—Hinduism, Islam, Christianity and Sikhism etc.—live together, sectional and religious training in schools is out of question. A moral and ethical education of a fundamental and universal character is, however, most essential. This should include elementary ideas of good and bad, attention to health and hygienic habits, clealiness of one's person and the surroundings, learning of crafts and a vocation useful for the individual's keep, selflessness, help of others, spirit of cooperation, hardwork, honesty, truthfulness, discipline, respect for teachers and older persons, kindness to children and the sick, love of mother- land, and a desire for building a new egalitarian society in which caste, class or colour of the skin do not play any part.

School and the Community. Only boarding schools have the chil- dren in their charge all the time; in most schools the child spends much of its time in the home and in the surroundings in which it lives. Further, schooling commences in India at the age of six or seven years and by that time the child's individuality and predilections have already taken some shape. Outside the school, it is most important that the school and the family should act in concert in the field of children's education. For this purpose teacher-parent meetings, meeting of parent's committees and participation of a parent's representive on various school committees including the management committee, are of the highest importance.

1. Adult Education. This is essential for the improvement of the individual, and vital for the development of the community and the country as a whole. Its relative cost is low and the economic return high and immediate. It should be accorded the highest priority. Its content should include 1 literacy, 2 development of skills to improve earning capacity, 3 education in health care, population control and eradication of evil customs, superstition and fear, and 4 the awakening of awareness to prevent exploitation and fight back social injustice. Its organization must be attempted on a massive scale by making use of the resources offered by the huge in- frastructure of the formal educational system as well as by the voluntary organizations like village panchayats, cooperative societies, youth and women's associations, trade unions, clubs and educated individuals with enthusiasm and commitment. All employers of labour—government or private should be under legal obligation to make their employees literate. Literacy brigades may be organised by closing down universities, colleges and high school classes for a year or two and by availing of the services of teachers, students and other enthusiastic persons for a speedy achievement of the goal. What has been said above about the education of the adults (21-59 years), applies equally to the out-of-school youth of age group 15-21 years. The educability of this group is greater and vocational train- ing has a special import for it.

2. Child Care Centres. What India needs desperately today is better

human material at all levels, than one sees in her in-feuding top leaders today. For building a New Man she must begin at the beginning and devote special attention to two categories of pepole —her women and her children.

Much has been talked and written about women's lib, in Western countries and more recently in India. But no liberation is possible, as Fidel Castro said, unless women are freed from the home and the kitchen chores. It should, therefore, be the endeavour of all women's organizations and all socially conscious individuals—both men and women in the country—to explain to the women and their husbands, how important it is for the country's economy and for their own development, for women to get out of the home and get involved in productive work. Towards achieving this end one must provide centres where infants and children of working mothers can be enroled and properly educated, when the mothers go out for work.

Childcare centres should be organized in India on the pattern they have been organized in Cuba where they are functioning with success. For a detailed account of the manner in which this has been achieved the reader is referred to Karen Wald's book 'Children of Che—Childcare and Education in Cuba'. In the integrated approach that is recommended the child's education is not separated from childhealth and childcare, and begins with better nutrition and childhealth care while the infant is still in the mother's womb and from the day it opens its eyes on the world outside. The Cubans have, for this purpose, ensured that all births take place in properly equipped and staffed maternity homes or hospitals and not in unhygienic city homes or dirt-floored houses in the countryside away from centres of medical care. This is as it should be.

During the period of gestation, mothers pay regular monthly visits to polyclinics, maternity homes or hospitals where their medical history is elicited; general and pelvic examinations made, records of weight, pulse, bloodpressure etc., maintained, and proper instructions regarding dict, exercise, medicines and other matters, issued. Childcare classes are held for all mothers, and both mothers and their husbands shown childbirth and childcare films.

The purpose of building childcare centres is two fold—first, to free women from the home and enable them to become happier, healthier, more productive and more complete human beings, and secondly, over and above the initial purpose of enabling them to leave their children in safe and suitable environments, to provide conditions for the development of the New Child who would eventually become the New Man with a developed sense of solidarity and collectivity with the people around him. Such a man will be unselfish and would identify himself with the group, even though he retains his own individual character. He would work with his compeers and produce things which he will share with them. He would respect all kinds of work, if that work serves the community, and regard the work of the labourer as important as that of a physician or an engineer. Such a man will help usher in a society in which there is no exploitation of man by man—a society in which there is not the kind of competition to go ahead so that the one in front puts out his foot to trip the one behind but there is desire on the part of everyone to help everyone else—a society where the pain of one is the pain of everyone and where an injustice to one hurts all.

The centres can be housed in existing spacious buildings belonging to the well-to-do people or in new buildings put up by offering employment to those who have no work, under the food for work programmes. The enrolment to the child care centres should be in the first instance restricted to infants and children—between the ages of 45 days and five years—of mothers who are either working or studying. With the expansion of facilities, enrolment can be extended to cover the entire population.

Infants and children are assigned different rooms depending on their age at the time of enrolment. Those who are enroled when they are barely 45 days old or a little older, are cared for in a separate room, each in its own crib. They are fed and looked after, by assistants or nurses wearing masks and sterilized gowns. Where they are a little older and able to crawl or sit, they are transferred to another room and put in play-pens with other children of their own age. The process of socialization begins in the cribs where they see and hear other children cared for, as they are cared for themselves but is intensified in the play-pens where they interact with one another and play with common toys. When they are able to stand or begin to walk, they are transferred to a different room with a large play pen or corral—the size of a small room and raised on wooden legs, so that they are looking out at the world, not up at it. It is in these pens that they develop their visual, auditory, manual, motor and verbal abilities. They play with the ball and other toys in the corrals and by the time they are able to walk, they are encouraged to do so up and down a ramp leading into the pen. At this stage all their activities are collective—bathing, changing, napping and eating. Milk, other food, books and stationery etc. are provided free to all.

As soon as they are able to walk, they begin playing games with other children in playing areas inside the building of the centre and learn to put away their toys in their proper places. When they are a little older they play games both inside the centres and the play areas outside attached to the centre. By the age of three they are able to dress and undress themselves.

Cleanliness and attention to hygiene, receive the highest emphasis at all levels. The toys used are washable and everytime a child places a toy in the mouth it is cleaned before another child handles it. All articles that can be boiled, are sterilized regularly.

From an early age emphasis is placed on learning through games and development of verbal skills such as story-telling, puzzles, poems, songs, dance, word games, puppetry and play acting. As soon as possible they are encouraged to engage in the use of clay, paint and work in the garden where they begin by watering and pulling weeds and later do all the work by themselves. For older children study is combined with work.

Collectivity is encouraged through group play, collective celebration of birthdays of all children born in one month, and emphasis on children learning from each other and helping each other. Children who do well are praised for good work and rewarded for it but greater praise is lavished on, and higher prizes offered to children who help others to learn.

Love of work and respect for the working people is inculcated in children in the childcare centres. The ancient divisions between manual and intellectual labour are pulled down by encouraging ability to perform a variety of skills. In most childcare centres, the children have a small garden plot and children relate themselves to the food they eat as the producers of that food. They plant, weed, water and harvest the vegetables and fruits which they will later eat. As all the childcare centres in Cuba, are sponsored by work centres, the children have an opportunity of visiting their parents in the factories or work centres, and this enhances their respect both for work and workers.

Childcare centres for pre-school education and care of children should be organised in India, as they have been in Cuba. The premier women's organisation—The All India Women's Conference has branches all over the country. These can be increased to cover all urban and rural areas according to need. The staffing and the supervision of the childcare centres should be the responsibility of the All India Women's Conference. There is no dearth of educated, non-working women in the country today. The All India Conference of Women should draw them into the educational system and make full use of this skilled work force. Women with high school and college education should be appointed to the posts of senior teachers and those with an education of sixth grade or more as junior teachers. All new teachers should study modern methods of childcare in special crash courses before they join duty at the centres.

Primary Schools. Gunnar Myrdal,[22] M. Blaug[23] and Amartaya Sen[24] have deplored the fact that primary education inspite of the highest economic return from investment in it, has been criminally neglected and that there has been inspite of very low economic return, a wasteful expansion in higher education in India. The rate of return on investment in primary education is found to be about 15 per cent. After middle school education the rate is 14 per cent, after high school 10.5 per cent and after a bachelor's degree in arts, science or commerce, a little less than 9 per cent. If 10 per cent is regarded as the minimum rate of interest acceptable, then the primary and the middle school education can be regarded as highly profitable and high school education worthwhile but not by a big margin. To obviate a misunderstanding Professor Sen adds that these rates of return relate to expansion of different levels of education. Says he, 'The intention is not to suggest that all university education is unprofitable at 10 per cent rate of interest, but only that the further expansion at this stage will be unprofitable, a reduction up to a point will make things better. The egalitarian process begun in the childcare centres must be continued in the schools and the primary education of 8 years duration, from the seventh year to the fourteenth, must be free and compulsory

[22]Gunnar Myrdal. 1968. Asian Drama, England.

[23]M. Blaug, P.R.G. Layard, and M. Woodhall. 1969. The Causes of Educated Unemployment in India, London.

[24]A.K. Sen. 1970. Aspects of Indian Economic Development, Ed. Pramit Chaudhary. 1971. London.

for all children. It should be as Gandhiji suggested imparted through the medium of a craft or vocation as already explained and be related to one's work in life.

Dr D.P. Chaudhary[25] working at the Delhi School of Economics has analysed inter-family, inter-village, inter-district aud inter-state data to show a positive correlation between levels of education and agricultural productivity. Both Gunnar Myrdal and A.K. Sen hold the view that educational differences do effect agricultural productivity, and schooling is a 'relevant constituent of a programme of agricultural expansion'.

In this context Professor Sen draws attention to three special aspects of the impact of education on agricultural production that have not received much attention so far. First, education by having more of it, although it increases the profitability of other factors of production of agriculture—fertilizer, better quality seeds, pesticide and water—is not just one more impact like the others. It affects the farmer's thinking process and his attitude towards other impacts. The educated farmer who can read hand-outs and pamphlets written by agricultural scientisits, is not only clear in his mind about the value of inputs but also makes better use of them than one who is not educated. Secondly, the impact of education on the use of inputs is not confined merely to individuals and families that have the advantage of schooling. It spreads to the neighbours in the village, to other villages and also beyond districts and states. Thirdly, school education has an indirect impact on the economic function through changes in the social and political elements in the system. It affects administrative factors concerned in securing credit, fertilizer, pesticide and irrigation facilities; it helps political organization of the village society; and finally it makes villagers conscious of their rights and enables them to resist social iniquities, and administrative abuse and corruption.

The per capita cost of primary education is the lowest, about one fifth to one third of secondary education, and one fifteenth to one thirteenth of the University education[26] and its economic return, 15 per cent as against less than 9 per cent of college education, is the highest. Yet it has been neglected in terms of the money spent on it.

[25]D.P. Chaudhary. 1968. Education and Agricultural Productivity in India, unpublished Ph. D. Thesis, Delhi.
[26]Gunnar Myrdal. 1968. Asian Drama, England.

Much more money needs to be spent on free and compulsory primary education. This can be done by economizing on wasteful expenditure on certain types of higher education as well as by general expansion of the budget.

Besides errors in the allocation of finances, certain other factors have stood in the way of progress of primary education. One of these is a complete failure to relate rural schooling to rural economic needs. Teaching of 3 R's and a general type of education in other subjects in the village school, has little or no meaning, if village children are not trained in scientific methods of farming and rural crafts or industry. At least half of the pupil's time must be spent in learning by doing, in the field or the rural workshop. The second non-financial failure of primary education is in the matter of dropouts. The ex-education minister, Mr Nural Hassan,[27] referring to the progress of primary education in the country, stated that the enrolment during the year 1975 was of the order 79 per cent and was expected to reach 82 per cent in 1976. Mr Nural Hassan's figures were impressive but also misleading. He informed the house about the numbers enrolled but said nothing about the drop-outs.

Studies undertaken at the Agricultural Economic Research Centre of the University of Delhi have disclosed that the tendency to drop out is very much sharper when the seasonal peaks of agricultural activity are reached. The study was confined to the states of Punjab and Uttar Pradesh and in both the number of drop-outs was significantly high, both at the time of the Rabi and the Kharif crops during sowing and harvesting. Many families require the help of the children at the time of the peak agricultural activity and short-time drop-outs during these periods often acquire permanency. A rearrangement of the school terms, the vacations and the time of examination in a manner such that sowing and harvesting fall during the period of the vacations, would help the children to pursue their studies as well as help in the fields during the peak periods. If and when primary education is made compulsory, a rearrangement of the school terms and examinations will have to be made if the farmer's interests and agricultural productivity are not to suffer.

I wish to reiterate in the end that the primary education I have in view for the country is the one Gandhiji recommended and has

[27]Speech in Parliament. April 1976.

been described earlier in this chapter. The education is free and compulsory and acquired through learning a craft or a vocation. Both girls and boys study together for eight years (Gandhiji recommends atleast seven years) between the ages of seven and fourteen, and instruction is imparted through the medium of the mother tongue Hindi in Hindi speaking areas and the regional language in other parts of the country.

Secondary Schools. Secondary schools exist mainly in urban areas—towns and cities. In larger cities as already stated there are two types of schools—schools for the rich and schools for the common people. Secondary education is a continuation of the primary education and is imparted in the same schools. The principal drawbacks of the secondary schools—the literary and general character of the education and the lack of relatedness to the business of living—have already been high-lighted.

Numerous proposals to restructure education have been made from time to time by educationists, economists, thinkers, the Planning Commission, members of various education commissions and political leaders but thanks to the vested interests of the entrenched ruling and the rich classes who stand to gain by the status quo, no recommendations for reform of education in general and of secondary education in particular, can be implemented.

An 11 year school—the higher secondary school—was proposed and introduced several years ago in Delhi, Madhya Pradesh and some other states. It did away with two years of training after the high school, and the intermediate examination. Under the scheme one year was added to the high school and another to the degree course, so that after the higher secondary a 3 years course was required for a B.A. or a B.Sc. degree. And what was the result? It did not help to alter the "general" or "literary" character of the education or make it job-oriented. It only helped to worsen and aggravate the employment situation by causing a further expansion of the university and higher education. Every one who passed the higher secondary examination was automatically enrolled for a 3 year degree course and according to the economist P.C.Malhotra in Madhya Pradesh, caused a 14 per cent expansion of higher education.

Mr Nurul Hassan, Education Minister in Indira Gandhi's cabinet advocated a 10+2+3 scheme originally proposed by the Education Commission for the whole country.

A framework[28] for the curriculum and the 10 year school proposed under the scheme was published and issued by the National
Council of Educational Research and Training, New Delhi. It
resembles closely the 10-year general secondary school curriculum
in the Soviet Union. It is claimed by its authors that it will improve
the quality and raise the overall standard of education in the
country, promote and improve the teaching of science and mathematics so urgently needed for industrial development, make education work-based and job oriented, and raise the cultural level of
the people by developing in them an aesthetic attitude. The time
allocated to each area of school work from class I—X is given
below:

Classes	Subjects	Time in hours & per month
I-II	First Language	25
	Mathematics	10
	Environmental studies (social studies & general science)	15
	Work Experience and the arts	25
	Health education and games	25
	Total	100
III-V	First language	25
	Mathematics	15
	Environmental studies (social studies)	10
	Environmental studies II (General science)	10
	Work experience and the arts	20
	Health education and games	20
	Total	100

The instructional time recommended in the lower primary
schools is 3 to 4 hours a day. The first language will be learnt

[28]NCERT. 1975. The Curriculum for the Ten Year School, New Delhi.

through environmental studies and games, mathematics will also be learned through work experiences and the arts, as well as through games. Hence work experience, arts and games are given 40 per cent share of the time. Without this, a changeover from bookish education and rote learning will be difficult to accomplish.

Class	Subject	Periods per week of 30-40 minutes
VI-VIII	First language	8
	Second language	5
	Mathematics	7
	Science (life science & physical sciences)	7
	Social Sciences (history, geography, civics and economics)	6
	Arts	4
	Work experience	5
	Physical education, health education and games	6
	Tolal	48

Class	Subject	Periods per week of 30-40 minutes
IX-X	First language	6
	Second language	5
	Third language	2
	Mathematics	7
	Sciences (life-science and physical sciences)	7
	Social Sciences (history, geography, civics, economics)	7
	Arts	3
	Work experience	5
	Physical education, health education and games	6
	Total	48

The instructional time including assembly and recess time in classes VI-X works out to six hours daily.

For evaluation as in the Russian general secondary school, there will be no pass or fail in any examination and there will be letter grading on a five point scale (A,B,C,D,E). For student and youth activities, once again, the Russian model of Pioneer Palaces is recommended.

The framework suggested above for the 10 stage itself suffers from a number of very serious drawbacks. First, as classes VIII and X may be terminal, the work experience from classes VI to X seems to be very insufficient and is not likely to prepare them and make them fit for taking on a job at this stage. It needs, therefore, to be considerably enhanced. Secondly, the number of subjects for study at the high school levels (classes IX and X) are far too many to be of any real use. The load of 'heavy syllabi and heavy subjects" must be lightened to make it reasonable and tolerable for the high school student. The science and other text books prepared under the direction of Mr Rais Ahmed, ex-chief of the NCERT, are extremely difficult and theoretical and pass over the heads of even brilliant students. Moreover, in the absence of equipment and practical facilities even in the best of schools in metropolitan cities, the charge that Indian teaching is theoretical and unrelated to the life of the community, will be fully proven. Thirdly, for students who ultimately wish to opt for arts or humanities, the emphasis should not be in the teaching of mathematics or physical sciences. This will not only prevent unnecessary and wasteful learning of subjects for which these students have a positive dislike and which have no relevance to their future lives, but also help to improve the qualities and standards of the other subjects which they need and for which they opt. Fourthly, there is an utter want of suitably qualified science teachers and other technical personnel, laboratories and workshops, and equipment even for schools in large cities, not to speak of towns and the rural areas. Provision of these facilities will not only take time but also require huge allocation of funds which the government somehow does not seem to be prepared to make. This is amply clear from the low priority which seems to have been accorded to education and specially primary and secondary education in the Congress regime both by the Planning Commission and the executive governments. For instance in the expenditure on education during the Fourth Plan (1969-74) there was a short fall of nearly Rs 100 crore compared to the original outlay, resulting in large cuts in the programmes for the expansion of primary and middle level (secondary) education. This happened even though the facilities for already over expanded university education outstripped the Plan target. The so-called up-dating of the Fifth Plan has the same story to tell. The size of the Fifth Plan in real terms of course shrank compared to the Draft Plan because of the fall in the value of the rupee. But the revised financial outlay of Rs 39,303 crore was still, marginally higher than in the Draft. However, an absolute cut was made in the allocations for projects under the minimum needs programme even in financial terms. The outlay on education was reduced by Rs 441 crore from Rs 1,728 crore in the draft to Rs 1,285 crore in the final version. Significantly the programme of primary education suffered the worst cut by as much as 45 per cent.

The Prime Minister of India, Mr Morarji Desai speaking in August 1977 at a conference of educationists in New Delhi, expressed his disagreement with the $10+2+3$ scheme. What I wish to emphasize is that even the 10 stage in the scheme is not free of serious blemishes which need rectification. At the present stage of our educational, social and economic development, the following measures will in my opinion prove rewarding the student's burden must be curtailed by cutting out unnecessary subjects and heavy syllabi, 2 academic teaching must be reduced to not more than 2-3 hours a day in the primary schools and not more than 4 hours a day in the secondary schools, 3 all children attending school must be apprenticed to farmers, fruit growers, food processors, spinners, weavers, dyers, launderers and dry cleaners, tailors, embroiderers, carpenters, furniture makers and workers in wood, masons, stone cutters, plumbers, electricians, glass manufacturers, workers in ceramics and plastics, shoe makers and other leather workers, makers of soaps, hair oil, dentrifices and other cosmetics, utensil makers and other metal workers, makers and repairers of simple machines, carpet and shawl makers, typing and shorthand establishments, teachers of music, dancing and fine arts, hair dressers, shopping establishments and trading centers etc., in the vicinity. Two or more hours of work daily, in addition to academic learning, will make these children employable and productive. Lists of qualified and acceptable teachers in every walk of life should be maintained by the state and placements of pupils made with the combined help of the parents and schools. The training on the job should be given equal importance if not more than that given to academic learning. In the foregoing scheme of education, the end of fifth, eighth and tenth years at primary or secondary schools are terminal and should enable the students to learn one or more callings and find suitable jobs.

While this should hold for the general primary and secondary schools in all neighbourhoods to which children both of the rich and the poor should go, there must be a number of other types of schools. Special Secondary schools for humanities should after class VIII, lay greater emphasis on the study of languages and literature; special secondary schools for arts, on drawing, painting, dance and drama; and special secondary schools for commerce on commercial subjects like accountancy, type writing and secretarial work. There should in addition be part time and evening schools to which the drop outs can return and complete their studies—polytechnics in all major cities would provide pre-engineering courses, and vocational schools higher training in particular trades. Those who qualify from the secondary schools, and do not opt for work at this stage will if they obtain the necessary number of A_S and B_S be admitted either to 2+vocational or to two-year pre-university courses in their special subjects. After a final screening depending on the number of A_S and B_S they secure in their pre-university years, they will be admitted to a 2 or 3 year university degree course or a professional school of engineering, medicine, law etc., or a teacher's training college.

Higher Education. A disproportionate overexpansion of higher education has taken place in the country during the past thirty years. It has been due as has been explained earlier, to a failure, to take into account the difference between the social and the private profitability of higher education, to the failure of leadership in withstanding political and regional pressures of unnecessary expansion, and to the inefficient and antiquated methods in fore-casting manpower requirements by the Planning Commission, in different sectors of the economy. There has been an immense overproduction of engineers, doctors and scientists, who have had to migrate to the United States and the United Kingdom in search of suitable employmemt.

The Estimates Committee[29] commenting on the brain drain of highly skilled personnel, quotes the results of an UNCTAD study to suggest that whenever a 'medical doctor leaves India to settle

[29]Editorial, Times of India, April. 1976 New Delhi.

in the United States, it amounts to a loss of Rs 3,30,000 for India and a gain of Rs 51,75,000 to the US. Similarly, the emigration of every scientist makes the country poorer by Rs 1,72,000 and the US richer by Rs 18,75,000. In 1972 alone 3,141 Indian doctors and scientists resettled in the US adding a staggering figure of Rs 656 crore to the wealth of the most affluent nation on earth. India is on this count alone giving far more in aid to the USA, than it is receiving from that country. This process the Estimates Committee states, will get institutionalised pretty shortly when the first ever regional centre for the transfer of technology among the underdeveloped nations is set up under the auspices of the United Nations Industrial Development Organisation, in this country.[30] Even before the setting up of the regional centre there has been a large exodus of Indian scientists and doctors to the countries of Asia and Africa. The Estimates Committee considers that a certain amount of compulsion will be necessary to 'ensure that persons with scarce skills are retained for service at home'.

The colossal figures for unemployment among arts, science, commerce, law, medicine and engineering graduates whose training-cost both to the individuals and the state is extremely high, is a pointer to the conclusion that expansion of higher education is not only at the present stage uncalled for, but needs a drastic curtailment. The money saved from this head and a further expansion of the budget can be then spent as Professor Sen has emphasized for making primary education free and compulsory.

Out of the School Education. A description of this aspect of education has already been given in the earlier paragraphs in which the need for training on the job and apprenticeship has been recommended as an integral part of the education. In some countries as for instance North Vietnam, this has been the practice for over two decades and half the children's time is spent in academic learning in school and half of it outside learning an art, craft or trade. Learning out of school can play a big role in eradicating adult illiteracy and in the continuing education of the individual. It is most unfortunate that professional educators have come to acquire a monopoly in education. Knowledge according to them is, what is dispensed in institutions of learning. Those who have studied in these

[30]UNIDO for the transfer of technology has already been set up in this country.

institutions know everything. Those who have learnt outside the institutions though they may know much more, 'do not know'. To know is to have diplomas or degrees. These are the tags, the labels, the hall-marks of learning without acquiring which no one need claim that he is educated or aspire for a top assignment or an office of ample profit and power. And yet people who have made great contributions to the fund of human knowledge will freely tell you that they acquired what they know and value most, more often outside than inside of an institution—from a friend, a poor relation an older person, or an expert under whom or with whom they worked; that they learned it while reading, listening to the radio or a tape, or viewing a film or the television; that they picked it up on the job or as an apprentice or while dismantling a machine. Ivan Illich[31] in his remarkable book classifies the organization of such educational resources in four groups:

1. Reference Services to Educational Objects—which facilitate access to things or processes used for formal learning. Some of these things can be reserved for this purpose, stored in libraries, rental agencies, laboratories, and show rooms like museums and theatres; others can be in daily use in factories, airports or on farms, but made available to students as apprentices or in off-hours.

2. Skill Exchanges—which permit persons to list their skills, the conditions under which they are willing to serve as models for others who want to learn these skills, and the addresses at which they can be reached.

3. Peer-Matching—a communications network which permits persons to describe the learning activity in which they wish to engage, in the hope of finding a partner for the inquiry.

4. Reference Services to Educators-at-Large—who can be listed in a directory giving the addresses and self-descriptions of professionals, para-professionals and free-lancers, along with condition of access to their services. Such educators, as we will see, could be chosen by pooling or consulting their former clients.

Similar views to Illich's on the out-of-the-school education, have been expressed by a large number of other writers. Alvin Toffler[32] is one of these. He writes, 'outside the schools, students would be taught skills by adults in the community. The design of secondary

---

[31]Ivan Illich. 1973. Deschooling Society, England.
[32]Alvin Toffler. 1970. The Future Shock, New York.

and higher education programmes would make use of "mentors" drawn from the adult population. Such mentors would not only transmit skills but show how the abstractions of the text-book are applied in life. Accountants, doctors, engineers, businessmen, carpenters, builders and planners might well become part of an outside faculty in another dialectical swing, this time toward a new kind of apprenticeship.

If learning is to be stretched over a life time, there is reduced justification for forcing kids to attend school full time. For many young people, part-time schooling and part-time work at low-skill, paid and unpaid community service tasks will prove more satisfying and educational.

It is hoped that the rulers, the educationists and other people in whose hands lies the future and the destiny of India, will ponder well and frame and institute a programme of education that will use all the out-of-the-school resources as well as a proper system of schools, to help build an egalitarian society in which no one will starve or go naked and every one live in reasonable comfort in clean and healthy surroundings both in the countryside and the town.

EIGHT

Health

Precious little has been done towards meeting the country's medical and health needs even after 30 years of attainment of independence by India. The responsibility for this rests squarely on the Congress Party and the Congress Governments that ruled the country during this period and the luminaries of the medical profession.

Students of history of medicine are fully aware of India's great contributions to development of the medical sciences. The earliest record of drugs and healing agents is found in the Rigveda. In the Atharvaveda there is a mention of nearly 450 herbal and other drugs. Chronologically the Vedas are much older than the Chinese herbals (2000 BC), the Egyptian Papyus Ebers (1,500 BC), the Greek books on medicinal plants (300 BC) and the Roman Galen (100 AD).

During the period of the Samhitas, Charak and Sushruta wrote monumental texts. Nagarjuna in his Ras-shastra for the first time introduced metals, particularly mercury, in the treatment of diseases. This was done by Paracelsus in Europe many centuries later. After Nagarjuna's Ras-shastra came Ashtanga Hriday and the famous treatise of Bhava Misra and a large number of Nighantus. These were great achievements.

After the industrial revolution in England and the British conquest of India a period of stagnation set in for us, whereas the European countries went ahead. They said goodbye to their authoritarian approach, while India continued to stick to its belief that everything indigenous or ancient was sacrosanct.

No wonder in the race for scientific and medical progress, it lost to the West.

Fifty years ago the modern doctor, although he was in a better position in regard to surgery and diagnostic aids, was not in a position greatly superior to that of a vaid so far as medical treatment was concerned. In his "armoury" he had hardly half a dozen effective drugs like aspirin, quinine, digitalis or neo-salvarsan.

But the situation today is completely different. During the past four decades a phenomenal progress, comparable only to progress in development of weapons of modern warfare or space travel, has been made in the development of new and effective drugs. These developments have been completely ignored by our political leaders either wilfully or due to ignorance.

We have today, to mention only a few, powerful and effective anti-infective agents like the sulfonamides and the antibiotics, anti-malarials, anti-convulsants, anti-diabetics, anti-depressives, analgesics, tranquilizers, hypnotics, hormones, vitamins and drugs for treatment and control of filariasis, tuberculosis, syphilis, gonorrhea and high blood pressure. These drugs bring relief daily to millions of human beings all over the world.

There is no justification for withholding these effective drugs from patients and treating them with the help of ineffective, inert, inelegant, bulky, unstandardised and unstandardisable Ayurvedic or Unani formulations. Treatment by these drugs of patients suffering from serious disorders which are now amenable to therapy by modern drugs, amounts to virtual murder of the poor and ignorant people by practitioners of a bullock-cart system in the space age.

As things stand, the medical and the health services of the country are in a bad way. Scant attention is paid to nutrition, supply of potable water, immunisation and other preventive measures, environmental hygiene, rural housing and social welfare programmes affecting women, children and the handicapped. It is a matter of profound concern that in the course of our Five Year Plans, whenever there were periods of financial stringency, the axe fell most heavily on social services and minimum welfare needs of the poorest sections.

Free medical care is today available to governors, ministers, judges, members of the houses of legislature and officers of the government—the very people who can afford to pay for it themselves. It is also available to the rich at the company expense. A few others who can afford to pay for it are those self employed people who have fabulous incomes often made by questionable means.

For the remaining among the self-employed with an income of Rs 1,000 per month or less, the question of affording adequate medical care does not arise at all. Our hospitals and dispensaries buy and stock expensive drugs but they are mostly used for the benefit of the influential and richer sections. Poor people seldom ever get them; they are asked to go and buy them from the market even when they are warded.

The bulk of the urban population and the entire rural population of the country has no access to modern medical care. It appears to me that our Government which is in theory committed to democracy and socialism, in practice, even in matters of education and health, makes a distinction between the elites and the under-privileged. We do not have one system of treatment for everybody.

We trick our masses and help strengthen the popular belief that Ayurveda, Unani and Homeopathy are good and independent systems of medicine. We hold back from them the truth that like Egyptian, Greek or medieval medicine, these also are only stages or steps in the development of modern scientific medicine, just as the present one may be a step to a more scientific and better system in the future.

Today modern scientific medicine is the best system for all the world and every citizen of India has a right to ask for it. A proof in favour of this is the large-scale use of modern medicine by the graduates of Ayurvedic medical colleges. Another proof if further proof is needed, is provided by a careful perusal of our daily newspapers. I have never read of a minister, a legislator or a prominent leader, when he is ill, being admitted in an Ayurvedic or a Unani hospital in Delhi inspite of the fact that there are Ayurvedic and Unani hospitals in the capital; they invariably go to Willingdon or Safdarjang hospitals or the hospital attached to the All India Institute of Medical Sciences.

Crores of rupees, in my opinion, are wasted yearly on running Ayurvedic colleges that train graduates who after passing out, use mainly modern medicines. Crores more are being spent by the CCIRMH in promoting unhealthy practices, in the name of research by a staff and an organisation without knowledge of research techniques or a scientific outlook. The only associations capable of promoting research in indigenous drugs are still the ICMR and the CSIR with the chain of laboratories in Lucknow, Calcutta, Hyderabad and Jammu.

After highlighting the sins of omission of our Government, I suggest a way out of the present impasse. On the eve of the October Revolution in 1917, Russia had 17,000 qualified medical men only.

After years of external aggression and civil strife, only 14,000 were alive by 1922. With the help of these and the available feldshers (a type equivalent to our compounders and dressers) Russia socialized its health services. The feldshers manned dispensaries in the rural areas and the qualified doctors not only supervised their task but also looked after the urban population. Preventive and curative work was combined in the same person.

We have 1,50,000 qualified doctors and over 200,000 vaids of which about 50,000 are graduates from our Ayurvedic colleges and have been taught modern subjects. My proposal is that all these men together with the available paramedical personnel be organised into a National Health Service providing free care to everyone, irrespective of the purse.

To achieve this, I suggest that the 200,000 Ayurvedic practitioners be attached to district medical hospitals in the country and imparted training for a period of one year in the diagnosis and treatment of common diseases. At the end of this period they should be awarded a proficiency certificate. This large number of duly trained men should be placed in charge of rural dispensaries. They should be paid well and their grade should not in any case be less than Rs 450-25-650-50-1200. The graduate doctors should also be available to help the rural medical officers.

With a strength of 3,50,000 medical men and our present population of about 62 crore, one doctor will be available for every 1,750 persons. This is a reasonable ratio. When Soviet Russia adopted the health plan they discontinued further training of feldshers who were gradually replaced by qualified doctors. If such a scheme is put into action, we should, like the Soviets, close down all Ayurvedic colleges and replace the vaids gradually by graduates and qualified medical men.[1]

I have so far criticised the leadership and the Central and State Governments. I would be showing a bias towards my own profession if I failed to point out that leaders of the medical profession have not taken sufficient interest in matters of health and medical care of the people. They have not provided a solution to the modern doctor's refusal to serve in the village, nor presented a

[1]M.L. Gujral. 2 May 1971. Times of India, New Delhi. The foregoing description of the Health Services is almost a verbatim report of the paper.

scheme for a National Health Service as operating in Britain or Russia.

The plan outlined by me helps provide doctors for the village in the framework of a National Health Service. It makes use of the services, of the trained vaid who would, if properly paid, take over where the graduate doctor refuses to go and also help provide the numbers required for the National Health Service.

I hope the "doyens" of the profession, whether in the Indian Medical Association, the Indian Medical Council, the Indian Academy of Medical Science, the Indian Council of Medical Research and the Director-General and the Directors of Health Services in the States and other eminent medical men will lead the way and throw in their weight in favour of the establishment of a National Health Service now.

NINE

Food and Agriculture

I

India like many third world countries has a hybrid or a dual economy—a large agricultural, subsistence sector, and a small modern industrial sector in enclaves round the urban centres. Agriculture contributes nearly half of the national income, provides livelihood for about 70 per cent of the people, supplies the bulk of wage goods to the non-agricultural sector and accounts for over 50 per cent of the export trade. The importance of the sector can be judged from a realization of the fact that years of good monsoon and good harvests have always been years of relatively lesser want and privation and that years of insufficient rainfall and droughts have invariably been associated with famines, and extreme hunger and destitution.

An adequate level of agricultural growth is imperative for a variety of reasons:

1. *To meet the increasing food needs of a growing population.* The population of the country has been increasing at a growth rate of 2.5 per cent per annum. Unless the food production increases, the needs of the growing population cannot be met even at the existing low per capita level of consumption both in respect of caloric and nutritional requirements. It is, therefore, important to step up the production of foodgrains, and a growth rate of atleast 5 per cent in agricultural produce is needed to feed the growing population. It is well known that as economic development takes place, the income elasticity of demand for food goes up and the people start consuming better and more food than before.

2. *To conserve valuable foreign exchange.* Large amounts of foodgrains have been imported from the United States during the past twenty years and are still being imported to feed the growing population and to check inflationary pressures. This has

cost the country hundreds of crores in precious foreign exchange which could be used for import of capital goods, scarce raw materials and components for the development of industry and economy as a whole.

3. *To increase employment potential.* Agricultural development would if properly carried out and combined with development of rural industries and rural works, eliminate or at least significantly reduce unemployment.

4. *To ensure growth with stability.* Economic development without proportionate agricultural growth is likely to lead to shortages of foodgrains and agricultural raw materials and engender inflationary pressures in the economy. This actually happened following the droughts of 1965-67, and the prices sky-rocketed between 1971-74 when the monsoons failed.

5. *To raise the level of industrial production and promote industrial growth.* Agricultural raw materials are needed for the development of industries, and shortages of raw materials are impediments in the way of industrial development. Professor Kuznets[1] considers the rise in agricultural productivity a required antecedent as well as concomitant of modern industrial growth. This view according to Lefeber[2] assumes great importance in under-developed countries where agriculture is the dominant sector and a demand for manufactured goods is the most likely alternative to industrial exports.

6. *To reduce the incremental capital-output ratio (ICOR).* For any targeted growth rate the overall investment in agriculture is less than in industry. As capital is not plentiful in the country, a major shift in favour of agriculture and rural development is not only the most effective way of promoting growth but also of improving the conditions of the poor, the majority of whom live in the villages. The only precondition is that investment in agriculture should be spread uniformly and not restricted to selected districts or rich farmers.

7. *To create a market for products of industries.* With the increase in agricultural production, the buying power of the rural population improves and they are enabled to absorb the produce of the industry.

[1]S. Kuznets. 1965. Economic Growth and Structure, New York.
[2]Louis Lefeber. In economic Theory and Planning Ed. Mitra, Ashok, 1974. Calcutta.

8. *To secure marketable agricultural surpluses.* Marketable surpluses are needed both for feeding the urban population as well as for providing raw materials for industry. In the absence of any adequate agricultural produce, shortages occur and prices of foodgrains as well as raw materials for industry and primary products for export, rise and create serious problems for the economy.

9. *To promote improvement in standards of living and general awareness.* An increase in the availability of foodgrains and consequently other meterial goods, improves the standard of living of the people including the educational and health standards. It thus contributes towards social and political education of the masses and a rise in the level of their awareness. It imbues them with a feeling of confidence in themselves, a sense of dignity and equality between man and man. They are better able to appreciate the causes that have hitherto kept them backward and under the heel of the exploiters and the oppressors. It also helps them to devise ways and means or measures for organisation and unity to counter their backwardness and to fight the injustices of the kulak.

10. *To reduce the disparity in incomes and wealth between the rich and the poor.* This may, however, be aggravated where the distribution of land is so unequal as in India. Inequality has actually been aggravated in the rural sector after the introduction of the new agricultural strategy in the late 1960s.

II

While the primary and the decisive role of agricultural economy cannot be denied or even matched, the attention paid to it by the policy makers, the planners or the bureaucrats has been scant. One of the most persistent criticisms of Indian planning has been its excessive pre-occupation with industry, especially heavy industry at the cost of agriculture which has suffered dire neglect due to the operation of a number of causes:

1. *Make-believe and delusory land reforms.* The first and the foremost cause of poor showing in agricultural and rural development has been the dire outcome of the meagre and halting attention given to the problem of land reform. For many years before India became free, her leaders kept on promising land to the tenants, share-croppers and landless cultivators. In 1936, Jawaharlal Nehru wrote:

'...the main drive in future will have to be a complete over-hauling of the agrarian system and the growth of industry. No tinkering with the land, a multitude of commissions costing lakhs of rupees and suggesting trivial changes in superstructure, will do the slightest good. The land system which we have is collapsing before our eyes and it is a hinderance to production and any large-scale operations. Only a radical change in it, putting an end to the little holdings and introducing organized collective and cooperative enterprises, and thus increasing the yield greatly with much less effort will meet modern conditions'.[3]

The story of the failure of the Congress governments to fulfil the promises made to the starving peasants in the courses of the liberation struggle and the half-hearted attempts to intro-duce and implement land reforms, is now common knowledge. During the British period, zamindars, jagirdars, inamdars and mahajans dominated the rural scene. They were bolstered up by the British and were the pillars of the colonial administration in India. After the British left, the erstwhile British props were taken over and adopted by the Congress to build, shore up and per-petuate their one-party rule in the country. Landlords, big farmers and usurers who were the biggest enemies of the country during the liberation struggle, overnight became patriots, joined hands with the Congress Party and became its "vote banks". Power in the village, district and state Congress Committees passed into the hands of the landlord and the big farmer. Due to their dominance in the Congress Committees at various levels and their links with the urban bourgeoisie which depended on them both for raw material and a substantial part of a market of luxury industrial goods produced in the urban industrial sector—they came to acquire power over the State Governments and the Chief Ministers, that has helped them to resist all attempts by the Central and the State Governments to legislate laws for land reform and to stall their implementation even if legislated.

In the early 1950s zamindari was abolished—at first in Bihar and Uttar Pradesh and then in other states of the Country. The surplus land over and above the ceiling enacted by law and large areas of privately owned forest land, grazing land and culturable waste was distributed among tenants and sharecroppers and nearly

[3]J.L. Nehru. 1936. Autobiography, London.

20 million tenants were brought into direct contact with the state. And yet the exemptions granted were so many, the loopholes in the legislation so numerous and the evasion of the law so easy that the old feudal exploiters turned themselves into "self-cultivating land-lords" and capitalist farmers and were able to retain hundreds of thousands of acres of land. What is more, a large number of the urban rich and even upper and lower middle class people who discovered that land was a safe and lucrative investment—industrialists, merchants, civil and military officers, shop keepers, doctors, engineers, lawyers, office clerks and petty officials—acquired or purchased land at throw away prices from the rich aristocracy who were in danger of losing it on account of the law on ceilings, or from poor peasants unable to hold it on account of poverty, illness, indebtedness or other reason.

At the 1959 session of the Congress held in Nagpur, a resolution was passed to strictly enforce the ceiling laws and to distribute the surplus land among agricultural workers for cooperative farming under the supervision of the gaon panchayats. It was recommended that technological and economic assistance should be extended to the cooperatives. Ten years later, in 1969 a Chief Minister's Conference was called to consider the problem of land reform. In 1971, a Central Land Reforms Committee was appointed. It fixed the upper limit of holdings but shelved the question of the floor. In July 1972 another Chief Minister's Conference met and laid down in detail, the ceilings for different types of land:

(*i*) For irrigated lands, whether state or privately irrigated and yielding two crops a year, the ceiling was fixed at 10-18 standard acres. If privately irrigated, the limit was not to exceed 18 acres; otherwise the limit was to be between 10-18 acres.

(*ii*) For irrigated land yielding one crop a year, the ceiling was 27 acres.

(*iii*) For other lands the ceiling was not to exceed 54 acres.

(*iv*) In special cases and hill areas and for land of the third category, rules could be relaxed. Before deciding the limits, however, the states were to consult the agricultural ministry.

The unit of application of the ceiling was a family of five—husband, wife and three minor children. If there were more than 5 family members the total land was not to exceed double the ceiling. Every adult son was to be an additional unit. The ceiling laws had a retrospective application from 24 January 1971 and after this no transfers were permissible. Exemptions were, however, allowed in respect of:

(*a*) Tea, coffee, cardamom, coconut and rubber plantations.

(*b*) Bhudan land, Cooperative banks, nationalized banks and for central, state and regional lands.

(*c*) Industrial and mercantile enterpises.

(*d*) Cooperative agricultural societies.

(*e*) Religious, charitable and educational trusts.

(*f*) Gaushalas and stud farms.

(*g*) Experimental farms up to 100 acres for sugar mills.

(*h*) Fruit orchards with limits as for dry lands.

Widespread and extensive exemptions allowed to rich and powerful sections of the population have made a mockery of the ceiling laws. But this is not the whole story. With the connivance and very often active support of the officials, even these laws are freely evaded and land divided among all the members of the family, young and old. Benami transfers to trusted relations and servants are common. Even unborn babies and domestic pets have land in their names. By such evasions and subterfuges, even the biggest landlords have been able to save and retain the entire land they possessed for their families.

Diverse other rules have been employed by rich farmers and landlords to impoverish the poor peasants.

The right of resumption for personal cultivation has been invoked to claim back once cultivable wastes developed at some cost and great effort by the poor.

The consolidation of holdings has enabled rich farmers to take away from tenants and share-croppers land which they were previously unable to farm due to the distance between the parcels.

The New Strategy of the 1960s has turned many a share-cropper, tenant and small farmer into a wage labourer. The tenants and the share-croppers have been ejected and the small owners have been forced to sell or lease out their plots to the big farmers.

The promise of "land to the tiller", held out to the peasantry in the course of the freedom struggle, remains unfulfilled after 30 years of Congress rule and the economic level of the deprived villager is no better today than it was before India became independent. If anything, rural poverty has been aggravated and the condition of the landless agricultural workers, small and marginal farmers, share-croppers, tenants and village artisans, has actually worsened. While the percentage of rural poor below the poverty line remains much the same, due to rapid growth of population, their absolute numbers have greatly increased. Consequently the numbers of destitutes and the deprived in the countryside is much greater today than before the Congress assumed power. And the ravenous and rapacious predators—the landlords and the big farmers, the usurers and traders, the city and the international bourgeoisie—continue to ravage the land, and pillage and plunder the primary produce, to-day as they used to, before the zamindari system was abolished.

In the wake of spiralling prices, run-away inflation and acute scarcities of essential commodities, a Task Force was appointed under the Chairmanship of Land Reforms Commissioner to con-sider de-novo the problems relating to land reform. The Report of the Task Force was submitted in 1973 and is an honest and out-spoken document of great value. It states: 'Enactment of progressive measures of land reforms and their efficient implementation call for hard political decisions and effective political support, direction and control. In the context of the socio-economic conditions prevailing in the rural areas of the country, no tangible progress can be ex-pected in the field of land reform in the absence of the requisite political will. The sad truth is that this crucial factor has been wanting. The lack of political will is amply demonstrated by the large gaps between the policy and legislation and between law and its implementation. In no sphere of public activity in our country since independence has the hiatus between precept and practice, between policy pronouncements and actual execution, been as great as in the domain of land reforms.'[4]
Again:

'In a society in which the entire weight of civil and criminal laws, judicial pronouncements and precedents, administrative tradition and practice is thrown on the side of the existing social order based on the inviolability of private property, an isolated law aimed at the restructuring of property relationships in the rural areas has hardly any chance of success'.[5]

The Task Force candidly admits that no radical land reforms are possible within "the political power structure obtaining in the

---

[4]Report of the Task Force on Agrarian Reform. 1973. Quoted by Balraj Mehta in Failures of Indian Economy, 1974. New Delhi.
[5]Ibid.

country", and therefore, in the place of land to the tiller or other radical measures, it suggests a much more modest approach for the fifth plan, in fact measures similar to those enacted earlier and implemented in the breach. The Task Force observes that after the zamindari abolition, hundreds of crores was paid in compensation to the zamindars. But whether or not abolition of intermediary rights conferred 'any new economic benefits on the tenants, is a moot point'. Ceilings on land holdings, tenancy reforms and redistribution of land, made small headway. According to the Task Force in some ways the position actually became worse. There were large scale evictions, voluntary surrenders of right on land and liberal exercise of resumption rights. In addition to the measures suggested earlier, the Task Force suggested the creation of a new set-up independent of the established revenue and administrative machinery, created expressly for and devoted exclusively to implementation of land reforms and vested with necessary powers to get round legal difficulties and other obstacles. It is difficult to understand why the Task Force was so naive that it did not realize that even the new set-up would not succeed in the absence of the political support which vested in the higher echelons of the administration—themselves substantial owners of land or having close links with the landlords and the rich farmers.

I would like to draw the attention of the reader to one final but important point that the Task Force made in its report. It stated that the land reforms upto the time of the submission of the report had been imposed from above and that 'the beneficiaries of the land reforms weighed down by crippling social and economic disabilities, had been passive, unorganized and inarticulate.' 'The Task Force' opined:

'In our view a certain degree of politicalisation of the poor peasantry on militant lines is a prerequisite for any successful legislative-administrative action for conferring rights and privileges on them'. How this politicalisation was to be achieved, the Task Force, however, did not say. It is obvious all the same that it would require a staggering programme of education, both free and compulsory education of school children, adult literacy and education for creating a social and political awareness.

Following the declaration of the emergency, the 20-point economic programme laid down that land ceilings decided by the Chief Ministers and the Central Government in 1972 should be implemented by 30 June 1976. The 1972 guidelines provided for ceilings between 10 acres and 54 acres depending on irrigation facilities and the kind and quality of land.

It was estimated that the implementation of the ceiling laws will release as much as 40 lakh acres of surplus land for distribution to landless agricultural workers preferably Schedule Castes and Schedule Tribes. At a conference of the Chief Ministers, a detailed step-by-step action plan was drawn up to implement the ceiling laws. It involved filing of returns, declaration of surplus land in the possession of land owners, take-over of the surplus land by the authorities and its distribution to those who work on the land but do not possess any.

The latest reports reaching the Union Government present a picture of the implementation which is not altogether assuring although the 30 June dead line had long been left behind. According to H.K. Dua,[6] the figures available in New Delhi in 1976, suggested that against the estimated 40 lakh acres, the state governments had by then declared only 25 lakh (2.5 million) acres as surplus. Out of this 14.83 lakhs had been acquired by the state governments from the land owners and only 8.5 lakh acres distributed among 6 lakh landless agricultural workers. The average size of the parcel was only 1.4 acres and there were numerous beneficiaries who had received not more than 1/3-1/2 of an acre. If holdings of less than 5 acres are barely economic, one would wish to know how the possession of these tiny patches would by themselves improve the economic status of the recipient. Even a partial solution of the land problem within the present political and economic set up, requires withdrawal of exemptions, complete elimination of the absentee landlord and the non-cultivating owner, the abolition of share-cropping and fixation of minimum wage for agricultural labour. Barring these all talk of land reform is a mere eye-wash.

2. *Lack of an integrated programme of land consolidation and complementary development work.* A plea for this even in the absence of a programme for radical land reform, has been made by Prof. B.S. Minhas. He considers the following points necessary for the success of the programme:

(*i*) Consolidation of land holdings must be made compulsory under the law.

[6]Indian Express. 6 November 1976, New Delhi.

(*ii*) Prior to actual consolidation, (*a*) the entire land in each village should be topographically surveyed and levelled to receive water wherever water is already available, *(b)* the irrigation channels and drains should be constructed for the entire village, (*c*) if there exists a potential for additional minor irrigation (underground or surface) works, these works should be constructed and rationally located from the point of distribution of watar, (*d*) in dry villages, without any potential for underground water resources, land levelling and contour bunding for soil and moisture conservation (and construction of storage tanks for collection of rain water) should be effected for the entire village or a group of villages at a time and (*e*) village and feeder roads should be properly aligned.

(*iii*) The survey, design and construction of these works should be entrusted to teams of surveyors, engineers, agronomists and administrators under the auspices of the state governments and the village panchayats.

(*iv*) Some part of the cost of this type of programme should be met by local contributions, which in the manner of consolidation fee today, should be collected, as a compulsory initial fee. In assessing each indivibual's contribution in the village, a considerable element of progression with respect to the extent of land held should be introduced. Peasants should also contribute in labour and draft power in the construction works.

(*v*) The developed land should be so distributed back among the owners that each one of them has his holding in one, or at most two compact pieces. An equitable and democratic procedure for such a programme of consolidation should be devised. One such procedure is discussed below. The lands of all holders having not more than, say 4 acres each could be realigned in a compact block on one side of the village for subsequent intensive development.

(*vi*) The maintenance and the care of the works constructed as part of this integrated programme could be the joint responsibility of the State and the panchayats. Adequate machinery for collection of current operating charges and other rates could be designed.[7]

Minhas then goes on to discuss the mechanism by which effective consolidation and land development can be achieved and also shows how the gains and costs can be allocated among the farmers.[8] The

[7]B.S. Minhas. 1974. Planning and the Poor, New Delhi.
[8]Ibid.

integrated programme of compulsory consolidation and complementary works on the lines suggested, says Minhas, would greatly
augment employment opportunities not only for rural labour, but
also in large numbers for a variety of technical personnel—engineers,
veterinarians, horticulturists and agricultural experts. Part of the
cost of the programme can be met:

(*a*) By reducing irrigation and power losses.

(*b*) By withdrawing subsidies made to rich farmers.

(*c*) And by imposition of an agricultural income tax as suggested
by the Planning Commission, K.N. Raj and others.

The programme suggested by Professor Minhas if implemented
would certainly be productive. But the question is, can it be implemented? Minhas himself acknowledged that it involved many difficult organisational problems as well as 'speedy and legislative
action to facilitate compulsory consolidation and mobilisation of
competent teams of technical workers to carry out the resources
development effectively in the field'.[9] He suggested that peasants
should also contribute in labour and draft power in the construction works. One would like to ask how tenants whose tenancy is
not secure and sharecroppers could be induced to cooperate and
help in a programme calculated to augment the profits of the
owners. His second suggestion regarding realignment of land of all
holders having not more than 4 acres in a compact block on one
side of the village for subsequent intensive development seems to
have undertones of cooperation or collectivisation. If this is so,
what is wrong with a similar development of the whole village?

Gunnar Myrdal too recommends complementary institutional
reforms and the use of improved technology but he rightly considers that these measures are possible only after an agrarian reform.
He is emphatic that tenants must be secure and should become
landowners, that absent landlords and non-cultivating cultivators
must be eliminated and that sharecropping must end. He considers
that institutional reforms in the presence of an inegalitarian system
of ownership and tenure, can only lead to greater inequality.[10] He
states:

'The one requirement any form of land reform should meet is that

[9]Ibid.

[10]Gunnar Myrdal. 1971. The Challenge of World Poverty, England.

it should create a relationship between man and land that does not thwart his incentives to work and invest. . . . Attempts to improve technology and to raise yields will never have great results if that relationship between man and land is lacking'.

3. *Low priority for the Agricultural Sector.* Inspite of talk of high priority for the agricultural sector in the plans and the emphases on self-sufficiency in food and rural development, the actual attention paid to agriculture and rural development by both the planners and the government, has been most niggardly. This view is held by Lipton[12] and many others including the present author and is borne out by the fact that the financial outlays in the Plans on agriculture which contributes nearly half the total national income, have been much smaller than the financial outlays on industries and mining which together yield only one sixth of the national income. In the First Plan the financial outlay on agriculture, community development, irrigation and flood control, was 31 per cent of the total outlay. It was progressively reduced to 22 per cent, 20 per cent and 17.4 per cent in the Second, Third and Fourth Plans. Those who hold the view that agricultural outlays during the Plans have been adequate and have not been dwindling, argue that the percentage figures do not give a correct picture of the financial outlays and that in absolute terms, the investments on agriculture, have been increasing during the successive plans—Rs 601 crore in the First Plan, Rs 950 crore in the Second Plan, Rs 2,110 crore in the Third Plan and Rs 5,410 crore in the Fourth Plan which ended in 1974.

Other arguments that have been advanced for the view that agriculture's share is in reality not so small as it seems are, first, that it has a low import content and therefore costs much less, secondly, because a much bigger share of non-agricultural investment such as money spent on primary health centres, rural education and housing, fertilizer, cement and tractor production, is in fact directed towards agricultural growth and finally the reallocation of resources within the agricultural sector may have been designed by the planners to obtain greater output and welfare for an agricultural strategy in which intensive farming has been done in selected districts and by rich farmers.

But all these arguments are fallacious. The real value of "imposing and large" financial outlays in absolute figures, have been neutralized by spiralling prices and run-away inflation. The low import content and consequently the low cost argument is countered by the fact that high prices and inflation, travel and spread among sectors and that private investors pay scarcity and not official prices for the imports. The argument that much larger share of non-agricultural investment has been directed towards agricultural growth holds equally well in the opposite direction that amounts invested in agriculture as for example in sugarcane and cotton crops, have helped in industrial growth. Lastly, agricultural spending by intensive farming of selected areas and rich farmers, is no argument for reducing the share of total outlay allocated to agriculture and exposing large areas to stagnation and, the bulk of peasantry to privation and pauperism.

As Pramit Chaudhury[11] points out there is a close link between the level of agricultural output and the net national product. Over a period of 25 years, the net national product approached or surpassed the 5 per cent level on seven occassions[12] and the years of growth of 2 per cent or less were also years of stagnation or falling output in agriculture. It is now being increasingly realized that the principal factor behind increased agricultural produce in particular years has been a benevolant rain god and not the increased use of superior technology or inputs. When the weather-god is ill-disposed, the land is ravaged by droughts and famines, and conditions of scarcity and acute hunger take a heavy toll. The question which needs to be asked is how long will India continue to depend on vagaries of nature for her supply of food and raw materials?

The gross cropped area in India at the end of the Fourth Plan in 1973-74 was estimated at approximately 169 million hectares (417 million acres). Out of this according to experts, irrigation facilities can be built up, for only 107 million hectares (264 million acres) or 63 per cent of the cropped area. In 1973-74 the cultivated area having irrigation facilities amounted to approximately 45 million hectares (111.15 acres) or approximately 26.6 per cent of the cropped area. This means that irrigation facilities can be extended to another 37 per cent of the area under cultivation. An irrigation Commission was set up by the Government of India in 1969 to review the progress of irrigation in the country. It took nearly three years to complete its work. Its report was placed before the Parliament on 4

[11]Pramit Chaudhary. 1971. Aspects of Economic Development, London.
[12]Ibid.

April 1972. It recommended 1 the setting up of a National Water Resources Council, 2 seven River Basin Commissions to formulate plans for the major river basins in the country, 3 a revision of water rates, 4 a revision of present laws for betterment levy, so that half the capital cost of the irrigation project is recovered from the beneficiaries, steps dealing with water-logging, drainage and flood control, 5 the construction and maintenance of field channels, 6 settlement of inter-state disputes and 7 expansion of irrigation facilities to 81 million hectares (200 million acres) or nearly 50 per cent of the cultivated area, at a cost of Rs 10,000 crore. The Commission was of the view that a countrywide irrigation grid was feasible.[13]

If Gandhiji's advice has been harkened early, if the Government and the planner's had not all along indulged in "speech day stuff and hortatory exercise", if the planner's words and the government's deeds had been matched and in reality 'highest priority given to agriculture and rural development, and if the advice of eminent foreign and Indian economists and recommendations made by important Commissions, had been given due weight and implemented, Indian agriculture would have lost its dependence on rainfall and import of foodgrains, and the economic condition of the country would have been surely different from what it is today and India would not have been among the half a dozen poorest countries in the world.

An impressive and formidable case for transfering Indian investible resources to agriculture is made by Michael Lipton.[14] He uses the "marginal capital/output ratio or K criterion" for allocating investible resources and concludes that as K is lower (about half) in agriculture than in industry, more resources should flow to agriculture.

The objection to the K criterion that it amalgamates different sorts of capital into a single capital/output ratio, instead of maximizing the yield on scarcer varieties of capital, is answered, first, by the fact that the foreign content for Indian industry is lower in agriculture than in industry, secondly, relative to industrial investment a higher proportion of the value of farm investment consists

---

[13]Report of The Irrigation Commission. 1972.
[14]Michael Lipton. 1968. Strategy for Agriculture, Urban Bias & Rural Planning in Streeton, P. & Lipton M. . The Crisis of Indian Planning, London.

of payments to unskilled labourers, and such workers would often be unable to get other jobs, especially in the agricultural slack season, when the expanded plans for minor irrigation works can be carried out; and thirdly, most farm investment has fewer moving parts, slower obsolescence and hence less depreciation.

A second objection to the K criterion that factory and farm investment are complementary and that factory investment can lower farm investment is also fallacious. For instance 'if steel from high-K steel works to produce tractors can augment yields from agriculture, so can extra irrigation of cotton soils increase the yield of cotton mills. Extra farm output thus permits general industrial expansion, both by freeing foreign exchange for raw materials and by reducing inflationary pressures on food prices'.[15]

A third objection to the K criterion that capital is not the only scarce resources and that the engineer/output ratio is important, is taken care of by greater economy of engineers and technicians in farm investment than in industrial investment.[16]

The long-haul case in favour of a low K for industrial priority associated with Nehru and Mahalanobis depends on two arguments —first, that the value of K is said to depend on the year in which extra output is measured, and the second, that a higher proportion of profit is saved than of wages. Both arguments have been demolished by Lipton with equal facility. In respect of the first, he cites evidence from Indian data to show that 'however many years after investment we choose to measure output, K in industry is at least $1\frac{1}{2}$ times K in agriculture'.[17] In respect of the second, he admits that a higher proportion of profits is saved than wages, and that the profit-to-wage ratio is higher in industry than in agriculture. But he adds that to use this as an argument against agricultural investment is to assume that the financing of investment depends on private saving alone.

One final objection advanced against transfer of more resources to agriculture is that it has low absorptive capacity for new capital and that it is getting as much investment as it can take. This is an old argument and has been trotted out right from the early 1950s. The fact is that properly organised agriculture has

[15]Ibid.
[16]Ibid.
[17]Ibid.

tremendous absorptive capacity and needs the implementation of programmes, recommended by economists like Gunnar Myrdal and B.S. Minhas mentioned earlier in this chapter and the recommendations of the Irrigation Commission of 1969. What is lacking is not the "absorptive capacity"; it is the political will to implement the programmes which go against the rural and the urban elites and the ruling party which derives its power from them.

And in the end, a few words about the targets of Indian agricultural planning for needs, outputs, inputs and resources. The target for output of foodgrains for 1970-71—119.8 million tons—was a modest one compared to the nutritional needs of the population but to achieve the objectives of self-sufficiency in foodgrains by 1971 and to sustain the planned level of industrial imports, new inputs— land and labour remaining the same—were far too meager with the result that the yearly growth of 4.3 per cent from 1966-67 to 1970-71, and the target of 119.8 million tons could not be achieved. The attainment of the target could have been possible with rises of 30 per cent in seed, 250 per cent in fertiliser and 17 per cent in irrigation outputs. Since these inputs and corresponding resources were not available, the level of output of foodgrains was 108.4 million tons, or 11.4 million tons short of the target for the year.[18]

4. *Lack of Incentives.* Incentives for hard work are important for everyone everywhere. In the rural setting in India, they are important for the absentee landlord who operates on land as a capitalist and a big farmer; for the middle farmer who owns a medium holding; for the small farmer, the share cropper, the tenant, the village artisan and the landless labourer. But the incentives in each case are not the same.

The landlord and the big farmer—who belongs to the upper-upper and the upper-middle class and provides bulk of the marketable surplus for the towns and cities—wants a high price for his produce and as low as possible a price for what he buys—seed, fertiliser, pesticide, irrigation and power facilities and labour. Low agricultural prices and high cost of inputs hurt him. He also clamours for cheap credit, support prices and subsidies. His persistent complaint has been that prices for foodgrains have been systematically kept low by control measures and by import of substantial quantities of food-

18Ibid.

grains even in years of bumper harvests.[19]

The farmer who has a medium sized holding, the medium-medium farmer, produces just enough to meet the food needs of the family and is left with a small disposable surplus, also looks for a high price to enable him to acquire other necessaries like shelter, draft animals, agricultural implements for traditional farming, clothes, medicines, fuel, soap and sundaries.

The medium-small farmer has no foodgrains to sell and is therefore not interested in a high price. The small-small farmer whose family needs are more than what he produces and who has in fact to buy from the surplus producer, is deeply hurt by high prices of foodgrains. And the great majority of rural households belong to the last two classes. It will, therefore, be appreciated that what are incentives to the big farmer are actually, highly inimical to the interests of the marginal and the small farmer.

The rich farmers plea that the government buy at a high price and sell at subsidised rates to the rural poor and the retail ration shops in the urban areas, is not acceptable to the authorities as it adds to the burden of public investment. As matters stand, private investment for improvement of land and agriculture by the rural rich, is already inadequate. They have been loth to invest due to a continuing and haunting fear of uncertainty regarding future legislation in respect of ownership of land or the size of the holdings. The share-cropper and the tenant have no incentive to invest money or more labour on land which he does not own and from which he can be ejected any moment. The incentive for the village artisan and the landless labourer is a good minimum living wage that will sustain him and his family, and a low price of foodgrains unless he is paid in kind.

5. *New Agricultural Strategy.* In 1959, a Ford Foundation team proposed a programme[20]— the Agricultural District Programme (IADP) to which food aid was tied. This was the precursor of the Intensive Agricultural Area Programme (IAAP), in which in 1966 the Food and Agriculture Minister, put before the Parliament a plan of self-sufficiency in food by the end of the Fourth Plan Period in 1973-74. The plan owed its origin, it appears, to his genuine con-

[19] K.N. Raj, in Mason, Economic Development in India & Pakistan.
[20] Agricultural Production Team Report on (Sponsored by Ford Foundation) India's Food Crises (1959).

version—through brilliant intermediaries like Raj Krishna and David Hopper—to the agro-economic ideas of J.W. Schultz.[21] In a television appearance to the BBC the Minister explained how over long years, the traditional farmer had learnt and made efficient use of traditional resources. But this had not solved the food problems of the country. A big rise in output, he said, was only possible from a massive infusion of a whole package of new factors and techniques, in limited, selected, well-watered irrigated areas. About 25 million acres or at the time of the initiation nearly half the area of the country, was proposed to be brought under intensive cultivation and the entire package inputs—high yielding better varieties of seed (HYV), chemical fertilisers, pesticides, irrigation and trained man-power—devoted to it. This area was expected to supply the extra food-grains required for achieving self-sufficiency at the end of the Fourth Plan. The Food Minister was quite frank in admitting that his expec-tation of extra production from outside the area chosen by him was only marginal. This clearly meant that there was no intention of introducing the new scientific approach for the benefit of the Indian farmer as a whole and that for years to come agriculture in general and specially in dry years and for poor farmers will continue to stagnate and even worsen, because the needs of the farmers out-side the selected areas would get lesser attention than before, under the new strategy. The only people who were likely to benefit from it were the rich farmers in selected areas who would afford to pay for HYV of seeds, fertilisers, pesticides, modern farm machinery and irrigation and power charges. The proposal, therefore, came under severe criticism right from the time of its presentation but as its drawbacks, limitations and failurers came to be known, the criticism became more trenchant.

The IAAF was launched in selected areas with assured irrigation from the Kharif season of 1966. Since then the area under HYV seeds increased from 1.89 million hectares in 1966-67 to 6.09 million hectares in 1967-68, 9.3 million hectares in 1968-69, 11.4 million hectares in 1971-72. In other words, there was a 9-fold increase in area under HYV seeds in just five years. Likewise there was a 3-fold increase in consumption of nitrogenous fertilisers between 1965-66 and 1973-74, a 5-fold increase of energisation of tube wells between 1965-66 and 1968-69, a 9-fold increase of long term loans. What

---

[21]J.W. Schultz. 1964. *Transforming Traditional Agriculture*, Yale.

was the outcome? There was a distinct impact on food production during the first three years. Weather-wise both 1964-65 and 1967-68 were good years but the total foodgrain output in 1967-68 was 6.6 million tons higher than 1964-65, a fact which has been attributed to the New Strategy. In 1965-66, the total foodgrains production was 72 million tons. In 1969-70 it reached a figure of 99.5 million tons and in 1970-71, a still higher level of 107.8 million tons.

The most spectacular increase was in the production of wheat. From the annual average of 11 million tons for five years before 1965-66, it rose to 18.7 million tons in 1968-69, 20 million tons in 1969-70, 23.3 million tons in 1970-71, and about 27 million tons in 1973-74. But it must not be forgotten that although there was a definite boost to production of wheat during these years, there was a decline in total foodgrains production in 1971-72, 1972-73, 1973-74 due to bad monsoons, providing thereby that good weather conditions by improving yields in dry farming areas were more important than New Strategy in the overall increase in food yields.[22]

What is, however, more disheartening, is that the earlier successes even in respect of wheat, were not sustained. A slowdown in the rate of progress—due probably to a saturation in the yield rates of HYV or perhaps exhaustion of soil due to rapid depletion of essential ingredients, was followed by actual deterioration. For example the total yield in Haryana, next only to Punjab in wheat production, steeply declined over the subsequent three years in about the same proportion in which it had increased in the preceding years. It showed a 7 per cent decline during 1974-75 and 1975-76, despite extra dosages of fertilisers used and crash programmes of supplying extra power to tube wells and releasing more water into canals during peak timings. The situation was further worsened by the appearance of rust disease which caused untold amount of damage to wheat crop in parts of West Punjab, Haryana and Western Uttar Pradesh.

Wheat is grown on only an eighth of the total cropped area of the country whereas rice is grown on one third of the total cultivated area. And there has been little or no impact of New Strategy on the production of rice and the coarse foodgrains. Viewed against the background of what has been said earlier, the initial euphoria even in respect of wheat, seems to be giving place to gloom and a

[22]Figures are from official sources.

feeling of dejection. The New Strategy has not been the herald of a Green Revolution as many including Subramaniam, the planners, the ICAR researchers, the Pearson and the Rockefeller Foundation Reports said, it was. The much hailed and greatly extolled Green Revolution proved counterproductive both in respect of production as well as distribution.[23]

First and foremost it softened both the Governmental and the planner's tensions and made them complacent. The need and the compulsion for even a half-way, ill-implemented programme of land reforms, received a serious set-back and went astray. A rational agricultural policy—provision of inputs like organic and green manures, irrigation facilities, cheap credit for seeds, implements or livestock and assured tenancy to small farmers on a countrywide scale—as inducement to intensive labour and greater production, was given the go-by and all resources and effort diverted to selected areas and rich agriculturists farming on the new capitalistic basis. The result for the country as a whole was unmitigated disaster. Agricultural production of small farmers in unselected areas all over the country, suffered seriously; tenants and sharecroppers were thrown out and ejected and small farmers compelled to sell their plots and reduced to the state of paupers and landless labourers. The only beneficiaries were the selected upper strata of farmers. They cornered all the inputs—HYV seeds, chemical fertilisers, pesticides, irrigation facilities and credit. Mr Subramaniam promised large credit facilities for agriculture and candidly admitted that the cooperatives alone could not meet the needs of the farmer. Two new agencies—The Agricultural Credit Corporation and subsequently the nationalized commercial banks, were proposed and pressed into service but not for the benefit of the small farmer who even earlier got little or no credit from the cooperative agencies. The credit only flowed to the selected rich.[24]

Secondly, the New Strategy increased the unbalance within the region and between the regions. Within the region it increased the disparity between the incomes of the rich farmers and the rural poor. The rich grew richer and the poor grew poorer. Unfortunately for agricultural and economic growth, the landlords and the

[23]For fuller exposition see Lipton, Michael in the Crisis of Indian Planning; Balraj Mehta. 1974. Failures of Indian Economy, New Delhi.
[24]Ibid.

rich farmers who made large fortunes after 1966, invested their savings in construction of palatial houses in the cities or in ostentatious expenditure in diamonds, gold and parties but not in productive investment. The greatly publicised socialist objective was rendered completely inane. Between regions the Strategy increased the inequality between the incomes of the Northern wheat producing States—Punjab, Haryana and Western U.P. and other parts of the country.

Thirdly, a point to note is that in-spite of the package of inputs and the introduction of new technology, no real break-through in agricultural production had been achieved. Before the New Strategy was instituted between 1949-50 and 1964-65, the compound rate of growth of foodgrains production in the country was about 3.4 per cent. As against this, in spite of huge investments the compound rate of growth between 1964-65 and 1974-75 was only 1.3 per cent.

Fourthly, the basic assumption in favour of the New Strategy that it will provide adequate and growing marketable surpluses, proved sheer balderdash.[25]

Landlords and big farmers with large holdings certainly took full advantage of all the subsidised inputs and incentive prices but never played ball regarding the urban and rural consumers' needs for marketable surpluses at reasonable prices. Their economic and political power and their alliance with well-off traders and merchants was deployed in their mutual interests and to the deterioration of the food and the economic situation of the country. The marketable surpluses rather than increase, began to show shrinkage, and procurement of foodgrains by official agencies fell. The Government was advised to take over the wheat trade in the 1973 Rabi marketing season. But procurement effort under the take-over scheme ran into difficulties. In the midst of its bewilderment the government set up a special Task Force to streamline the procurement effort. The Task Force offered new incentives in the form of priority entitlement of inputs and credit at concessional rates to producers of marketable surpluses in the surplus wheat states of Punjab, Haryana and Uttar Pradesh, to induce this section to part with their surplus grain to the government agencies at the fixed procurement prices.

The Agricultural Prices Commission had been asked to announce

[25]Ibid.

its procurement policy before the rabi sowing—1973—and not at the time of harvesting as was being done—to make the producer aware of what he might expect for his labour. The commission held that the producer was getting a fair price for his inputs and labour and there was no case for upward revision of the price. Yet it was persuaded to add an emergency premium of four rupees per quintal as a special incentive to stimulate production in the rabi season to offset the shortfall in the previous Kharif season, at a time of rising prices in the open market. The APC was in the face of sharp strains in the food economy after the wholesale trade take-over, being pressurised to submit its report on price policy for the Kharif season for the 1973-74 season. It was made quite plain to the Commission that the procurement prices for the incoming kharif cereals would have to be substantially marked up. In its incertitude and perplexity, the government lost sight of everything except the incentives and even the cost of incentives was ignored and not worked out. At the prevailing level of procurement and distribution prices, the subsidy for wheat amounted to Rs 18.50 per quintal and Rs 16.50 per quintal in respect of rice. With the off-take as high as 1.2 million tons per month, the monthly burden of the subsidy to the government was nearly Rs 22 crore, which amounted to nearly Rs 270 crore during the year as against a provision of Rs 130 crore in the 1973-74 budget. The wholesale take-over of the kharif crop was dropped. The kulak-trader lobby was victorious and jubilant.

One could list many more reasons for the failure of the New Strategy and the HYV seeds. The new varieties were less disease resistant and required pest control measures and organisation which had not yet been built up. They were soft and unpalatable. The seed farms were finding it difficult to meet the targets for the requirement of the new varieties. Scarcity of complementary fertilisers was substantially reducing the turn out from the new seeds. Many improved varieties produced stalks which were not satisfactory for fodder. Their price relative to the price of the traditional varieties tended to fall as their demand was less. Many varieties yielded only enough to justify the higher cost of fertiliser if water was constantly and accurately available and proved uneconomic under less controlled conditions which rose both from power failures or from shortages of fertiliser or credit.

The New Strategy was not the breakthrough that had been promised to the nation. It helped to raise significantly the economic status of a small section of the farmers but in all other respects, its efforts were deleterious. The agricultural production did not increase except in years of good rainfall, the marketable surpluses remained low and uncertain, and the foodgrain prices sky-rocketed with a galloping and a run-away rate of inflation. The New Strategy was consigned to the limbo of oblivion and there was concern once more for the little man—the small and the middle peasant—if not in deeds, at least in official pronouncements.

6. *Under utilisation of labour.* Agricultural yield per acre, in India, is only one fourth that of Britain or Japan, and one of the lowest in the World. Seventy per cent of her total population living in the villages practice agriculture and the country has a colossal agricultural labour force. Yet the country is not able to produce sufficient food to meet the needs of her population even at the prevailing low levels of calorie and protein intake. This is a measure of the low productivity of her labour force in the agricultural sector.

The level of productivity of the Indian worker, to whatever sector—agricultural, industrial or service—he may belong, is beyond doubt extremely low. The output of workers in organised industry due to considerable absenteeism and a low level of efficiency, compares very unfavourably with workers in industrialised countries. In the unorganised industrial sector, a carpenter, a brick-layer or a metal worker in Kashmir, Uttar Pradesh or Bihar, has less than half the daily output of a similar worker in the Punjab or Haryana. In service industries, a white collar clerk, for that matter even an officer, does not work for more than two hours a day. The remaining part of his office hours he spends in idle prattle or in tea rooms and caffetaria. As a result files which are marked urgent, take weeks or even months to move. What is true of workers in government offices, is equally true of teachers in schools, colleges and universities. There are 105 universities and 20 deemed universities, more than 100 medical colleges, and almost a similar number of engineering colleges and institutes in the country. There are in addition a large number of degree colleges. The number of teachers on the staff of these institutions runs into hundreds of thousands. But what is their productivity? Even the text books used in these places of learning are written by foreigners and imported mostly from England and America. In most cases the professors and other faculty members read out notes which they prepared ten or more years earlier and which they continue to dictate year after year. They have very few, if any, original contributions in the form of research papers or books of lasting value in fields of literature, philosophy, social or natural sciences. The Indian student even at the university level, loves to be taught, and has no concept of education as a learning process in which he can lose himself for hours on end in the library or other places of learning. Both Indian teachers and students are inordinately fond of holidays and the number of holidays the Indians have, when combined with vacations and Sundays, leaves them little time for productive activity. A foreigner when he looked at the list of holidays for a particular year was surprised and asked in amazement 'when do the Indians work'? But I am digressing.

Let me get back to productivity in the field of agriculture. According to Gunnar Myrdal, 'work practices in agriculture are not labour-intensive but labour-extensive'.[26] The labour input per worker in terms of man-hours is low, and of low efficiency. The low yields per acre are, therefore, largely a consequence of an under-utilisation of labour force, or in other words an increase in labour input through increased duration and efficiency of work, would raise yields even without any technological innovation or additional investment except work.[27] Emphasising underutilisation of agricultural labour force, Dantwala remarks, 'There is so much scope for the wider application of known techniques, involving hardly any additional capital investment, that in the initial period, at any rate, progress can be rapid'.[28] Another distinguished economist, S.R. Sen, elaborates this point further: '...differences of yields are noticeable not merely as between different areas but also between different groups of farmers. In the same area, the best farmers are known to have produced yields per acre several times higher than those produced by average farmers. ...In fact...the difference between the best and the average is much wider in India than in technically advanced countries. This is both an index of the backward character of Indian agriculture and a measure of its potentiality for development'.[29] Gunnar Myrdal draws attention to the fact that a large

[26]Gunnar Myrdal. 1971. The Challenge of World Poverty, England.
[27]Ibid.
[28]Ibid. Dantwala quoted by Myrdal.
[29]Ibid. S.R. Sen quoted by Myrdal.

part of the labour force does not engage in any work at all. Most of the workers who do work, work only for short periods per day, week, month and year, and not very intensively and efficiently. Poverty and low yields, he states lead to malnutrition and undernutrition in its turn impairs willingness and ability to work, leading to the establishment of a vicious circle.[30] According to Myrdal, additional labour inputs—building roads, bridges, irrigation canals, soil conservation terraces, ware houses for storing crops, draining ditches, wells and tanks and labouring on afforestation and pasture improvement—can be considered investment because it promises to increase future yields. Such work is highly labour-intensive and requires few resources to complement labour beyond those locally available.

Other uses of the villager's spare time—construction of school buildings, dispensaries, privies and gutters, cleaning wells for drinking water and other household uses, paving of village streets to do away with dust and mud, manufacturing simple furniture, killing rats, or merely washing the children and keeping flies away from the eyes—relates more directly to consumption. These highly productive undertakings of surplus labour in the service of consumption, have been characterised by late Professor Ragnar Nurkse as a "disguised saving potential". Why this huge saving potential has not been utilised by any third world country is attributable first, to the difficulties involved in the distribution of costs and benefits between land owners who harvest all the gains but neither toil themselves nor pay those who work and toil but do not own, and secondly, because organisation of the labour force for collective undertakings meets with 'strong resistance from established work practices, founded on the system of land ownership and tenancy which itself holds down the quantity and quality of individual inputs of labour'.[31] A widespread impression has been created and allowed to exist that in third world countries with surplus agricultural power, improved and modern technology is likely to aggravate the low level of utilisation of labour. But this is altogether false. Improved technology contrary to the belief held, does not decrease the demand for labour. Except for mechanisation—and intermediate innovations and techniques that do not displace human labour can be devised—improvements in preparing the soil, sowing, weeding

[30]Ibid.
[31]Ibid.

and caring for the growing crop, increase the demand for labour.

7. *Faults and failures of education.* The role of lack of education or mis-education in perpetuating underdevelopment and poverty, and the beneficial effects of free and compulsory primary education have been fully described in the chapter on education. The report by the Education Commission that 'attempts to train for vocational competence in agriculture at primary and lower secondary levels have failed and further efforts should be held in abeyance',[32] is in the opinion of M. Lipton unduly pessimistic and un-warranted. He calls attention to the facts that little is known about the comparative performance of farmers with different types and levels of agricultural training and that schooling in agriculture is often oddly designed and not available until the child is twelve, and cautions against root and branch attacks on agricultural schooling based on such programmes.[33]

The Gandhian view of learning by doing and of basic education round a craft, and his approach and solution of the problems of rural poverty and unemployment, have been discussed widely throughout the body of the work and especially in the chapters on Gandhian economy, technology and education.

M. Blaug, Gunnar Myrdal and A.K. Sen have written about the highest economic returns from investment in primary education. These views are fully described in the Chapter on education. Professor Sen recommends free and compulsory education of 8 years duration between the ages of seven and fourteen years, imparted round the medium of a craft or a vocation and related to one's work in life. He states categorically that the glib traditional view to regard formal education including literacy to be unimportant from the point of view of productivity, and to argue that all that matters is traditional wisdom of the peasant, has been successfully challanged in a number of studies and notably one made by Dr D.P. Chaudhary in which he analyses inter-family, inter-village, inter-district and inter-state data to show a positive correlation between levels of education and agricultural productivity.[34]

[32]Education Commission Report, 1964-66.
[33]Michael Lipton. 1972. The Crisis of Indian Planning, London.
[34]D.P. Chaudhary. 1968. Education and Agricultural Productivity in India. Unpublished Ph.D Thesis. Department of Economics, University of Delhi.

Among the foibles of the Indian character particularly of the poorer strata are an indwelling sense of servility; a deep-rooted belief in the law of Karma and a pitiless, inexorable destiny; and infinite capacity to put up with hunger, squalor, deprivation and disease, and inherent debasing laziness; a lack of ambition to improve one's standard of living and the will to resist and fight back social injustice. The poorer strata in the village, according to Myrdal, are neither educated nor organised and staggering educational effort including social and political education is needed to overcome these drawbacks. It is obvious that the ruling party has been deliberately depriving masses of this much needed education. This task in my opinion should have been taken up and fulfilled by the opposition parties of the left but they have unfortunately failed to discharge their responsibility.

8. *Malnutrition and Ill-health.* No precise data are available regarding the influence of malnutrition and ill-health on agricultural productivity but this must be considerable. The per capita availability of cereals is very low. The per capita consumption of pulses which constitute the poor man's protein, is less today than it was two decades ago. The cooking oils are expensive and in short supply. Dairy products, eggs, fish, meat, poultry, nuts, fresh vegetables and fresh fruit are expensive and available only to those in the upper brackets and almost exclusively in the urban areas. Malnutrition is, therefore, rampant both among the workers and the peasants. People who do not get enough to eat, naturally lack the energy to produce and are unable to put in a full day's work. It is a vicious cycle of circular causation. Insufficiency of food causes malnutrition which in turn results in low productivity.

Another factor of great importance which seriously affects level of agricultural production is the high incidence of sickness in the countryside. This results from lack of clean potable water, bad housing, insanitation and prevalance of bowel diseases—diarrhoeas, dysentery and worm infestations. The reappearance of malaria in a big way is another source of anxiety. The number of man hours lost as well as reduced efficiency, have a very adverse effect on productivity. This is further aggravated by lack of health and medical facilities in the rural areas. Almost 80 per cent of the population of the country lives in the rural areas but only 11 per cent of the total number of qualified doctors in the country, attend to their needs. The remaining 89 per cent look after the 20 per cent population living in the urban areas.

9. *The Decline of the Indian Village and the brain drain.*
Another factor of importance which has adversely affected the
growth of agriculture and rural development, is the continued
migration of all talent from the countryside. The rich farmer who
cornered most of the credit and other benefits flowing into the
rural areas, invested the large fortunes he made, in large villas in
the cities. The students from rich and middle class homes who
migrated to the cities for secondary and higher education, never
went back to the village. And in the absence of a reverse flow of
educated youngmen—engineers, doctors, scientists, educationists and
social workers—the countryside has been depleted of all talent. This
brain drain from the rural to the urban areas has been even more
damaging to the country's development and economy than the
brain drain to developed countries from the urban areas. No wonder
both agriculture and rural development have languished.

III

In the first section of this chapter, I have described at some
length the reasons why an adequate level of agricultural growth is
imperative for the country. In the second section have been described the causes that have contributed to a poor growth of the
agricultural sector. In the third and final section I shall consider the
ways and means by which shortages of food can be met, and produce of agricultural raw materials for industry and export, stepped
up to meet the country's needs. In a way, at least indirectly, I have
already discussed these measures while considering the impediments
to agricultural and rural development in Section II of this Chapter.
I shall now consider some of these measures more directly.

After the achievement of independence, the promises made to the
farmer were quietly forgotten. A Zamindari Abolition Act was
introduced and passed in 1951 but it left plenty of exemptions and
loopholes. The ceiling laws enacted from time to time were evaded
with impunity. While a "soft state"[35] did not implement and enforce the ceilings fixed by law, it did not even enact for the lower
limits, or floors of the holdings. The result was that government
and other lands declared surplus were distributed among the land-

[35]Gunnar Myrdal. 1971. Challenge to World Poverty, England.

less families in fractions of less than an acre. Many time the holdings were as small as half or even a third of an acre. These mini-holdings can neither benefit those who acquire them nor the growth of agriculture in the country. But they are certainly in the interest first, of the ruling party whom they can help to win the support and the vote of about 20 to 30 per cent of the landless families and the poorer sections and secondly, of the absentee landlords and big farmers increasingly engaging themselves in a capitalist mode of production. The land reforms introduced by the state governments have been gradually but decisively, changing the pattern of agriculture from a feudal but simple type to a capitalist and more complicated one and have only aggravated the poverty of the weaker sections of the people. Gunnar Myrdal has railed at these reforms and called them "mini-reforms or an outright sham". He considers that reforms introduced in parts and bits and implemented half-heartedly or not at all, intensify and feed the forces of resistance and that small and gradual reforms evoke greater resistance than a large and rapid push against prevailing attitudes and institutions. From his study of conditions and trends in India he became more and more convinced that it was easier to carry out a big rapid change than a series of small gradual changes "just as a plunge into cold water is less painful than slow emersion".[36]

Elsewhere in this book we have referred to Jawaharlal Nehru's pre-independence speeches and writings against reformism and gradualism. He said, 'in India only a revolutionary plan could solve the two related questions of the land and industry as well as every other major problem before the country', and even quoted from the War Memoirs of Lloyd George who wrote, 'there is no graver mistake than to leap the abyss in two jumps'. Myrdal feels that if Nehru, 'had not been satisfied with continually spelling out the radical ideals in speeches while postponing the social and economic revolution, but instead had inaugurated vigorous political action, for their speedy realisation, India's history would have been different'.[37] He wonders 'what would have happened if Gandhiji had not been assassinated right at the start of India's independence era' and 'what position he would have taken, for instance on the shelving

[36]Ibid.
[37]Ibid.

of the land and tenancy reform through a nationwide pattern of collusion and corruption'.[38]

Upto the end of first quarter of the nineteenth century land in India belonged to the village. It was commonly tilled and its produce divided among the members of the community.[39] The revenue was paid by the village community in one unit and not by individual cultivators. To enhance its revenue income, the East India Company scrapped the old system and made direct arrangements with each individual cultivator. Both Sir Charles Trevellyan and Sir Charles Metcalfe admired the village constitutions of India. The latter desired that they should never be disturbed and dreaded everything that had a tendency to break them up.[40] Gandhiji who was greatly distressed by the break-up of the village constitutions and the ruin of the village economy in the interest of India's British rulers, knew fully well that the key to the country's economic development lay in the recovery and the improvement of the Indian village which in turn depended on the development of agriculture and rural industries. In his mature wisdom he proposed that land should once again belong to the village, that it should be cultivated jointly and that the produce be shared by those who worked on it.

It is my firm belief that Gandhian approach to land reform with minor alteration due to passage of time, can transform agriculture and rural development in India within a period of five to ten years. As a matter of fact the Chinese Commune System is so similar to the Gandhian approach that I have reasons to believe that the Chinese Commune System may have been influenced by Gandhian thought. The Chinese initial priorities as in the Soviet Union were urban industrialisation with heavey industry as its base, consumer goods industry and agriculture. But as this did not work, the emphasis was shifted to agrarian policy which made use of cooperative principles and applied them to farm conditions in China.

The Chinese Commune System has four components: 1 The Work Team, 2 The Brigade, 3 The Commune, and 4 The Science Team. The commune production plan is an integral plan of the State Plan and is finalised after a long two-way traffic at the level of the district. The brigade plan is similarly finalised at the

[38]Ibid.
[39]Karl Marx, Das Capital.
[40]See Chapter on Gandhian Economy.

commune level and the work-team plan at the level of the brigade. The work-team is responsible for the execution of the agreed plan. The commune production plan settles the kinds and amounts of output for the duration of the year; the amount to be marketed and specially the sales to the State; the gross income; the members earnings; and the allocations for investment. The size of the communes varies but the largest have about 75,000 inhabitants.

Four features which constitute the backbone of the commune system are:

1. The entire strategy of balanced social and economic development based on farming.

2. The peasant unit of production is endowed with political and administrative powers and brings together industry, agriculture, commerce, education and military affairs.

3. It fuses at all educational levels, scholastic and manual work, eradicating the cultural cleavage between the peasant and the intellectual and prevents officialdom from hardening into a privileged caste. It curtails radically the output of neo-mandarins from the social system and bypasses the arrogance of the Soviet managers. It provides for an enormous effort of in-training and an upgrading of the performance of workers on the job. It promotes relationship of mutual aid and raises the level of the socialist consciouness. It helps in the spread of an ascetic morality which is essential in the early stages of development of an economy and results in a marked reduction of corruption.

4. It recognizes the need to limit population growth in the interest of speedy economic development and social growth.

High praise has been lavished on the Chinese decentralized economy by Tara Chand Gupta who visited China for a second time after two decades in 1976. Similar approbation of the Chinese achievements has come from a team of journalists including Nikhil Chakravarti who visited China in 1978.

A modified Gandhian Plan for agricultural and rural development which resembles the Chinese Commune System is outlined below:

The land in it will belong to the village and farmed jointly. Families will have their own houses or plots on which to build, and a small patch for growing vegetables for their own use. The total area of these patches shall not exceed 10 per cent of the cultivable area of the village land. Areas for the village school, a dispensary, a meeting hall, village cooperatives and workshops according to need, and a play ground shall also be set aside. After deductions for tax, investment funds for sub-blocks and blocks, and for work days earmarked for infra-structure work, amounting to approximately 20 per cent of the farm output, the balance will be divided among the families according to the work they put in.

Special groups will be set up for fishing, fruit growing, bee-keeping, poultry farming, pig raising, dairying, industrial crops, food processing (bottling, canning etc.), weaving carpet making, hosiery, tailoring, and making hand made paper, soap, dentrifices, hair oils, toys, bakelite and plastic articles like combs and mugs, glass ware, pottery, metal utensils, and simple machines etc., introducing industry into the heart of the village. The older people who cannot engage in more strenuous jobs in farms, factories, land, building and road development etc., will contribute by spinning cotton, woollen or other yarn. No one will remain idle and both efficiency and full employment will be ensured.

About 1,000 persons living in a village or a group of villages will constitute a work team. Ten work teams will make a brigade and ten brigades a block or a commune. About fifteen blocks or communes will make a district with roughly a population of a million and a half. India's 630 million people live in about 400 districts in 22 states and 9 Union territories. For purposes of economic development the districts—under the overall control of the state and the Union Governments—will be more or less autonomous. The administrative and the law and order machinery of the districts will remain as at present. But each district will have separate Chief Production Managers for agriculture and industries. After making a survey of the skilled personnel, the districts will be allocated by the States, managers, economists, statisticians, research workers, educationists, accountants, auditors, engineers, scientists, technicians and others according to the population and the size. All efforts will be made to avoid undue dislocation of the personnel, who will then be formed into teams.

The four components of the organisation will be the work teams the brigades, the blocks and the science teams. The block production will be an integral plan of the States and the Union Plans, and will be finalised after long and two-way consultations at the level of the block, and the work-team plan at the level of the brigade. The work-team as in the Chinese experience will be responsible for the execution of the agreed plan.

The eight pillars on which the Block Production Plan wlll stand will be:

1. Personal freedom.
2. Absence of fear.
3. Unselfish behaviour.
4. Mutual help.
5. Peasant base and decentralization.
6. The political and administrative powers.
7. The blending at all levels of scholastic and manual work.
8. The need for population control.

It was Gandhiji who conceived the idea of a decentralized rural economy for India. It was Mao who after his failure with the Russian way, put this into practice and made of it a success story. The present plan is a fusion of the Gandhian theory which could not be implemented because Gandhi was assassinated soon after independnce, and the Maoist practice. It, however, believes in the Gandhian values of personal freedom, humanism, truth and non-violence.

Gandhi was a plebian and a man of the masses but he was human and made mistakes. The biggest mistake he ever made, however, was when he chose and groomed a patrician who was completely opposed to his policies as his political heir. India will have cause to rue that decision for a long long time. Had he chosen diffe-rently—a humanist socialist like himself, a J. B. Kripalani, a Narendra Dev or a Jaya Prakash, India would have kept out of the capitalist net and developed painlessly on the path which he had outlined for the country and on which Mao successfully built the Chinese economy and power.

2. *Complementary Institutional and Other Reforms.* In the absence of a radical land reform and rural development as outlined under the previous heading, these reforms will benefit only the upper strata of farmers. Extension of irrigation facilities wherever possible to all areas where dry farming is practised and its full utilisation, use of improved technology and better inputs, will be of immense value in increasing yields.

3. *Increase of outlay for agriculture and rural development.* As has been pointed out in section II of this Chapter, the outlay on agriculture and rural development has been too meagre. This has hampered the growth not only of agriculture but also of the indus-

trial sector and the economy as a whole. This must be stepped up by investing less in large scale consumer industry at the present stage of country's development and utilise the savings for agriculture and rural development. The capital output ratio in the agricultural and rural sector being low and the import content negligible, much smaller capital investment can go a long way.

4. *The power structure.* I have repeatedly called attention in these pages to the existing power structure and the tripartite alliance between the rural rich, the ruling elite in the cities and the multinational foreign companies. This unholy alliance has right from the start, stalled land reform and rural progress, and blocked the implementation of even those measures which have been from time to time legislated.

The Congress Party's record of achievements is most dismal. It has made promises ad galore at the time of elections and never kept one. It has shown concern for the poor farmer and distributed its bounties—irrigation facilities, electric power, inputs and credits —among big farmers in selected areas. It has bragged about educational reform and completely neglected primary education. It has boasted about rural and poor man's housing and promoted the construction of multi-storey buildings, 5-star hotels and luxury villas. It has encouraged manufacture of air conditioners, refrigerators, electric kitchen appliances, perfumes, cosmetics and hundreds of varieties of textiles for the use of one or two per cent of the country's elites but has done precious little to produce articles of common household use which the weaker and poorer people need and can afford. It has promoted the manufacture of small cars for the elites and neglected manufacture of buses for public transport. It has levied excise, sales and other indirect taxes which hurt the poor and given tax exemptions and subsidies to the corporate sector. It has expressed lip sympathy for the poor and allied itself with Birlas, and Dalmias. There has been an immense gap between its pronouncements and performance and this will continue so long as this power structure is not demolished. No effort has been made during the two years the Janata Party has been in power to alter this power structure.

TEN

Industry

I

Relationship Between Industry and Agriculture. There is an intimate relationship between agricultural development and the development and growth of industries. Unless the agricultural sector is substantially modernised and improved, there is bound to be stagnation or extremely slow development in the industrial sector. In the short run, due to a heavier outlay in one sector, the relationship may be competitive but in the long run it is complementary. Industrial growth depends upon agriculture in a variety of ways: 1. the latter supplies foodgrains for the urban area, 2 furnishes raw material for industry, 3 provides markets for the growing industrial sector and 4. as W.W. Rostow the author of Stages of Economic Growth, observed in a lecture delivered in New Delhi at the institute of Economic Growth in April 1963, is the basic working capital for industrialisation—working capital in the most direct sense of agricultural raw materials for processing, and working capital in the large sense of either serving to generate exports or preventing to dissipate foreign exchange in imports of foodgrains and other agricultural products.

Early Developments. In early times India was industrially more advanced than West European Countries. This finds mention in the records of foreign travellers who visited the country in those times, and is borne out by the Indian Industrial Commission which reports:

'At a time when the west of Europe, a birthplace of modern industrial system, was inhabited by uncivilised tribes, India was famous for the wealth of her rulers and for the high artistic skill of her craftsmen. And even at a much later period, when the merchant adventurers from the west made their first appearance in India, industrial advancement of this country was, at any rate, not inferior to those of the more advanced European nations'.[1]

Mogul Period. During the Mogul period industry in India was fairly well developed and its products commanded wide foreign markets. The European trade in cotton goods began in this country in the beginning of the seventeenth century. They bought cotton fabrics in exchange for billion and sold these in South East Asian countries where they bought spices for the European markets. Gradually Indian made cloth became popular in European markets as well, and large quantities of cotton and silk fabrics, indigo and saltpetre were bought by the Portuguese, the Dutch, the French and the English traders. Early in the eighteenth century, the British obtained from Farukh Sayeer, a great grandson of Aurangzeb, a firman exempting their trade from all duties. In 1707 Aurangzeb died and in the chaos that followed there ensued a struggle between the European powers for supremacy in India. In this struggle the English worsted the other powers by virtue of their superiority in sea power and the support which they received from the government at home. Within half a century of Aurangzeb's death, the English acquired mastery of Bengal and by stages, of the whole of the country.

The industrial organisation during this period is best described under 1 rural industries and 2 urban industries. The former were carried on in the cottages of the villagers who made coarse cloth and other necessaries for their own use. In the urban areas master craftsmen produced fine and superfine cotton and silk fabrics, woollen shawls, silver and gold ornaments, wood carvings, inlay work and articles of high artistic value. They worked on their own account and in kārkhānas (workshops), were financed by traders, merchants and bankers, and patronized by the rulers. The superfine cloth and other articles of luxury produced in the urban areas enjoyed a wide market—in South East Asia, Middle East, African coastal towns and England. From the middle of the seventeenth century onwards the import of Indian muslins and fine fabrics by England and its export of bullion increased phenomenally and an agitation was set on foot against the East India Company which was accused of inflicting an injury on the British nation. Prohibitory laws were, therefore, enacted against the use of printed calicoes in England and high tariffs were imposed to restrict their import.

[1]Report of The Indian Industrial Commission. 1966-68.

The principal factors which led to a decline of the Indian industries are:

1. *The Impact of the Industrial Revolution.* One of the most important causes of the decay of Indian industries was the Industrial Revolution which began in the second half of the eighteenth century and was in almost full swing by the first quarter of the nineteenth century. The invention of the spinning jenny and the steam engine set in motion forces that helped in the utilization of mechanical power in industrial development. The loot from India which followed in the wake of the victory of the battle of Plassey in 1757, provided Britain with the capital she needed for the Industrial Revolution. The assumption of Diwani in Bengal in 1765, established for her permanent markets for British woollens, metals and other machine-made goods. The first industry in Britain to be revolutionized was the British textile industry. Its products were in the first instance crude and not comparable in quality with the artistic Indian hand-made fabrics but after a series of innovations their quality improved. The big advantage the machine-made products had over the Indian goods, was their reduced cost of production. This enabled the British to displace Indian goods from the foreign markets and later on even from the home market. The Indian craftsmen could not sell their ware, were driven out of work and for lack of other occupation, fell back on land.

2. *India's colonial status.* Britain's growing economy required raw materials for the industrial development and markets overseas for her manufactured goods. Both these objectives were achieved through a disruption of the old Indian economic system and introduction of new economic norms. The khadi produced in the villages was both coarse and expensive than the mill-made cloth from Lancashire. The super-fine cloth made by the urban craftsmen was no doubt artistic and superlative in quality, but could not compete with the mill-made cloth in cost. With the gradual disruption of the Indian industry and with the development of railways and communication system in India, vast markets for British manufactured goods opened up in remote and interior regions. India's role became from now on, one of a producer of raw materials and primary goods for the industrial machine of Great Britain. Her industrial development was prevented or deliberately slowed down when it could not be prevented altogether.

3. *Heavy and prohibitive import duties on Indian Goods.* The Industrial Revolution created a powerful industrial and manufacturing class in England but up to 1813, the cotton and silk goods produced in India could be sold in England at a price 50 to 60 per cent less than those manufactured in England. Heavy duties were, therefore, imposed on goods imported from India to protect the English industry and to prevent the Indian goods from flooding the English market. The Indian goods thus lost their markets in England and were increasingly diverted to the rest of Europe, Africa, America and West Indies. In 1840, the East India Company made a petition to the British Parliament to remove these prohibitive duties. As the manufacture of cotton textiles in India had already died out, Chairman of the Committee of the House of Lords, allowed the petition in respect of cotton manufactures but denied the relief and justice that was sought in respect of silk goods, the manufacture of which was last to die out, and which were still competing with silk goods made in England.

4. *The High-handedness of the company gamāshtas.* The Gamāshtas or agents of the Company were invested with wide powers which they abused for their own advantage. Artisans and craftsmen were forced to accept low and un-remunerative wages and sell their products at unduly low prices. The invidious behaviour of the Gamāshtas often led to corporal punishment of the artisans, and harassment and oppression of all kinds. The economic outcome of the East India Company's hurtful and nefarious policy was almost total abandonment of their calling by the weavers, leading to widespread unemployment and the decline of the industry.

5. *Primary-products economy.* With India's industrial economy destroyed, the East India Company was interested in improving the quality of the primary products and in encouraging the export of raw materials like cotton, silk, hides, oilseeds, jute and dyestuffs which were needed for the promotion of England's industrial growth. India thus entered a period of industrial decay and dependence upon agriculture and improvement in this sector if any, reacted very adversely on industrial development. The increased income from agriculture and the higher purchasing power of the farmer augmented the volume of foreign imports.

6. *Abolition of company's trade monopoly.* In 1833, the East India Company's monopoly of Indian trade ceased and with this there was a considerable inflow into the country of private enterprise

which had a profound effect on the course of India's industrial development. Unlike the East India Company which traded in goods produced in India, the new merchant class endowed with a special commercial ability, came in search of markets for goods manufactured in England.

7. *Loss of court patronage.* In pre-British times, the Nawabs and the Rajahs were great patrons of arts and artistic wares. With their disappearance from the scene this patronage ended and this had a very adverse effect on the Indian handicrafts.

8. *Disorganisation of guilds.* The British rule enfeebled the organisation of the guilds which supervised the quality control of the products. This resulted in marked deterioration and decline in value of the goods produced.

9. *Increase of transport facilities.* The ease of ocean travel, the opening of the Suez Canal and the construction of railways in the country opened up the interior and enabled easy penetration of the home market by English goods and large-scale production and export of foodgrains and raw materials from the country.

By 1875 Indian handicrafts were almost completely destroyed and the edifice of her cottage industries lay in ruins. The men engaged in these vocations were thrown out of employment. The predatory character of the British capital interests had given way to free trade which invariably favours the richest and the most powerful nation and competitive forces were being relied upon to capture the Indian like other world markets. India was from then on, an agrarian appendage of Imperial Britain.

II

Evolution of Modern Industry. Modern industry had its beginnings in this country in indigo plantation which came up towards the end of the eighteenth century. Later on tea and coffee plantations were developed as the return from the export of these commodities was extra-ordinarily high. From the very outset the plantations were owned, managed and controlled by Europeans. The manufacturing industry in India was started in the 1850s but its real progress commenced after 1875. In the next two decades cotton and jute industries were reasonably well set. The British never intended India to develop an industrial economy and the first steel mill in Jamshedpur was the outcome of the courage and the vision of the great

Parsi entrepreneur, Jamsetji Tata. On the whole industrial development in India before World War I, was slow and lop-sided in
character.

Development between War Years. In the period between the two
wars and especially between 1922 and 1939, considerable progress
was made in industrial production. The production of steel ingots
increased from 1.3 lakh tons in 1922 to 10.42 lakh tons in 1939 and
of cotton goods from 1,714 million yards to 4,016 million yards;
production of paper and paper board increased from 24,000
tons to 67,000 tons and of sugar from 24,000 tons to
9,31,000 tons. The output of match industry increased from 16
million gross to 22 million gross. Other items which recorded
large increases during this period are cement, glass, vanaspati and
soap; and manufacture of several varieties of engineering goods
was also begun. The total number of factories increased from 2,936
in 1914 to 11,613 in 1939 and the number of workers employed in
them increased from 950,000 to 1,750,000,

Development during Second World War. During World War II,
India was an important supply base for the needs of the Allied
Armed Forces for Middle East, South East Asia and Far East. In
pre-war years, whereas there was plenty of idle capacity in her
plants, during the war the industrial production received a big fillip
and was limited only by the available spare capacity of the existing
plant and machinery. Many industrial establishments were working
at full capacity and in two or three shifts. New industrial enterprises set up for the first time were 1 ferro-alloys liks ferro-silicon and
ferro-manganese, 2 non-ferrous metals and metal fabricating industries such as copper, copper wire and cable, and copper sheets, 3
mechanical industries like diesel engines, pumps, transport and
electrical equipment, machine and cutting tools, sewing machines,
and bicycles, 4 hydrogenated oil, 5 chemicals like caustic soda,
chlorine, super-phosphate, power alcohol, synthetic resins, plastics
etc., and 6 plant and equipment for new industries. There was a
rapid expansion of small scale industries all over the country and
new sources of supply were created. All those who set up industrial enterprises during the war years, were given assurances of
government help and patronage after the war ended.

The war gave a big boost to industrial growth in volume, diver-
sity and capital accumulation but due to its inherent drawbacks—
war time diversion of resources for defence production, comman-

deering of iron and steel, and cement, statutory control of cotton and jute goods and strict control of production and distribution of sugar and other commodities—the economy suffered in a number of ways :

1. The capital equipment of pre-war industries was put to heavy strain. There was continuous deterioration of plant and machinery due to working of extra shifts in several industries.

2. There was acute scarcity of consumer goods including durables. This was aggravated by currency expansion which led to serious inflation, hoarding, black marketing and profiteering. The business class made fabulous profits and the masses were hard hit.

3. The war-time controls—rationing, permits, quotas, licenses—introduced widespread corruption in the economy.

4. Considerations of cost of production, priorities, location and regional balances were total casualties.

Recession between 1945-48. In August 1945, when the War ended much of the industrial equipment was almost completely broken down and out of gear. Replacements and imports of capital goods were not easy and preternaturally delayed as both the victor and the vanquished nations with their industrial machines shattered, were engaged in rebuilding their own economies. The only country that came unscathed out of the war was the USA. She had her order books full with requirements from Europe and Japan. Consequently in 1946, there was a fall in production of essential items like iron and steel, cement, cotton textiles and sugar etc. The shortages were further aggravated by countrywide out-break of strikes, internal commotion and bottlenecks in transport and distribution.

In 1947 came independence and the partition of the country affected industrial development unfavourably. It involved 1 loss of raw materials like long staple cotton, jute, gypsum, rock salt etc., 2 loss of markets for manufactured goods, 3 import of foodgrains which should have saved valuable foreign exchange, 4. migration of artisans and technicians to Pakistan, and 5. expenditure of thousands of crores of rupees which could have been profitably spent for developmental purposes, on defence.

Widespread communal disturbances and violence, mass immigration of minorities and resettlement of refugees put heavy strains on the financial and the administrative machinery of the country, and economic development received a serious set-back.

In December 1947, a tripartite conference was called and agreed on a 3-year management labour truce. The new incentives—the passage by the Constituent Assembly in February 1948 of a bill to establish the Industrial Finance Corporation, the tax exemptions in the 1948-49 budget and the cheap credit, revived the economy somewhat and in 1948 industrial production showed a definite improvement over the previous year.

Industrial Policy. On 7 April 1948, the Resolution on Industrial Policy was adopted. It lay down the broad objectives of the government in the field of industry, demarcated the spheres of private and public sectors and stressed the need for stepping up production of capital equipment and essential consumer goods for export so as to strengthen the economy internally and to increase foreign exchange earnings. A year later on 6 April 1949, a detailed statement was made regarding government policy in regard to foreign capital and its repatriation. The government made it clear that it did not propose to impose on foreign interests any restrictions that were not applicable to any similar Indian enterprises.

Both the Industrial Policy Resolution of 1948 and the decision on foreign enterprises, ignored the views that Gandhiji had been putting forward before the nation for nearly three decades. The former was a repudiation of his policy of decentralized village economy in respect of consumer goods and the latter of his Swadeshi programme. Now that Gandhi was removed from the scene, Jawaharlal Nehru who considered Gandhian economy a regression to primitivism and the past, was free to project his own contrary policy of building a large-scale consumer goods industry which as later events have shown, has proved disastrous not only for growth but also for the solution of the problem of unemployment.

Recovery in 1948. Recovery in Indian industrial production registered in 1948 was maintained in 1949 and 1950 and most of the industries recorded substantial increase in output. The increase in output in respect of iron and steel, cement, electrical goods and diesel engines was particularly substantial. In respect of cotton, jute and sugar industries, due to shortages of raw materials, the output declined. The official general index of industrial production (base: 1947-100) rose to 106.3 in 1949, 105.2 in 1950 and 117.4 in 1951. In 1951 output in cotton, jute and sugar industries which had shown a decline earlier, also improved. Factors which contributed towards the rise in production included, 1 fewer man-hours lost,

2 establishment of some new industries, 3 installation of additional units in some industries and expansion in others, 4 better availability of essential raw materials due to liberalisation of imports 5 upward revision of prices of pig-iron, steel and cloth to meet the higher cost of raw materials and replacements of machinery, and 6 continued improvement in transport.

In March 1950, the Planning Commission was set up to make an assessment of the material, capital and human resources of the country and to investigate the possibilities of augmenting such of these resources as were found to be deficient in relation to the country's requirements. It was asked to formulate a plan for the most effective and balanced utilisation of the country's resources on a priority basis and to indicate the factors which were tending to retard economic growth. In July 1951 a Joint Consultative Board on Industry and Labour was set up to deal with nationalisation and related problems. In September 1951 the State Financial Corporation Act was passed to enable state governments to set up their own Financial Corporations to assist small-scale and medium enterprises and also the Tariff Commission Act to enquire into the claim for protection of Indian industries by establishing a Statutory Tariff Commission. In October 1951 was passed the Industries Development and Regulation Act for regulating industries as a corollary to planned development.

III
INDUSTRIAL DEVELOPMENT UNDER THE PLANS

First Five Year Plan. The First Five Year Plan was published by the Planning Commission in December 1952. It was a transitional Plan intended to rehabilitate the Indian economy which had been hit hard by World War II and the Partition of the country. It aimed at agricultural growth to meet first, the deficiencies of foodgrains and raw materials created by the partition and secondly, to create the necessary economic overheads like power and transport for future industrial needs of the country.

The total outlay on industrial development was Rs 557 crore. Out of this Rs 94 crore only was in the public sector as against Rs 463 crore in the private sector split into Rs 233 crore on expansion programmes and Rs 230 crore on modernisation and replacements.

During the First Plan period, production increased by 39 per cent or about 8 per cent per annum. Production of capital goods increased by 70 per cent, industrial raw materials by 34 per cent and finished consumer goods by 34 per cent. The index of industrial production (base 1960) rose from 54.8 in 1951 to 72.7 in 1955. Targets set for the period were achieved for paper, paper board, sewing machines and bicycles. Production of cement increased by nearly 2 million tons and there was a substantial increase in the output of general engineering goods, and heavy chemicals. A number of public sector enterprises—Hindustan Machine Tools, Sindri Fertlizer Factory, Chittaranjan Locomotive Works, Integral Coach Factory, Hindustan Cable Factory, Newsprint Factory, Penicillin Factory and Indian Telephone Industries were launched.

In respect of certain industries like steel, aluminium, fertilisers etc., there were shortfalls and the targets could not be achieved. Yet, despite a very modest investment over the Plan Period, the overall industrial production increased substantially and an infrastructure of power, transport and several other facilities, was built up.

The Second Plan. The Second plan launched in 1956 aimed at laying the industrial foundations of the country by building up a number of important and basic industries. The total outlay on industrial development during the Plan Period, was envisaged at Rs 1,094 crore split into:

1. Rs 759 crore to be invested in producer goods industries— Rs 463 crore in the public sector and Rs 296 crore in the private sector.

2. Rs 156 crore to be invested in industrial machinery and capital goods industry. The share of public sector was to be Rs 84 crore and that of private sector Rs 72 crore.

3. Rs 179 crore of the consumers goods industries; out of this the public sector allocation was to be Rs 12 crore only and the private investment to the tune Rs 167 crore.

The above figures show that the public sector was assigned a higher responsibility for the development of producer and capital goods industries, and the expansion of the consumer goods industries was to be in the private sector. What is important to remember is, that the public sector was to invest 98 per cent of its allotted funds for the development of the producer and capital goods industries whereas the private sector was to invest only 68 per cent of the funds allocated to it, for this purpose. The share of the consumer goods industries in the total funds allocated to the public sector was thus only 2 per cent whereas it was a substantial 32 per cent in the case of the private sector.

If the reader bears in mind, 1 that the private sector is highly profit-oriented and yields quick dividends, 2 that this sector engages in large-scale production of items like super-fine fabrics, pharmaceuticals, cosmetics, household electrical appliances and consumer durables which only an infinitesimal minority of the people can afford, 3 that large-scale industrial production of consumer goods in a few urban enclaves has stood in the way and prevented the growth of decentralised village industries to serve the needs of the vast majority of people living in India's 600,000 villages, 4 that this in turn has led to mass-scale rural unemployment and under-employment, and loss of buying power, 5 that consequent limitation and exhaustion of markets has put a stop on economic growth and national income and brought about stagnation in a country where the population has been growing at an increasingly fast rate, 6 that stagnation in the economy has led to scarcities which have engendered hoarding, black marketing, profiteering and inflation, 7 that inflation has made the poor more indigent and the rich, richer, 8 that this has led to wide disparities of income and wealth between the rich and the poor, and to concentration of wealth in a few industrial houses and families and, 9 given them political power which makes them the virtual rulers of the land, he will be in a position to appreciate and assess the damage that India has suffered through a faulty allocation of resources and investments, and the wrong turn that Jawaharlal Nehru gave to the Indian economy soon after independance.

The impressive achievement of the Second Plan was the development of the iron and steel industry and the establishment of the three large steel plants at Rourkela, Bhillai and Durgapur in the public sector and the expansion of capacity of the Tata Iron and Steel Mills, Indian Iron and Steel Mills and of Mysore Iron and Steel Works in the private sector. Manufacture was undertaken of several new items like machinery for cement and paper plants, compressors, boilers, tractors, motor cycles and scooters. Rapid progress was made in the production of consumer durables like fans, radios, bicycles and electrical goods, and in some heavy industries like machine tools and heavy engineering industries. There was expansion of capacity of essential producer goods like cement, fertilisers and heavy chemicals, and modernisation and re-equipment of jute, textile and sugar mills.

There were short falls in several industries such as steel, fertilisers, newsprint, dyestuffs, soda ash, cement, chemical pulps, sulphuric acid, pig iron, refactories, sewing machines, railway wagons and cotton textile machinery due to foreign exchange shortage which began in 1956, and non-availability of machinery and equipment, and technical know-how from foreign collaborators in time. The performance of small-scale sector was poor and that of exports as against export targets unsatisfactory.

Despite the short falls, the Second Plan period was a time during which a favourable infra-structure was built for industrialization of the country and dependence on imports of machinery and capital goods was reduced very substantially. The index of industrial production (base 1960) rose from 72.7 in 1956 to 100 in 1960.

Third Plan. The pressing need of the Third Plan (1961-66) was to lay the foundations of rapid development during the succeeding 15 years, if long term objectives in respect of growth and levels of employment, were to be achieved. It was, therefore, considered necessary, first, to continue with the establishment and expansion of basic capital and producer goods industries with special emphasis on machine building industries and secondly, on the acquisition of related skills, technical know-how and design ability, so that in the succeeding plan periods, the growth of economy in the fields of power, transport and minerals, would become self-sustaining and increasingly independent of outside help. Whereas the long-term objective was the emphasis on the production of capital goods and raw material intermediates, the industrial programmes in the Third Plan period aimed also at providing fully for essential need of the people and in a limited measure for a wide variety of manufactured goods including even semi-luxury and luxury articles. The role of cottage goods and small-scale industries was conceived as one of providing larger employment opportunities and of increasing the supply of consumer goods.

Theoretically industrial expansion in the Third Plan was governed by the Industrial Policy Resolution of 1956, and the role of the private and the public sector were conceived as complementary and supplementary to each other. In practice, however, numerous changes were made in it, to favour the private sector. A highly profitable programme of manufacture of dyestuffs, plastics, pharmaceuticals and cosmetics was reserved for the private sector and made complementary to a programme for the manufacture of basic subs- tances and intermediates—which were not profit yielding—in the public sector. Fertilizer production which was previously reserved for the public sector was thrown open to the private sector and in the case of pig iron, the policy was relaxed to allow establishment in the private sector, plants with a much higher capacity than was permissible earlier.

The total financial outlay for the industrial sector in the Third Plan, was Rs 2,570 crore. Of this, Rs 1,520 crore were in the public and Rs 1,050 crore in the private sector. A sum of Rs 425 crore was allotted for the development of small-scale and village industries.

During the Plan period notable progress was made in the produc- tion of new items like watches, time pieces, radio valves, diodes and transistors, cameras, magnets, microscopic slides, hydrau- lic presses, tax-metres, micrometres, roller bearings, potassium permanganate, heavy water and some other chemicals. Progress was also made in the reduction of import content by manufacture of raw materials, components and spares for machine tools, auto- mobiles, electric motors, transformers, switch gears etc. Substantial addition was made to the existing capacity by starting new units for manufacture of machine tools, metallurgical and engineering goods, petro-chemicals, oil refining, fertilizers, ship building, loco- motive and wagon building, aircraft manufacture, drugs and pharmaceuticals. The production of cement machinery increased from Rs 6 million to Rs 49 million, of sugar machinery from Rs 49 million to Rs 77 million, of cotton textile machinery from Rs 104 to Rs 216 million, of pulp machinery and paper machinery from nothing to Rs 16.8 million and of machine tools from Rs 70 to Rs 244 million. The output of petroleum products increased by 48 per cent, of basic metals by 49 per cent, of metal products by 57 per cent, of transport equipment by 50 per cent, of electrical machinery by 71 per cent and non-electrical machinery by 82 per cent.

The industrial progress on the whole was uneven. It increased by 8 to 9.5 per cent during the first four years but only by 4.5 per cent in the final year of the Plan, giving an annual average increase of 7.9 per cent against the anticipated 11 per cent. There were serious shortfalls sometime amounting to as much as 30 to 60 per cent or more, and physical targets were not achieved in a large number of industries. Shortfalls were to the tune of 60 per cent or more in respect of alloys, zinc, stainless steel, mining, machinery, fertilizers, sulphuric acid, newsprint and paper and between 30 and 50 per cent in respect of iron ore, steel ingots, caustic soda, tractors, sugar machinery, woolen fabrics and commercial vehicles.

The Third Plan had flopped and the principal reasons for its poor performance were 1 the China and the Pakistan wars, 2 shortages of foreign exchange, 3 cessation of AID flow, 4 shortages of power and transport, 5 inflationary pressures in the economy, and 6 unprecedented droughts leading to shortages of foodgrains and raw materials.

If the Third Plan was a flop, the three years following it, were a period of unmitigated disaster. From 1 April 1966, the country was on a Plan holiday. There was a sharp deceleration in industrial growth—0.2 per cent in 1967 and 0.5 per cent in 1968—due to a variety of causes: 1 strains in the economy following the Indo-Pakistan war of 1965, 2 cessation of aid flow, 3 foreign exchange difficulties, 4 under-utilization of capacity in several industries, 5 political instability and fall of Congress Governments in the States following the fourth general election, 6 disturbed industrial relations resulting in strikes, lockouts and gheraos, 7 failures of monsoon and shortage of foodgrains and industrial raw materials, 8 devaluation of the rupee, 9 reckless spending on current consumption and unproductive investment by the Government, 10 indiscreet use of resources including bank credits for building inventories, hoarding and speculation in commodities by private sector, 11 price hikes and inflationary pressures, 12 fall in domestic savings, 13 decline in the ratio of net investment to the net domestic savings, and 14 fall in the share of capital formation expenditure.

In September 1967, Professor D.R. Gadgil was appointed the Deputy Chairman of the Planning Commission. After taking over he decided to postpone the commencement of the Fourth Plan, as the economy was in a precarious condition.

In 1968 the rainfall was good and with an adequate production of foodgrains (98 million tons) and raw materials, industrial production recovered somewhat. In the following year, 1969-70, the Fourth Five Year Plan was launched.

Fourth Plan. The year 1969 was an ominous time for the Fourth Plan to get started. The objectives of "growth with stability" and "progressive achievement of self-reliance", remained only on paper.

As the plan has already been considered in the chapter on Congress Socialism and the Plans, we shall in what follows confine ourselves to some aspects of the industrial sector only.

Out of a total outlay of Rs 24,882 crore for the Plan, the outlay for the industrial and mineral sector was Rs 5,198 crore—Rs 3,238 crore in the public sector and Rs 1,960 crore in the private and cooperative sectors. The share of the village and small industries was a meagre Rs 298.45 crore. The projected overall rate of growth was 5.7 per cent per annum, 5 per cent annually for agriculture and 8 to 10 per cent for industry. The rate of domestic savings of 8.8 per cent in 1968-69 was expected to rise to 13.2 per cent, of investment from 11.3 per cent to 14.5 per cent and of per capita income at current prices from Rs 558 to Rs 643 in 1973-74. Particular attention was to be paid to the production of fertilizers, metals, petroleum products and machinery.

The performance during the Plan period was extremely poor and there were shortfalls all along the line. The growth rate was 5.2 per cent in 1969-70, 4.2 per cent in 1970-71, 1.7 per cent 1971-72, 0.6 per cent in 1972-73 and 6 per cent in 1973-74. The average rate of growth was 3.5 per cent against the anticipated rate of 5.7 per cent. The most important reason for a low rate of growth of the GNP and a poor performance on the industrial front was the failure of the monsoon and an inadequate production of foodgrains and raw materials between 1972 and 1974. The rate of agricultural growth was 5.1 per cent in 1969-70 and 5.3 per cent in 1970-71 but it declined by 1.7 per cent in 1971-72 and 5.1 per cent in 1972-73. The output of foodgrains was 99.5 million tons in 1969-70 and 107 million tons in 1970-71 which was a bumper year. In 1971-72 the production fell to 105.2 million tons and in 1972-73 it further fell to 95.2 million tons. In the final year of the Plan it rose to 103.6 million tons—a figure 3.4 million tons short of the 1970-71 figure and 11.4 million tons short of the target of 115 million tons for that year. The target achieved was only 1.6 per cent against 5 per cent envisaged in the Plan.

That bad harvest years are invariably years of hardship for the masses and difficulties for the Indian economy as a whole, that the economic welfare of her people depends at least in the initial stages on an abundant and secure agricultural growth and that this growth must be freed from the capriciousness of the rain god—are lessons that Jawaharlal Nehru or his daughter never imbibed. If they had, they would have concentrated on expanding the country's irrigation potential to its very limits. This they never attempted or did. The question to which one wants an answer is, how long it will take the new "Gandhian rulers" of the Country to achieve this much desired objective?

The rate of growth in the industrial sector was well below the Plan target of 8 to 10 per cent. It was 6.5 per cent in 1969-70, 3.7 per cent in 1970-71, 4.5 per cent in 1971-72, 5 per cent 1972-73 and 0.5 per cent in 1973-74.

In none of the other sectors were results satisfactory. The rate of domestic savings which reached its highest level of 11.1 per cent in 1965-66 declined for two successive years and then went upto 8.2 per cent in 1968-69. It was 8.6 per cent in 1969-70, 9.4 per cent in 1970-71, and 10 per cent in 1971-72. The target figure of 13.2 per cent in 1973-74 could not be achieved. The rate of investment much like the rate of domestic savings touched its peak of 13.4 per cent in 1965-66. It continued to decline in the succeeding 4 years. It was 9.3 per cent in 1969-70, 10.5 per cent in 1970-71, 11.5 per cent in 1971-72, and the targeted rate of 14.5 per cent at the end of the Plan period could not be achieved. How can the economy grow, the question has been asked, if the rate of productive investment continues to fall? There were bottlenecks in respect of transport and serious shortfalls in power output.

The factors that coutributed towards the failure of the Plan include 1 the failure of monsoon and the shortage of foodgrains and raw materials, 2 the Indo-Pakistan war of 1971 and the cost of looking after 10 million refugees on the Eastern border, 3 the price hike in crude and petroleum products, 4 excessive deficit financing and monetary expansion, 5 diversion of finances from productive investment to adhoc current consumption, 6 price hikes and runaway inflation, 7 acute shortages of essential goods, 8 under, utilization of capacity, 9 shortage or irregular supplies of power, 10 transport bottlenecks, 11 unsatisfactory industrial relations and management problems, and 12 political turmoil.

Fifth Plan. In 1973 for reasons enumerated above the economic condition of the country was pretty grim. Foodgrain and other shortages, rising prices and hyperinflation were causing hardship everywhere. In Gujarat and Bihar they were manifest as agitations by at first students and later the people. In December 1973, Dr B.S. Minhas resigned from the Planning Commission on the ground that the Draft Fifth Plan targets were utterly unrealistic and impossible of achievement.[2] In 1974, after the increase in oil prices, fertilizers and foodgrains created a balance of payments problem of large proportions, the situation reached a breaking point and was further complicated by the rail strike.

Jeremiah Novak, a columnist for the Asian Mail (USA), in a series of three revealing articles,[3] describes Indira Gandhi's difficulties during this period and the events that led her up to the emergency. She approached the International Monetary Fund—World Bank, for aid to finance her balance of payments deficit and to revamp the country's shattered economy. Before committing aid it is the custom of these agencies to stipulate that the recipient country must prove that it has a policy that would stabilize the economy. This was achieved for Indira Gandhi, Novak writes, by the V.K. R.V. Rao—P.N. Dhar proposal outlined in a book published in October 1973.[4] The policies which the proposal recommended— money supply reductions, wage freezes, increased imports, strong exports and freezing of private capital—it is said, fitted neatly into the IMF—World Bank categories. In fact as C.H. Hanumantha Rao of the Indian Economic Growth (IEG), who was asked by P.N. Dhar to brief Jeremiah Novak stated, 'the V.K.R.V. Rao—P.N. Dhar package had been developed with a view towards the negotiations'.[5]

As is well known the IMF and the World Bank aid consortia, act in consonance. The IMF makes sure that the recipient country adopts policies which will "stabilise" its economy and promote its exports so that the basis for repayments to the World Bank consortia can be laid. Foreign loans have to be paid for, out of export earnings. Furthermore the aid-to-India consortium, Novak states, due to prodding by Daniel Moynihan, insisted that Indira Gandhi give up her quasi socialist policies and adopt those more in tune with those of the aid-giving Western countries.

Her need for economic aid and the political turmoil created by the movement led by Jaya Prakash Narayan, it seems, left her no choice. Like her father before, she agreed to all the conditions imposed by the IMF- World Bank aid consortium. On 1 May 1974, the IMF issued a press release which said interalia, 'The fund had

---

[2]The full story is related in the chapter on Congress Socialism and the Plans.
[3]Times of India, New Delhi. 1, 2, 4 July 1977.
[4]V.K.R.V. Rao. 1973. Inflation and India's Economic Crisis, New Delhi.
[5]Ibid.

agreed to the purchase by the Government of India of the equivalent of SDR 235 million (One SDR-approximately 90 US cents). . . .
On 20 May 1974 the Far Eastern Economic Review signalled the
results in its press release to suggest that India's economy was
about to have an "overhaul."[6]

In May 1974, Indira Gandhi mercilessly crushed the railway
strike. In June 1974, the World Bank sanctioned its loan to India.
In July 1974 she announced at Bangalore School of Social Studies
headed by V.K.R.V Rao her new policy impounding dearnes allowance and profits, increasing the bank rate and curtailing severely the
supply of money. Novak adds, however, that Bangalore was only the
tip of the ice-berg and to implement the IMF stabilization programme, Indira Gandhi had to increase exports, unshackle industry of
its fetters, decrease taxes in the higher income brackets to defuse
black money and to re-invigorate the agricultural sector—in other
words as P.N. Dhar put it, "to open up the economy along Western
lines". But Mrs Gandhi, Novak, says never announced at Bangalore
or anytime thereafter that she had switched over to the Western
model of development. This she couldn't, first, because she was still
telling people that she was wanting to help the poorer sections of the
people and build a socialist society but "some people" were stand-
ing in her way and preventing it, secondly, because her Party was
"socialist" and she did not dare tell it that she had relinquished
the socialist path and lastly, because she still needed CPI support.

The Bangalore speech and the new anti-inflationary policies had
an adverse effect on the workers plight. It is true that prices began to
come down by September of 1974, but the wages fell faster and the
level of unemployment rose. The fall in prices was the consequence
of the loss of buying power of the workers and the poorer sections
due to wage and D.A. freezes and changes in the bonus policy.

But even as there was a fall in prices and improvement in exports,
a good part of the IMF-India programme was stalled by the political situation, and by the courts on technical grounds. The situation
as it existed towards the end of 1974 and the first half of 1975, has
been admirably summarized by Ruddar Datt and K.P.M. Sundharam.
They write, 'Attempts to control prices since the Bangalore speech
in July 1974 had borne fruit and the general price level was falling,
but the government could not take advantage of the situation and

[6]Jeremiah Novak. 1 July 1977, Times of India.

consolidate its control over inflation. By June 1975 the economy was poised to take a deep plunge. The various steps taken by the government against tax dodgers and smugglers were thwarted by the courts on technical grounds. The many welfare measures the government brought . . . did not succeed due to the opposition of the vested interests. It was indeed heartbreaking for the government, as it was not allowed to implement any worthwhile economic measures. . . . superimposed over these economic problems was political instability arising out of the revolt of the opposition and the internal dissensions in the ruling party'.[7]

Ruddar Datt and Sundharam, it appears, saw clearly how what was begun in Bangalore as the IMF—India programme, needed the emergency for its full implementation. P. N. Dhar said that Bangalore and the 20-point programme were related. Novak agreed and added, 'So were the IMF-World Bank programmes and the emergency. For the Bangalore policies and the crushing of the rail-road strike were among the major causes of the increased political agitation of 1974-75 and both were related to the IMF-World Bank loans and the V.K.R.V Rao—P.N. Dhar programme'.[8]

The movement led by Jaya Prakash Narayan was already making it most difficult for Indira Gandhi to implement the IMF—World Bank- V.K.R.V. Rao—P. N. Dhar programme, when the Allahabad High Court judgement struck and swept her off her feet. For a person who 'expects everybody to minister . . . to her comforts . . . and is remarkably casual and indifferent to others',[9] who loves power inordinately and wants to stick to it at any price, Indira Gandhi had no choice. On 25 June 1975, without even consulting her cabinet colleagues or the Congress Working Committee, she imposed internal emergency on the country. She needed it both for her court case and for the implementation of the IMF-India programme. Novak adds, 'made bolder after the emergency, she then

[7]Rudder Datt and K.P.N. Sundharam. 1976. Indian Economy, New Delhi.

[8]Jeremiah Novak. 1 July 1977, Times of India, New Delhi. Approximately three months later V.K.R.V. Rao issued a rejoinder in which he said 1 he had not read Novak's articles earlier, 2 P.N. Dhar had nothing to do with the proposal in his book, copies of which had been sent to the Prime Minister, 3 he was not aware of the negociations with World Bank-IMF which is quite possible. (There is no reason why he should have been.)

[9]J. L. Nehru Letter to his sister Vijaylakshmi Pandit.

implemented a western-backed population programme. Mr P. N. Dhar, Mr V. Ramachandran and Mr C. H. Hanumatha Rao were not responsible for her population programme. "The sterilisation programme came purely from the Aid-to--India consortium", one of them told me. . . . Nearly everyone on the Indian side of the programme objected to the sterilisation programme and blamed Mr Sanjay Gandhi, "who is too much influenced by World Bank— IMF and the Foundation people."[10]

The Fifth Five Year Plan should have been started on 1 April 1974 but due to spiralling prices and economic instability, it had to be deferred. In 1974-75 signs of revival of industrial production became visible. The index of industrial production went up by 2.5 per cent as against a decline of 0.2 per cent in 1973-74. In 1975-76, the production picked up and improved to 5.7 per cent but still fell short of the annual target of 8.2 per cent for the fifth plan. Significant increases in production were achieved in the public sector specially in some basic industries like steel, coal, cement, non-ferrous metals and power generation. But private sector lagged behind and the decline was particularly marked in industries like passenger cars, consumer durables and textiles.

The curbs on industrial licensing introduced after the exposures of the Hazari and Dutt Commission reports (1967 and 1968) were removed soon after the Indo-Pakistan war of December 1971 and relaxation of industrial policy was announced in respect of 72 priority industries. In 1972, regularization of unauthorised capacity of 65 industrial units was announced. In 1973, industrial units were permitted 100 per cent expansion on the plea of diversification. On 25 October 1974, in step with its new economic policy (NEP), the government announced further changes liberalising industrial licensing policy and 21 industries were delicensed. The government also permitted unlimited expansion beyond the licensed capacities to foreign companies and monopoly houses in 30 other important industries. Among other concessions extended to large industrial houses were taxation cuts on the lines of the Wanchoo Committee report, investment rebates and subsidies. The industrial houses never had it so good and they amassed large fortunes. The motive for this largesse to big industrial houses appears to have been the promotion of growth. The objective of prevention of concentration of

---

[10]Jeremiah Novak. 2 July 1977. Times of India, New Delhi.

economic power had for the time being at least taken a back seat.

Between October 1974 and March 1976 the prices fell by about 15 per cent due partly to a good harvest in 1975-76 and partly to a fall in demand of essential goods, consequent on wage and D.A. freeze and loss of buying power of the poorer sections. But the prices began to rise once again after March 1976 and in six months between March 1976 and October 1976 rose by 11.5 per cent undoing all that had been achieved in the previous 18 months.

In October 1976 the National Development Council met. It had met three years earlier in 1973. The Fifth Plan document which was collecting dust all this time, was finalized. But the goal of self-reliance or the net zero aid by the end of the Plan period was given the go-by, the sights were lowered and the overall growth rate targeted at 4.37 per cent, which is lower than what Minhas had proposed. The total outlay was raised to Rs 69,300 crore. Table 1 below indicates the distribution of invesment outlays in the Draft and the finalised Plans.

TABLE 1
Distribution of Outlays

	Investment in Crore	
	Draft Plan	*Final Plan*
Agriculture and allied programmes	4,944.08	4,643.09
Irrigation and flood control	2,804,84	3,449.18
Power	6,076.65	7,293.90
Industry and Mining	9,031.11	10,200.60
Education	7,110.62	6,881.43
Social and economic services	5,286.80	4,759.77
Hill and tribal areas	500.00	450.00

A cursory glance at the table reveals that there is reduction in outlays in respect of important sectors like agriculture, education, social and economic services, and allocation for hill and tribal areas. Even in respect of irrigation, power and industry where the outlays were stepped up in the final plan document, if the price-rises and the fall in the buying power of the rupee are taken into consideration, there is a marked reduction in outlays.

In the third year of the plan (1976-77), due mainly to a bumper harvest but also to measures against tax dodgers and smugglers, enforced discipline, improved industrial relations etc., the industrial production showed a sudden spurt. Industrial production increased by 10 per cent, something which had not happened for over a decade. The gross national product, however, increased by less than 2 per cent compared with 8.5 per cent in the previous year. As the rate of growth of population is around 2.5 per cent, the per capita income declined. According to the economic survey for the year by the Finance Minister of the Janata Government, the agricultural production declined by 5 to 6 per cent compared to a 15.6 per cent increase in the previous year. Prices rose by 11.6 per cent and money supply by 17.1 per cent adding to inflationary pressures. Exports rose by 23.2 per cent to Rs 4,980.6 crore while imports declined by 6.8 per cent to Rs 4,908.2 crore leaving a trade surplus of Rs 72.4 crore as compared to a deficit of Rs 1,722.4 crore in 1975-76. Net invisible receipts, particularly inward remittances were buoyant and foreign exchange reserves rose to Rs 2,863 crore at the end of the year. But this result was achieved at the cost of investment for growth.[11]

The spectacular increase in exports was due to the new export policy and the concessions to the exporters. They created scarcities at home even in respect of food articles like onions, potatoes, tea, coffee and oil seeds, and essential producer goods like cement. As a result the prices of these commodities rose and created hardships for the poor and the middle class people. Those who made big gains out of people's misery were the exporters. Some foreign companies like Phillips India exported their goods at less than half the cost price in India to their branches abroad where they were sold at exorbitant prices. Phillips India made enormous profits from their export deals but the country lost tremendously in the bargain.[12] The decline in imports during the year was essentially due to a marked reduction in the imports of food and fertilizers which was, however, partly offset by rise in the imports of cotton and edible oils. External assistance according to the survey declined in 1976-77 to Rs 1239 crore from Rs 1747 crore in the previous year. The employment in the organised sector increased by 5.20 lakhs or 2.6 per cent in 1975-76 due mainly to an increase of 4.7 lakhs in the public

[11]The Economic Survey presented to the Parliament by H.M. Patel Union Finance Minister on 13 June 1977.

[12]These disclosures came out in a case of a license application by Phillips before Justice Nain of the M.R.T.P. Commission.

sector but the number of job seekers on the live registers of employment exchanges in the country increased by 4.8 per cent to 9.77 million at the end of December 1977. This was, however, less than half the increase in 1975-76. The total number of educated unemployed also rose from 48 lakhs in 1975 to 51 lakhs in 1976. The picture is on the whole a gloomy one and the economic survey shows that the Congress Government's claims that its economic policies were helping the poor or that the emergency had yielded economic gains across the board, were false and fraudulant.

IV

Industrial Stagnation. Significant progress in industrial production was made during the 15 year period from 1951 to 1966. During the First Plan period industrial production increased by 39 per cent or about 8 per cent per annum. The index of industrial production (base 1960) rose from 54.8 in 1951 to 72.7 in 1956. In the Second Plan period, the index of industrial production (base 1960) rose from 72.7 in 1956 to 100 in 1960. During the first four years of the Third Plan, industrial production increased by 10 per cent per year but in the final year 1965-66, the rate of growth fell to 4.3 per cent, the average annual rate being around 9 per cent.

Towards the end of 1965, India was involved in a war against Pakistan and its economy received a severe set back. The year 1966, it would appear was a watershed in respect of the growth and development of the industrial sector. From this year onward till the ignominious fall and exit of Indira Gandhi, the Country's economy stagnated and made no progress whatsoever. In 1966-67 the rate of her industrial progress slumped to a paltry 0.2 per cent and in 1967-68 it was a mere 0.5 per cent. The country was on a Plan holiday. In 1968-69, the industrial production recovered somewhat but as the production of foodgrains was 3 million tons less than in the previous year, the commencement of the Fourth Plan was shelved for another year. In April 1969, the Fourth Plan was launched and the industrial target set at 8 to 10 per cent. In 1969-70, the first year of the Fourth Plan the rate of industrial growth was 6.8 per cent but in the following year it fell to 3.7 per cent. In 1971-72 and 1972-73, it slightly improved to 4.5 per cent and 5 per cent respectively but in the last Plan year 1973-74 it was no more than 0.5 per cent. The average annual rate for the Fourth Plan as a whole was only 3.3

per cent. In the first year of the Fifth Five Year Plan (1974-75), industrial growth was still low at 2.5 per cent. In 1975-76, it rose to 5.7 per cent with significant growth in the public sector. Production in the private sector specially in the manufacture of passenger cars, consumer durables and textiles languished. In 1976-77, the public sector picked up and the growth rate rose to 10 per cent but the private sector showed little or no improvement. The rate of growth in GNP due mainly to decline of agricultural production was less than 2 per cent.

Whichever parameter one takes into account, the stark reality of stagnation stares one in the face. Let us take the figures for the national and the per capita income for the past 25 years. The national income figures at constant prices, are comparable but conceal the population effect. To eliminate the effect of growth of population, per capita income is calculated. The following two tables show the movement of national and per capita income in two series from 1950-51 to 1960-61, and from 1960-61 to 1973-74.

TABLE 2

Movement of National and Per Capita Income during 1950-51 to 1960-61 (Conventional series) at 1948-49 prices

Item	1950-51	1955-56	1960-61
		(Rs Crore)	
Net National Product at constant prices	8500	10480	12730
Per Capita Income (Rs)	247.5	267.8	293.3

Source: Central Statistical Organisation.

TABLE 3

Movement of National and Per Capita Income from 1960-61 to 1974-75 at 1960-61 prices (New Series).

	1960-61	1965-67	1966-67	1967-68	1971-72	1973-74	1974-75
Net National Product (in crores)	13294	15021	15243	19171	19299	19724	20075
Per Capita income (in rupees)	306.3	310.4	307.9	329.2	348.4	340.1	341.4

Source : Central Statistical Organisation.

A perusal of the figures in the two tables shows that the national product per capita at 1948-49 prices increased from Rs 247.5 in 1950-51 to 293.3 in 1960-61 in the first phase giving an average rate of growth of 4.58 per cent. In the second phase from 1960-61 to 1974-75, the national product per capita at 1960-61 prices increased from Rs 306.3 in 1960-61 to Rs 341.4 in 1974-75 yielding an average rate of growth of only 2.5 per cent. A closer examination of the figures for the last 7 years shows that the rate of growth for these years is less than one per cent and the per capita income for 1971-72 is actually higher than the income for 1974-75.

An interesting recent article brings out the decline in the per capita output and income of the agricultural population. In the 'fifties, both per capita output and income in the rural areas increased slightly from Rs 197.80 (at 1960-61 prices) in 1950-51, the pre-plan year, to a near all time peak at Rs 219.20 in 1960-61. But since the early sixties, despite a continued increase in the agricultural part of the plan outlay, which doubled (1960-61 prices) from Rs 254 crore in 1961-62 to Rs 510 crore in 1976-77, the agricultural per capita income has gone down steadily except for spurts in years of good monsoon and rich harvests notably, in 1964-65, 1970-71 and 1975-76. Thus the gains recorded in the fifties were more than wiped out by 1976-77, when the per capita output and income was Rs 196.50 or Rs 1.30 lower than in the pre-plan year, over 25 years ago'?[13]

TABLE 4

Components of capital Formation in India at current prices. Percentage of Gross Domestic Product Annual Average

	I Plan	II Plan	III Plan	1966-67 to 1968-69	1969-70 to 1972-73
1. Gross domestic capital formation	10.0	14.2	18.8	17.7	17.1
2. Depreciation	3.6	4.6	5.5	5.4	5.4
3. Net Domestic Capital formation (1-2)	6.4	9.6	13.3	12.3	11.7
4. Net capital inflow	0.4	2.9	2.9	2.0	0.8
5. Saving (3-4)	6.0	6.7	10.4	10.3	10.9

Source : C. S. O. : Estimates of Capital Formation.

[13]Shenoy, B.R. 21 June 1977. Times of India, New Delhi.

Savings depend upon incomes and capital formation and investment upon savings. The Central Statistical Organisation of the Union Government prepared estimates of gross capital formation for the period 1950-51 to 1972-73. Table 4 brings out clearly the components of capital formation in the Indian economy.

The gross domestic capital formation rose on an average from 10 per cent of GDP during the First Plan to about 18.8 per cent during the Third Plan but declined to 17.7 per cent during the Annual Plans (1966-67 to 1968-69) and further to 17 per cent in the first four years of the Fourth Plan. The net domestic capital formation (NDP) closely followed this trend. From 6.4 per cent in the First Plan it rose to 9.6 per cent in the Second and 13.3 per cent in the Third Plan. Thereafter it declined to 12.3 per cent in the period 1966-67 to 1968-69 and to 11.7 per cent in 1969-70 to 1972-73.

As for savings, the net domestic saving (NDS) is the sum of the savings of the corporate sector, the government sector and the household sector. A study of table 5 shows that the share of corporate sector in the total net domestic saving is very small and has fluctuated between 3 and 8 per cent of the total savings depending upon the level of profits in the corporate sector. The share of the government sector in the total saving was 18 per cent during the First and the Second Plans. It rose to its peak of 29.5 per cent in 1965-66 and then slumped to 17.7 per cent in 1971-72. It was 22.5 per cent in 1972-73 and 1973-74. The decline in government saving during the Fourth Plan period was due first, to the decrease in surpluses generated by the public sector, and secondly, to increase in government expenditure in the form of wages, salaries and raw material costs as a consequence of continuously rising prices. The major share of the savings is accounted for by the urban household sector. Its share in the total saving moved up from 48 per cent to 58 per cent. The rural household sector, however, showed a decline due first to an increase in the size of the urban areas and secondly, to the impact of efforts to increase savings in the urban areas. The sharp increase in prices during 1973-74 and 1974-75 eroded a major part of the savings of the household sector which slumped to 58 per cent in 1974-75.

In the decade 1967-77, industrial production stagnated and suffered but not the big business. According to Ranjit Sau, the big business never had it so good. The assets of the medium and large public limited companies (having paid-up capital of Rs 5 lakhs or more) nearly doubled in eight years between 1966-67 and 1974-75 (Table 6). Among them the bigger ones did far better. The total assets of 20 celebrated Big Business Houses multiplied by 150 per cent—from 2,080 crore in 1967-68, to Rs 3,515 crore in 1972-73, then to Rs 5,110 crore by 1975-76.

TABLE 5

Sector-wise Share of Savings in the Indian Economy

	Per cent of National Income				Per cent of Total Saving		
	Govt.	Corpo-rate	House-hold	N.D.S.	Govt.	Corpo-rate	House-hold
I Plan Period	1.2	0.5	4.9	6.6	18.0	8.0	74.0
II Plan Period	1.6	0.4	6.5	8.5	18.0	5.0	77.0
1961-62, 1962-63	2.5	0.7	6.3	9.5	26.3	7.4	66.3
1963-64	3.1	0.8	8.1	12.0	26.0	6.9	67.1
1964-65	2.7	0.4	7.6	10.7	24.8	4.3	70.9
1965-66	3.2	0.4	7.2	10.8	29.5	4.0	66.5
1966-67	1.8	0.4	5.8	8.0	21.8	6.5	71.7
1967-68	1.0	0.2	6.8	8.0	12.7	3.1	84.2
1968-69	2.0	0.2	6.2	8.4	23.8	2.4	73.8
1969-70	2.2	0.4	5.9	8.5	25.7	4.6	69.7
1970-71	2.2	0.6	7.3	10.1	21.6	6.1	72.3
1971-72	2.0	0.5	8.9	11.4	17.7	4.7	77.6
1972-73	2.8	0.4	9.4	12.3	22.5	3.1	74.4
1973-74	2.7	0.7	8.7	12.1	22.5	5.4	72.1
1974-75	3.5	0.9	7.4	11.8	29.7	7.7	62.6

Source : Reserve Bank of India Bulletin, 1974-75.

'Profits swelled even more. If assets had grown at the compound rate of 7.62 per cent per annum, gross profits of medium and large companies as a group increased much faster by 11.33 per cent. Thus starting with Rs 660 crore in 1966-67, profits rose to Rs 1,680 crore in 1974-75'.[14]

In the race for the top position among the business houses, till 1966-67 the top position was held by the Tatas. After this date, however, Birla's gradually came up and are now challenging the Tatas. The Mafatlal group which ranked tenth in terms of assets, moved up to the third position and the JK group after going down to the eleventh place in 1966-67, gradually moved up to the fourth

[14]Ranjit Sau. 9 April 1977. Economic and Political Weekly, Bombay.

TABLE 6
Medium and Large Public Limited Companies

Year	RBI Coverage (Per cent)	Total Assets	Net Sales (Rs Crores)	Gross profits	Share of wages in output (Per cent)
1960-61	70.1	3,631.6	3,413.8	363.8	66.78
1965-66	72.1	5,990.7	5,660.0	603.4	64.11
1966-67	72.1	6,784.5	6,331.2	662.6	62.77
1967-68	72.1	7,292.5	6,839.6	630.0	65.66
1968-69	72.1	7,735.9	7,424.1	655.9	66.49
1969-70	72.1	8,280.8	8,252.9	791.6	64.51
1970-71	80.0	8,744.8	8,399.2	833.1	63.57
1971-72	80.0	9,432.5	9,814.8	981.3	61.16
1972-73	80.0	10,007.3	10,892.2	1,033.8	63.16
1973-74	80.0	11,122.7	11,694.5	1,246.8	61.14
1974-75	80.0	13,187.9	14,790.9	1,682.8	57.60
Annual Growth rate since 1966-67 (per cent)		7.62	9.72	11.33	—

Source: Compiled by Ranjit Sau from RBI Bulletin, Various issues (E.P.W.).

position in 1972-73. There have been similar fluctuations in the fortunes of other houses too. The question which has been posed is, whether the rise of Birlas and other houses to their present position, is in some way related to their political alignment?

Facts and figures are presented to show that in the decade 1967-77, 1 the medium and the large public limited companies thrived, 2 the foreign controlled rupee companies which actually are members of the group of medium and large companies as defined by the Reserve Bank of India, were quite ahead of the average in the group and their assets and profits were higher by 8.40 per cent and 1⅔ per cent respectively, 3 the records of the branches of the foreign companies were surprising in that the total assets did not rise but gross profits kept on mounting at the annual rate of 6.06 per cent, 4 the small public limited companies lost ground and were driven to the wall, their total assets and gross profits having declined from Rs 439.8 and Rs 37.2 crore in 1965-66 to Rs 364 and Rs 19.7 crore respectively in 1973-74, and 5 while assets and profits of the middle and the big industrial houses were rapidly mounting, the share of wages in output per cent (see table 5 last column) was not only stagnant but actually shrinking.

In 1960-61 the wage output ratio was 66.78 per cent but by 1974-75, it dwindled to 57.50 per cent. As the volume of unemployment both in urban and rural areas increased during this period, the decline in real terms of the workers wage meant a loss of buying power and shrinkage of the market for consumer goods. If such is the case, the buyers of goods which swell the assets and profits of the medium and the big industrialist must come, apart from the overseas buyers and the city elites, from the rich farmers. In fact there has been a symbiotic alliance between the kulaks and the large industrial houses, in other words between "Wheat and whiskey".

Dr Ashoke Mitra, former economic adviser to the Government of India and now West Bengal Finance Minister told a press conference in New Delhi that West Bengal had witnessed a 40 per cent decline in industrial production during the period between 1965-66 and 1976-77 and over 30 per cent from 1972-77. Jute, textiles and heavy engineering which comprise over 60 per cent of industrial production, showed a precariously declining trend. Along with the decline in production, the rate of investment in industries also went down although Gross National Product (GNP) during the period went up by 7 per cent due to agricultural production and commercial activities. He further said that unemployment increased from 9 lakhs in 1971 to 1.8 million in 1976. In the rural sector 30 per cent of the agriculturists remained landless and the size of the holdings of the share-croppers became smaller. Also, as the majority of the population spent its income on foodgrains only, there has been tangible shrinkage of industrial demand.

What is true of West Bengal is in a way true of the rest of the country. Stagnation both in industry and agriculture stalks the land.

ELEVEN

The Choice of a Paradigm

I

The malaise which started in the early 1960s and plagued Indira Gandhi's regime was attributed by different people to different causes:

1. Indira Gandhi's Government attributed it to natural calamities—war with China, wars with Pakistan, failures of monsoon, price hike in oil and increasing cost of raw materials, components and capital goods from developed countries—and the basic assumption underlying its explanation was that such difficulties were transitory and beyond the control of the Government.

2. The monetarist school held that the production crisis or stagflation was due to an unsually large increase in money supply. Consequently, 140 economists suggested a scheme which came to be known as "Semibombla", (Scheme of the Economists for Monetary Immobilisation through Bond Medallions and Blocked Assets). It was bitterly critised by an equal number of economists who argued that, 1 the authors of "Semibombla" had failed to understand the causes working behind the monetary veil, 2 the monetarists had failed to appreciate the significance and extent of black money operating in the country, 3 the rate of profit of consumer durables was so high that the ten per cent rate of interest proposed by the monetarists, was hardly likely to induce the holders of black money to voluntarily offer their money holdings or near money assets in exchange for bond medallions, 4 the implementation of the scheme would lead to the erosion of the faith of the people in bank deposits, and lastly, a drastic reduction in money supply may bring down the prices for the time being but would have a disastrous effect on growth.

3. Among other causes to which writers on economic subjects

have attributed stagnation are 1 a tax policy in which the burden of taxation has fallen not on the urban rich and the well-to-do farmer on whom it should have, but on the common man and the poorer classes, 2 failure of capital formation consequent on inability to mobilise resources through savings, 3 allocation of resources in favour of luxury consumer goods industry rather than on essential wage goods, 4 emphasis on growth and not on employment, 5 excessive deficit financing, 6 failure of industrial licensing policy, 7 capital-intensive technology in a country with a rapidly increasing surplus labour force, 8 inefficient administration by civil servants and 9 corruption at the highest levels and deliberate encouragement of hoarding, blackmarketing, profiteering and smuggling for the purpose of building Party funds to win elections and keep in power.

No one can deny the importance of the aforementioned impediments in the path of economic growth but the fact to bear in mind is that many of them stem from the choice by India of a wrong paradigm.

II

Professor Kuznets, based on the historical growth patterns which operated in West European countries, equates development with urban industrial growth.[1] A.K. Bagchi, motivated by Kuznet's treatise, presents the essential elements of "foundations of capital growth", and voices his misgivings with regard to their relevance in the economic growth of poor and undeveloped countries today.[2] Professor Louis Lefeber who shares Bagchi's views emphasises that the essential elements of the historical growth experience in either capitalist or socialist industrial nations are not basically dissimilar. He says, 'development requires the transformation from a state of rural, agricultural development to the dominance of an urban industrial sector. As urban industrialization accelerates, the relative share of agriculture in the total labour force and in the national product, decreases. Higher wage rates motivate migration from rural to industrial urban areas which, together with capital investment in agriculture, increases the average productivity of labour in agricul-

[1]Simon Kuznets. 1971. Economic Growth of Nations, Cambridge, Mass.
[2]A.K. Bagchi. August 1972. Economic and Political Weekly, Bombay.

ture to levels approaching those obtained in industry. When and why the ball begins rolling is more difficult to pin-point and here the experience of socialist and capitalist countries may be very different. But the pattern of sectoral change has been the same for all nations which are currently developed : a continuous absolute and relative growth of sectors unrelated to agriculture with a concomitant population transfer from rural to urban areas'.[3]

According to Lefeber, in most of the countries of Latin America, South and South East Asia and Black Africa, the above described pattern has been accepted as the paradigm for development, but it is not taking hold as the special conditions which prevailed in the nineteenth century in the now developed industrial countries of the West, and in the twentieth century in the USSR, and which made the above transformation possible, do not exist any more. And if these conditions are neither present, nor possible to duplicate, development based on the Western model, has hardly any chance of success.

The conditions that favoured the development of Western nations have been described by Bagchi. They were, first, large-scale migrations and secondly, capital transfers. The migrations were again of two types. The first category resulted in the ruin of the trade, and decay of arts, crafts and industry in densely populated countries under foreign yoke, like India and China and their displacement by the ruling whites. The second category included sparsely populated countries like North America, Australia, New Zealand, South Africa etc., colonized by white settlers. These helped to reduce population pressures at home, opened up new continents for exploitation, and provided the supply base of West European industrialization. And while the loot from the densely populated, conquered countries was transferred home for the development of European industries, capital from Europe was exported overseas to countries settled by white immigrants. The net result was a continuous and unceasing capital transfer throughout the nineteenth century from densely populated colonies and possessions to white-settled sparsely populated countries. There is a further difference. The capital not transferred to Europe by the white traders but invested in non-white colonies was invariably tied either to raw material extraction[a]

[3] Louis Lefeber (1974) in *Economic Theory and Planning, Essays in Honour of A.K. Dasgupta*, Ed. Ashok Mitra, London.

[a] A.K. Bagchi, *August 1972, Economic and Political Weekly*.

or the export interests of the white rulers; its control was also exclusively in white hands. As against this, in sparsely populated countries settled by the whites, in addition to skills, education and other resources which the white men took with them and over which they had control, capital exported from Europe was invested in a variety of enterprises and not always tied to raw material extraction or the export interests of the capital exporting country; the control was also largely in the hands of the residents of the capital-importing country.

Bagchi concludes that the parasitic mode of growth of the developed countries in the nineteenth century, is not replicable in the underdeveloped countries of today, as the conditions under which it took place—large scale migrations and capital transfers—do not exist any longer.

Professor Thomas E. Weisskopf of Harvard University is of the view that the capitalist model is unsuited for the economic growth of the poor countries. It is, on the other hand, likely to perpetuate underdevelopment in three important respects. First, the increasing integration of the world capitalist system will tend to heighten the economic, political and cultural subordination of the poor countries to the rich. Secondly, capitalist institutions within the poor countries will tend to aggravate rather than diminish inequalities in the distribution of income and power. And thirdly, capitalism will be unable to promote in poor countries a long-run rate of economic growth sufficiently rapidly to provide benefits to the whole population or to reduce the income gap between the rich countries and the poor.[4]

The same view is projected by Josef Pajestka, the noted Polish development economist. He divides the countries of the world, into three groups—the developed countries or DCs, the socialist countries or SCs and the underdeveloped countries or UCs. The West European group of DCs, historically shaped as the core of the dominant metropolis of the world and has developed mechanisms and forces which enable it to maintain self-sustained progress. It has benefited both from internal drives including human factor and progress in science and technology, and from external factors of exploitation of colonies and the poor countries which it still continues to do. It has at its disposal a vast economic, political and

---

[4]Thomas E. Weisskopf. 1972. In Economics And World Order. Ed. Jagdish N. Bhagwati, London.

military machine to enable it to maintain the status quo. The second group or the group of the SCs has developed within the framework of the Western civilization, as a response to the social injustice of the capitalist system. Development in these countries began from a much lower level. They have, like the DCs benefited from the internal drives but unlike the DCs, the external factors have been unfavourable and even hostile. Inspite of these handicaps, however, the growth in the SCs has been phenomenal and actually higher than that in the DCs. The SCs like the DCs have developed strong political and military machines, ensuring their unthreatened further development. The underdeveloped countries or the UCs are the largest of the three groups, the least homogeneous and the most unorganized. All of them are hopelessly poor and afflicted with hunger, malnutrition and degrading living conditions. The internal disparity between the incomes of the rich and poor is enormous, the surplus and increasing labour force remains unutilized, the educational and technical skills are low, and low economic levels make saving and capital accumulation difficult and check both human dynamism and activity. The inner urges for development are not strong, the external factors are unfavourable and hostile. And the prospects for reducing the gaps between the DCs and the UCs are minimal.

It is not possible for these countries to aspire to the form of social and economic life existing in the DCs. Their main target should be to solve their own problems such as doing away with hunger, poverty, great social and economic inequalities and degrading living conditions which hinder the development of human creative abilities. This is hardly likely within the capitalist framework due to absence both of internal drives and favourable external factors and is possible only by adopting the socialist model of which the main ingredients are 1 mobilization of internal efforts and resources, 2 awareness of the masses and assurance of satisfaction of their needs and aspirations and 3 active planning with imposition upon the economy of structural and institutional changes conducive to development. For this to happen the Party which rules the country must have both the political will and the capability to implement the Plan.[5]

[5]Joseph Pajestka. 1973. In Economics and World Order. Ed. Jagdish N, Bhagwati, London.

III

The paradigm that helped in the growth of Western developed nations is thus of no value for the development of poor nations today. This has been shown beyond the shadow of a doubt in China where the Chinese following the Soviet example began by emulating their development model but gave it up in less than a decade and fell back on a decentralized model. It has failed to work in India where Jawaharlal Nehru impressed by the success story of the Western Capitalism in the nineteenth century and more especiaily in the post-war years, accepted the model on which they had built their affluent society. He was, it appears, also impressed by the views of economists like Prebisch[6] and Kuznets who equate development with urban industrial growth. Jawaharlal Nehru, however, failed to take into account that the conditions under which the developed countries 'took off' in the nineteenth century, did not exist any longer for the benefit of the underdeveloped countries. There were no vacant lands to settle for the growing populations of the poor countries and no capital transfers in their favour, and in the absence of the aforementioned conditions, the paradigm for development had also to be different.

Simon Kuznets points out that the existence of demand for industrial products is a requirement of modern industrialization, and that if it is not from abroad, it must come from domestic sources.[7] He further observes that in 'less developed follower countries, a modern industry can hardly be built on the expectation of gaining a foothold in foreign markets that have already been developed and occupied by the earlier pioneer countries.[8] The prospects for building on external demand are rendered even darker by the protectionist policies of rich countries. A second precondition to industrial growth, according to Kuznets, is the need to meet the increased demand for agricultural products that industrialization

[6]Raul Prebisch. 1959. United Nations, Economic Survey of Latin America. The doctrine he expounded favours industrialisation at the expense of development based on raw materials and staple production, because the demand for food is believed to be income elastic and the change in international terms of trade between the industrial and primary products has at times favoured the former.

[7]Simon Kuznets. 1965. Economic Growth and structure, New York.

[8]Ibid.

induces. It was met by England in the nineteenth century from import of food but in the absence of external sources, it has to come from domestic increases. Kuznets believes that the rise in agricultural productivity is both a requisite antecedent as well as a concomitant of modern industrialization. And if this is so, how are we to bring about this initial rise ?

In an underdeveloped country like India where both land and capital are in short supply and where there is superabundance of labour, this can come only from a more efficient and a more intensive cultivation of land with a view to enhance significantly the produce from a unit of cultivable land. This can be achieved by radical land reforms, larger financial outlays, full and speedy expansion of irrigation facilities, improved dry farming, higher and better inputs, cheap and easy credit and deployment of other measures recommended in the chapter on agriculture. But even this is not enough. There may exist a demand for more food and there may be increase in output of foodgrains and a favourable supply position following a good monsoon or use of modern technology and yet hunger may stalk the land as is happening today. There are more than 18 million tons of foodgrains in the government stores but people's stomachs are empty. Both demand and supply for food and essential goods are necessary. But they are not enough. Something more is needed to bridge the distance between the buffer stocks and the hungry mouths. And this is the buying power. In a free market economy the returns to owners of capital (including skills) and land are much larger relative to the share of unskilled labour. And the more labour-abundant an economy is, the smaller is the share of the lowest deciles in the GNP. Hence there is an urgent need for income redistribution.

Redistribution on an adequate scale can be effected only by increasing the demand for labour through the provision of new and improved work opportunities and by improving the conditions of self employment. The additional employment created must not be of the "make-work" (digging holes and filling them up) type as it could be in the case of Keynesian underconsumption; it must be goods and income-producing work. Louis Lefeber writes:

'Social justice and structural conditions in the economy require improvement in the distribution of income, and growth in the incomes of the lower income groups. But these can be brought about only by increasing employment and work opportunities at higher returns than the market can yield. Since the primary opportunities for the productive use of unskilled labour can be found in rural and agriculture-related activities rather than urban industrial or service employment, the focus of development effort must be shifted from urban industrialization towards rural transformation. But there are no competitive market processes which can bring about the required change; hence the market must be in some of its basic functions, replaced by government or community action. Hence the need for a new paradigm for development'.[9]

An egalitarian, self-reliant paradigm of decentralized rural transformation was spelled out for this country by Gandhiji long before independence came. It is unfortunate that Jawaharlal Nehru considered it a regression to the past and rejected it in favour of the Western paradigm which has landed us in a blind alley. The Gandhian paradigm has been described in detail in chapters on Gandhian economy and agriculture and there is no need for me to describe it over again. It is, however, necessary to point out that its emphasis is on rural transformation and it does not depend on foreign aid which in the form and the niggardly amounts in which it is given (.25 per cent of GNP of DCs), only perpetuates underdevelopment and the conditions for which it is sought. It does not abandon or relinquish urban industrialization, first, because the new farm technology needs heavy industry inputs like petrochemicals, cement and steel, and secondly, because cottage industries, decentralized consumer goods industries, and processing and other activities ancillary to agro-industrial growth, must have their inputs. In the Western paradigm agriculture played a supporting role to urban industrialization; in our paradigm the roles are reversed and urban industrialization must serve the needs of rural transformation.

The paradigm may not build an affluent society which Jawaharlal Nehru dreamed of, but will surely take care of the problem of unemployment and provide the minimum living standard that people in this country urgently need. After their failure with the Soviet version of the Western paradigm, the Chinese made a success

---

[9] Louis Lefeber. 1974. In Economic Theory and Planning. Essays in Honour of A.K. Dasgupta, London. Ed. Ashok Mitra.

story of the paradigm of rural transformation which Gandhiji had enunciated much earlier. If the new government which swears by Gandhian economy, translates it promises into actions,[10] there is no reason why India should not succeed where China has.

[10]Due to its in-fights and non-performance, the Janata Government fell on 15 July 1979. It has left the country in utter chaos of the economy in shambles.

TWELVE

Choice of Technology

India is a large country with a long sea-coast and land border to defend. She has a dual economy with a large traditional sector and a small well developed modern sector in urban enclaves. She has a colonial past and before the development of modern industries in the West, Indian manufactured goods—muslin, calicoes, silk and woollen fabrics, artistic ware—were in great demand, and had world wide market. After the Industrial Revolution, her village economy was wrecked and her arts and crafts systematically destroyed.

To serve the interest of her British masters, she was turned into a producer of raw materials that England needed, and a vast market for manufactured goods she produced. The growth of an indigenous industrial sector was, therefore, out of question and adroitly suppressed. India is short on capital. She has an enormous largely unskilled and idle labour force. Any technology-mix, therefore,—for no single type of technology will do for all sectors of her economy—will have to be specifically tailored to the human and material factor endowments of the country as a whole and its various regions.

India is poor, shockingly poor. More than half her people live below the poverty line. She is poor because she does not produce. She cannot produce unless her people work. Some of them are habitually lazy and must be coerced to work but most of them do not work because there is no work for them. In a family consisting of the husband, the wife and three or more children, there is generally only one working member, one bread winner. This is hardly satisfactory. Unless the earning member is in the upper income bracket and has a very high income, families with one working member in these days of escalating prices, barely manage to keep their noses above water. It is for this reason that young and educated men and women prefer to seek matrimonial alliances with educated and employed mates. When both husband and wife earn, the incidence of taxation is lower, the expendible income greater and the standard of living higher. Gandhiji was for full time employment for all persons of working age group. Nay more, he even wanted production by childern of school age. In his scheme of free and compulsory primary education built round a craft, children between the ages of 6 and 14 years, where expected to produce essential consumer goods which the State was to purchase from the school and market on its behalf. Gandhiji belived in bread labour. He stood not for mass production but for production by the masses. In his scheme of decentralized economy and agricultural and rural development, all that the inhabitants of the village needed, was to be produced in the village itself or in a neighbouring village or centre. Foodgrains, vegetables, fruit, milk, egg, fish, jaggery or gur, processed foods, edible oils, cloth, shoes, soaps, hair oils, combs, tooth brushes, tooth powders or pastes, mirrors, glass or plastic ware, pottery, brass and aluminium utensils, hand-made paper, simple household furniture, sanitary brick houses, simple tools and machines—and many more things that a villager needed, could be made in the village homes, or cooperatives. It is true that the decentralized village economy of Gandhiji's imagination could not provide for a life of luxury. But then he was not aiming at building an affluent society on the West European or American models. He was wanting to build a society in which no one exploited anyone and everyone's food, clothes and other necessaries of life, were taken care of.

In 1908, when he wrote his "Hind Swaraj," he was an uncompromising critic of all machines and declared himself against them in no uncertain terms. But since then there was a gradual and imperceptible shift in his opposition to machines. By the early 1920s he had moved a long way from his original position and he welcomed small machines that made labour less arduous and life less difficult. He was, however, still opposed to large-scale consumer goods industry which led to exploitation of man by man and threw millions out of employment. He was against the displacement of human labour which was so abundant in the country, the destruction of human beings and human personality, improverishment and decay of the villages, an undesirable urbanization leading to rise of urben unemployment and growth of slums and shanty towns, and finally the enslavement of man by the machine. For him, the development of agriculture and rural industries, was the only solution for the problems afflicting the millions living in the villages.

The experience of past 30 years has shown that large-scale consumer goods industry in the private sector in urban enclaves, is incapable of solving the unemployment problem of the country. This is made clear by the table given below:

Growth of Employment in Organized Sector in India

| | In Lakhs | | |
	1	*2*	*3*
	Public	*Private*	*Total*
1961	70.50	50.40	120.90
1966	93.78	68.10	161.88
Average Growth Rate	6.6	7.0	6.8
1967	96.34	66.80	163.14
1968	98.02	55.20	163.22
1969	100.95	65.30	166.25
Average Growth Rate	2.5	—1.4	0.8
1970	103.74	67.00	170.74
1971	107.31	67.70	175.1
1972	113.05	67.70	180.75
1973	119.75	68.50	188.25
1974	124.86	67.90	192.76
Average Growth Rate	4.70	0.80	3.20
1975	128.38	68.00	196.38

Source: Reserve Bank Bulletin, February 1975.

A perusal of column 2 in the table shows that the number of persons employed in the private sector in the year 1966 is 68.1 lacs. It fell to 65.20 lacs in 1968 and gradually increased to 68 lacs in 1975. The Ace industrialist G. D. Birla recently stated that the employment situation in the organized private sector had shown no improvement during the past seven years. The number of people employed in 1970 was 67 lacs and it is 68 lacs in 1977.[1] In fact the number employed in this sector is still 0.1 lac less than it was eleven years ago in 1966. The annual growth rate of employment in the

[1]G.D. Birla. Speaking at the Golden Jubilee Session of the FICCI in May 1977.

private organized sector was 7 per cent between 1961 and 1966 or the Third Plan Period. It fell to—1.4 per cent during the period of the Annual Plans, 0.8 per cent in the Fourth Plan period and zero per cent during the fifth Plan period upto May 1977.

Taking the entire organised sector, the employment growth rate was 4.5 per cent during 1961-75. In the context of full employment, this rate of growth is highly unsatisfactory and calls for a reorientation of national policies.

Industrialization accelerates growth and Jawaharlal Nehru was impressed by its results both in the Capitalist West and the USSR. He failed to realize, however, that the circumstances under which growth had occurred in these countries, were not present in the under-developed countries which had only recently won their political independence. He also forgot that real agrarian reform as the history of Western Europe illustrated, was an essential pre-requisite for successful industrialization. After achievement of independence the country was launched on a programme of economic development in which the half hearted land reforms that were legislated were stalled, and the most profitable sector of the economy—its commanding heights—left in the care of private predators and the country's meagre capital frittered away. Scarce capital generated within the country itself, and all foreign AID which should have been utilized first, for the development of defence, heavy and basic industries, and secondly, for the development of agriculture and rural industries, was squandered in the manufacture of non-essential luxury goods in the private sector. Expensive plant was imported and thousands of unnecessary collaboration agreements entered into with foreign firms. Many a time these agreements were for projects for which both plant and know-how were available in the country. If thousands of crores of rupees and precious foreign exchange had not been wasted in import of expensive plant, in acquiring foreign technology, in collaboration agreements favouring foreign companies and countries, in producing items of luxury for the elites—if a major part or some at least of this capital were spent on the promotion of agriculture and decentralized village economy—illiteracy, ignorance, backwardness and a dehumanising poverty would have been things of the past, the standard of living of the people would have improved and the shape of things much more agreeable than it is at present.

Similar views on technology and related subjects to those held by Gandhiji have been expressed by a number of distinguished foreigners and Indians. We shall consider some of these in the following paragraphs.

Harrison Brown wrote in 1954 what Gandhiji would have fully endorsed: 'I imagine a world within which machines should function—solely for Man's benefit, turning out those goods which are necessary for his well being, relieving him of the necessity for bearing physical labour and dull routine and meaningless activity. The world I imagine is one in which people are well fed, well clothed and well housed. . . . In the world of my imagination there is organization but it is as decentralized as possible and compatible with the requirements for survival. There is a world government but it exists solely for the purpose of preventing war and stabilizing population and irrevocably restricted. . . . In the world of my imagination, the various regions are self-sufficient and the people are free to govern themselves as they choose and to establish their own cultural patterns. All individuals have a voice in the government and individuals can move about when and where they please. . . . At least if we try to create such a world there is a chance that we will succeed'![2]

The British philosopher, Bertrand Russel writing about underdeveloped countries like India, pointed out that 'electricity and motor transport have made small units of industry not only economically possible but even desirable. . . . When a rural industry flourishes, it should be gradually mechanised through electricity but left in small units. In those parts of the world in which industrialization is still young, the possibility of avoiding the horrors we have experienced still exist. India, for example is traditionally a land of village communities. It would be a tragedy if this traditional way of life were to be suddenly and violently exchanged for the greater evils of urban industrialization. . . . The rivers of the Himalayas should provide all the hydro-electric power that is needed for the gradual mechanisation of the village industries of India and for the measurable improvement of physical wellbeing without either the obvious disaster of industrial slums or the more subtle loss and degradation when age old traditions are too rudely broken.[3]

[2]Harrison Brown. 1954. The Challenge of Man's Future.
[3]Bertrand Russel. The Authority and Individual.

The celebrated writer Aldous Huxley made a powerful plea for decentralization and urged inventors and technicians to apply the results of pure science for the purpose of increasing self-sufficiency and political independence of small owners, working either on their own or in cooperative groups concerned with subsistence and supply of local markets.[4]

The Nobel Laureate, Gunnar Myrdal, author of the monumental three volume "Asian Drama", has expressed his agreement with Gandhiji on several important issues affecting the under-developed countries. He shares Gandhiji's views on equality, development of agriculture and rural industries, unemployment, urbanization, hardwork, manual labour, learning by doing, self-reliance and discipline. Like Gandhiji, he believes that the employment effects of industrialisation could not be expected to be large for decades ahead, that is until the region was much more industrialized.[5]

The English Nobel Laureate in Physics, Professor Blacket emphasized that in most parts of Asia, the problem really was to devise new technologies which make man-power more efficient without much capital expenditure.

The same point is made by the Dutch economist and Noble Laureate, Professor Jan Tinbergen. He writes, 'I would like to suggest that, by and large at this moment you will find the widest range of choice in the industries that are oldest in the history of mankind. Thinking of agriculture, of construction, and textiles, I think it can be said that these have been with mankind from the start on their way without capital. Some of these activities have been indeed done in a labour intensive way and these methods are, therefore, known. This raises a question, however, whether or not further research could show that in some of the modern industries, modern and advanced methods which nevertheless would be more labour intensive could be discovered. . . . It may be that research activities have been so much in the hands of the rich countries that it is their interests that have been served most. Their interest, of course, was to replace labour by capital but now that so many countries are coming up, for which it is of interest that capital be replaced by labour, if only temporarily, I wonder whether a sustained effort should not be made by engineering profession to find labour inten-

[4]Huxley Aldous. 1950. Science, Liberty and Peace.
[5]Gunnar Myrdal. 1968. Asian Drama, England.

sive methods, not antiquated ones, but new ones using all the insight that we have both in men and machines'.[6]

R. B. Gregg, a Western admirer of Gandhiji has listed a large number of advantages that accrue to the economy from decentralization of consumer goods industries. These include full employment, eradication of poverty, diminished cost, utilization of local raw materials, freedom from exploitation, reduction of risks due to fire and theft, avoidance of transport costs and delays, absence of strikes and lock-outs, reduction of inequality, decrease of urbanization and its accompanying evils, reduction of mental tension and improved body health.[7]

Dr E. F. Schumacher, a noted English economist was invited to India in 1961, in the capacity of a consultant on rural development. He was profoundly impressed by Gandhian economic thought and the Gandhian Plan of decentralization and production by masses. He thought that 'the economics of gigantism and automation were leftovers of the 19th century thinking and totally unrelated to the problems of the day'. He said, 'An entirely new system of thought is needed, a system based on attention to people and not primarily on attention to goods'. He recommended the conscious utilization of man's enormous technological and scientific potential for the fight against misery and human degradation, that is a fight in contact with actual people, with individuals, families, small groups, rather than states and other anonymous abstractions. And this presupposes a political and organizational structure that can provide this intimacy'. Seeing in decentralization a new way of life with small comprehensive groups he added, 'We must learn to think in terms of an articulated structure that can cope with a multiplicity of small scale units. If economic thinking cannot grasp this, it is useless. If it cannot get beyond its vast abstractions, the national income, the rate of growth, capital, capital-output ratio, input-output analysis, labour mobility and capital accumulation have no meaning. If it cannot get beyond this and make contact with human realities of poverty, frustration, alienation, despair, break-down, crime, escapism, stress, congestion, ugliness and spiritual death, then let us scrap economics and start afresh'.[8]

[6]Jan Tinbergen, Essay in Regional and World Planning (NCAER, New Delhi).
[7]R.B. Gregg. A Philosophy of Indian Economic Development, Ahmedabad.
[8]E.F. Schumacher. 1966. Roots of Economic Growth.

Dr Schumacher professed the need for developing what he called an Intermediate Technology,—a technology which would use local skills and raw materials and serve the needs of the local people. Such a technology was to be better than the traditional technology in use but not so modern as to throw things completely out of gear. The intention was to adapt science and newer knowledge to the conditions prevailing in the village and to help people do things better than they were doing before. It was to be labour-intensive and a more optimum man and machine-mix than the labour saving devices developed in the West where capital was in plenty and labour scarce. It was in the final analysis a technology most relevant to the environment and for that reason likely to be most productive and efficient.

Since the concept of Intermediate Technology was first introduced a number of variants,—convenient, alternative, micro, appropriate, convivial—have been introduced, pointing to the awareness of the need for a new technoloy more relevant to the economies of poor countries. A popular modification in India of Schumacher's Intermediate Technology is the concept of "Appropriate Technology" suggestive of the concept that any technology has in the ultimate analysis to match the factor endowments of the environment. Such a technology must vary from region to region depending on its stage of development and be dynamic and vary from one period of time to another since what is appropriate today may cease to be so in a few years as skills and resources develop.

The widespread awareness of growing regional imbalances and the problem of acute unemployment, induced the Indian Government to set up in the Ministry of Industrial Development an Appropriate Technology Cell for identifying suitable technologies in important sectors of economy. The Cell made a study of select sectors of the economy with the intention of finding out how Appropriate Technology could be applied in practice. As a result of this study, the Cell was able to identify several areas of suitable formulation and implementation of the New Technology. These areas are:

1. Leather including tanning and leather products.
2. Scaling down large sized plants (steel, sugar, cement, paper).
3. Food processing and preservation.
4. Agricultural tools and implements.

5. Ceramics including pottery.
6. Roads and building Construction.

The last though one of the most distinguished foreigners whose views I propose to consider, is Ivan Illich who has aroused world wide attention as a formidable critic of some of society's most cherished institutions—organised religion, the medical profession, the school and tools. His thoughts on social and economic organi- zation are in many ways close to those of Gandhiji. He advocates the use of simple or convivial tools which can be easily used by any- body and are least controlled by others. They are individually accessible, work-intensive and best suited for decentralized pro- duction. As examples of such tools he mentions motorized push- carts, bicycles and tri-wheelers for which multilane highways are not needed and which can operate at a speed of about 20 miles per hour on country roads built to rural standards but covered, to diminish drag. Scores of small, hand or power driven tools which make work less laborious and wearisome but do not displace human labour and promise full employment for the rural millions in under- developed countries, can be designed, built and maintained by people trained on the job.[9]

Illich regards modern industrial tools and unlimited, cancerous production, as threats to life on this planet. He is disturbed by the ruthless plunder and exhaustion of the planet's natural resources which were built up over a period of hundreds of millions of years, and by the pollution of the biosphere. He deprecates monopoly and total control of professional doctors over health care, of teachers with academic tags over education, of professional architects and builders over house building and of undertakers over funerals. Illich divides the present world into those who do not have enough and those who have more than enough. The former are pushed off the road by the latter who ride the cars. His preference is for a society whose members will have just enough. It may not be an affluent society but its members will not be hungry, ill-clad or ill- housed. He is against overpopulation, excessive consumption, and waste which pose serious problems and call for urgent solution.

I will now refer the reader to the opinions on the subject under

[9]Such tools are at present being made in village workshops in Punjab and Haryana.

discussion of a few eminent living Indians. The first and foremost among them is Mr Jaya Prakash Narayan, the Chief architect of the Congress Socialist Party (CSP) who, nurtured the socialist movement in the company of Acharya Narendra Dev, Dr Ram Manohar Lohia, Ashok Mehta, Achyut Patwardhan and others. A brave freedom fighter, in 1942 he scaled the high wall of the Hazaribagh jail, escaped from prison and became a legend. He was captured, taken to Lahore Fort jail and subjected to cruel torture. On his release from prison in 1946, he leapt into fame and received a hero's welcome wherever he went. In 1948, together with many others he broke away from the Congress, and the Socialist Party was formed. In the early 1950s he gave up politics and joined the band of Sarvodaya workers. A devoted follower of Gandhiji, he cherishes dearly the Gandhian values of simplicity, austerity, personal freedom, equality, hardwork, honesty, truth and non-violence. He is fearless, unassuming, selfless and without any personal ambition. He has a cheerful disposition and is loving and affectionate. A socialist, a humanist, a democrat, he prizes civil liberties and is a friend of the poor. An illustrious patriot, a brilliant thinker, a convincing speaker, Jaya Prakash Narayan is an honoured and popular leader. He is an ardent advocate of decentralized rural economy and has suggested that politics should be kept out of Panchayat Raj. He was greatly attracted by Dr Schumacher's proposal of an Intermediate Technology and his thesis that "Small is Beautiful", as propounded in his book of the same title. J. P. has referred a good few times to Schumacher's technology in his 'Prison Diary'. Millions of his countrymen hope and pray that the "wounded soldier" will live for many more years and guide the country and the world at large, towards the goal for which Gandhi lived and died.

Simple and austere in his life style, and full of wit, wisdom and satire in his speeches and writings, the oldest living conferere of Gandhiji, J. B. Kripalani, has become a symbol of fearlessness. He is a true Acharya, has written a biography of Gandhiji, and never tires of advocating the Gandhian way. In numerous speeches delivered in different parts of the country, he has been telling people that India can solve its problems of unemployment only by going back to Gandhiji's constructive programmes. Speaking at a function organised by the Tamil Nadu Congress Committee (O) for unveiling the portrait of the late K. Kamaraja, he said that Gandhian programmes were comprehensive and covered every aspect of human life—decentralization, self reliant village republics. swadeshi, nai talim (basic or new education), full employment, egalitarianism, humanism and the welfare of all. He emphasized the need for hard work and said, 'If only there was a scheme to make all the roads in the country into Pucca ones, it would increase employment tremendously while helping the villager to move his goods'.[10]

Ashok Mehta, a prominent founder of the CSP was close associate of Narendra Dev, Jaya Prakash and Lohia. He was a member of the National Executive of the Socialist Party and later of the Praja Socialist Party. He accepted the post of Deputy Chairman of the Planning Commission in Jawaharlal Nehru's Government and held the assignment of the Deputy Chairman and the Minister for Planning under Indira Gandhi. Sometime after devaluation of the rupee, he was dropped from the cabinet and when the Great Divide came in 1969, he stayed behind in the Congress (O) of which he became Chairman. His numerous books[11] on socialism bear the stamp of Gandhiji's influence on his mind. In his "Studies of Socialism" (1956), he recommends the Gandhian plan of economic development for the country. In his latest book a whole chapter "Vision of Gandhi" he elaborates the Gandhian values of love of man, Satyagraha, abhaya, ahimsa, sādhna, aparigrāha and nishkāma karma, and the Gandhian remedies for eradication of poverty and unemployment.[12]

S. N. Aggarwal, or (Shriman Narayan) who died recently, had a long association with Gandhiji and is the author of the Gandhian Plan based on decentralization and self-reliant villages. The amount allocated in Shriman Narayan's Plan to agriculture and village development is 48 per cent and more in keeping with the importance of the sector. The amount of 10 per cent earmarked for edu-

---

[10]J.B. Kripalani. 16 January 1977. Speech at TNCC (O) Headquarters in Madras.

[11]Ashok Mehta. 1951. Democratic Socialism, 1956 Studies in Socialism; 1977. Reflection on Socialist Era.

[12]Satyagraha. Gandhi described satyagraha as the active force of love, faith and sacrifice.

Abhaya means fearlessness.

Sadhna is fight for evil within self by pure means; evil in society can be fought with same weapons.

cation is also much higher than that allocated in the Five Year Plans. But more important than the allocation for education is the quality and nature of education proposed. Gandhiji himself who wrote a forward for his Book,[13] stated that the author 'had not misrepresented him in any place'.

II

The configuration of India's industrial map has changed considerably during the past three decades. As Indira Gandhi herself admitted at a meeting of the National Development Council in October 1976, mistakes in economic policy had been made. First, under the policy of New Strategy in agriculture, the needs of the small and the marginal farmers were ignored, and largesse in the shape of high yielding varieties of seed, fertilizers, pesticides, low and subsidized irrigation and power rates, and cheap and easy credits provided to rich farmers in selected and irrigated areas. This not only adversely hit the small and marginal farmers who were forced to lease out or sell their small plots to the kulaks and were in the process reduced to the status of landless labourers but had an adverse overall effect on agricultural production. Mrs Gandhi justified the strategy and the concessions to the "not so poor" by the then Agriculture Minister, Subramaniam, by saying that they were required to boost agricultural production during a period of food shortages. Secondly, she agreed that some industries that were hardly necessary, had been set up, but they were there, and there was no going back on them.

The country at present needs a technology-mix that will effectively meet the needs of :

1. Agriculture, cottage, village and small industries.
2. Profit-oriented luxury and other goods industries in the private sector.
3. Public sector industries under schedules A and B of the Industrial Policy Resolution of 1956, such as arms and ammunition, atomic energy, space and satellite technology, iron, steel and other metals, heavy machinery, heavy electricals, aircraft, air and rail transport, shipping, telephone, telegraph, generation

[13]S.N. Aggarwal. 1944. Gandhian Plan.

and distribution of electricity, radio and television transmission, machine tools, chemical industry, antibiotics and other essential drugs, fertilizers, synthetic rubber, carbonization of coal, chemical pulp, and road and sea transport.

The Janata Government which took office two years ago, committed itself to eradication of poverty and unemployment within a decade, through improvements in items listed under the first head, i.e., agriculture and development of cottage, village and small industries on Gandhian lines. The technology for production of essential goods in village homes and cooperatives and traditional artistic wares, is well known. There are talented craftsmen all over the country who produce ware of great artistic skill,—shawls, carpets, handloom fabrics, embroidered sarees, chicken table-ware, sandalwood and brass articles, mother-of-pearl, ivory and brass in-lay work, lacquered and carved furniture and hundreds of other articles—which are prized by connoiseurs in this country and other parts of the world. They should be encouraged not only to produce these objects but also to train more craftsmen for revival of the dying handicrafts. The technology should be constantly improved to reduce costs, to increase productivity and to better the quality of the goods produced as suggested by Gandhiji, R. B. Gregg, E. F. Schumacher, Ivan Illich, Jan Tinbergen and the appropriate Technology Cell of the Government or others.

There are plenty of scientists, engineers and technologist, and design and commercial artists in the country who can be usefully employed to help in this direction. Incidentally this would also help solve the problem of uneducated unemployment.

For industries listed under the second and the third heads, viz., the profit oriented luxury and other goods industries in the private sector and the Schedule A and B industries in the public sector, our efforts have been in the past greatly influenced by the thinking of advanced countries, instead of being based on objective considerations of what would be best in our own interests. During the past 25 years we went about in a big way and entered into collaboration agreements with hundreds of foreign houses and tens of foreign governments, sometimes for enterprises in the private sector which should not have been set up at all, many times for simple projects for which local know-how was available but the use of foreign brand name or association, guaranteed high profits and sales to the collaborating parties and harmed the interests of the Indian entrepreneurs who were on their own.

A. S. Rao has deprecated borrowing of advanced technology on a number of grounds :

1. It is capital intensive and involves import of expensive plant.
2. It needs the services of highly paid foreign experts.
3. It is unsuitable under conditions of abundant labour.
4. It is ineffective from the long term angle unless a base has been built up which can absorb it, analyse it, understand or adapt it, and innovate on it. Because of this factor of inadequate absorption India bought several large turn-key iron and steel plants from different countries. It was not necessary. We should have bought only one and designed the others ourselves.
5. Projects in which borrowed advanced technology is used, suffer from another serious drawback concerned with replacements and maintenance. The country continues to depend for spares on the suppliers of the original plant and after sometime the bills for these are exorbitant under the plea that these are out-moded spares, no longer stocked by them because of new models having supplemented the old ones.
6. The most serious drawback of borrowing technology is that it induces intellectual lethargy, buying technology becomes a habit and an easier and a more manageable means than develop one's own.
7. Imported technology dragoons us to errors and pitfalls—wasteful consumption, depletion of natural resources, pollution, man-independent automation and alienation of the youth—pitfalls which can be avoided.[14]

During the past 25 years India has trained in her university science departments, research institutes, engineering colleges and technology institutes, a sufficiently large force of scientists, technologists and engineers. Many of them have received higher training abroad. With the large industrial infra-structure which she has come to acquire and the ample natural resources she has, she is in a position to satisfy all her need of manufactured goods indigenously. India possesses today a sufficiently high level of technology

[14]A.S. Rao. 1976. Mainstream, Republic Day Issue, New Delhi.

and expertise and except in the rarest of instances we should not buy or import technology. Through an intelligent approach to learning from other's knowledge and experience and using our own technological talent, we can go a very long way. 'The technology pioneered stage by stage, in our capitalist industry', writes Joan Robinson, 'is available to be copied in so-called backward countries. It does not have to be freshly invented'.[15]

There are important lessons we must learn from our own past experience of thirty years and from the experience of other nations. First, as Joan Robinson says in respect of North Koreans, every one in this country should abstain from consuming luxuries till the time a tolerable standard of life for all is secured. If and when this is possible, a large share of resources will become available for development of agriculture, power, irrigation and rural industries. For this to begin or happen, some hard policy decisions will have to be taken by the ruling party. There should be no further expansion of the luxury goods industries. They should be taken over by the State and the profits used for purposes of development. Along-side of the adoption of these measures the use of luxury goods by the people should not only cease to be a status symbol but also carry with it a social opprobrium. Secondly, we should avoid all "hazards of concentration". Single large units and economics of scale may reduce costs of production but need large capital investment, managerial skill of a very high order and a complex technology. The disposal of effluents and other wastes poses serious problems of pollution. A breakdown of the unit is fraught with dislocation of supplies for the entire region supplied by it. What is more, the financial gain in cost of production may be swallowed by the problems of distribution and transportation.

A decentralized economy is best suited to our needs as it requires very little capital, is labour-intensive, utilizes local raw materials, requires the use of simple (intermediate, appropriate or convivial) tools, is self relaint and does not depend on imports of foreign aid, is egalitarian, does not produce regional imbalances, involves no transport costs and is most advantageous from the defence angle.

Before I close this chapter, I wish to reiterate that technology,

[15]Joan Robinson. 1974. In Economic Theory and Planning Essays, in Honour of A.K. Dasgupta Ed. Ashok Mitra, London.

and research and development (R & D) as they have evolved in the West, are not germane to our needs. Their technology is capital intensive. Their research is undertaken at the corporation level and "linked to want-creation, product-differentiation, labour-saving and raw-material-saving-and-displacing innovation",[16] which by economizing on raw materials and use of synthetic materials, work against the interest of countries that produce primary products. None of these is relevant to our needs. We must evolve our own appropriate or convivial technology and the research and development in our universities, engineering and research institutes must not be wasted on "esoteric and irrelevant problems fashionable in the academic circles in the West",[17] but focussed on improvement of our tools both for a decentralized rural economy and for our basic and heavy sectors. In the latter context I commend to Indian technologists to emulate the examples of the Japanese and North Koreans, rip open imported machines and copy and improve on them.

[16]J.N. Bhagwati. 1972. Economics and World Order, New Delhi.
[17]Ibid.

THIRTEEN

Foreign Aid

Foreign aid without doubt could be a factor of great importance in furthering the economic development of the poor countries of the third world, only if it was given 1 liberally, and 2 with the genuine desire and objective of raising the living standards of that major portion of the human race which today lives in subhuman conditions of abject poverty. A world in which there exists a stupendous economic gap,—a gap which is increasing with each passing year—between the rich and the poor and within nations, cannot for long remain free from explosive situations, conflicts and collisions. To make it free from confrontation between the rich North and the poor South and to promote social harmony Jagdish N. Bhagwati counsels that foreign aid both financial and technical be stepped up.[1] He 'considers that everything within the realm of feasibility needs to be done to accelerate the growth of the underdeveloped countries and even if aid flows were economically not productive, they would seem to be imperative purely from an income-distributive point of view, if the international polity is to be characterized by social harmony and a sense of justice in the teeth of the widening gap'.[2] As regards the level of the aid flows, he quotes from the impassioned document produced by the celebrated Soviet Academician Sacharov:

'In the opinion of the author, it is necessary to have a tax on the developed countries equal to 20 per cent of the national income for the next 15 years. The introduction of such a tax would automatically lead to a significant decrease in expenditures for weapons. Such joint aid would considerably help to stabilize and improve the

---

[1]Jagdish N. Bhagwati. 1972. Economics and World Order, London.
[2]Ibid.

position of most under-developed countries; it would limit the influence of extremists of all types . . . Mankind can develop painlessly only by viewing itself in the demographic sense as a unit, as one family without divisions into nations except from the point of view of history and traditions'.[3]

If the purpose of the aid flows is as it should be, both productive and income-distributive, then according to Bhagwati the question of "absorption" by poor countries of flows even as high as 20 per cent of the income of the developed countries, does not arise. But if the game of the "absorptive capacity" must be played and aid flows absorbed only through productive uses, it should not be difficult to absorb 5 to 10 per cent of the GNP from rich nations for massive programmes of development in the poor countries. It is quite likely that studden injections of large capital flows from rich to poor countries, would create some "structural" problems especially in respect of skilled manpower, but these can be got round in a few years by proper training under technicians from the developed countries. Bhagwati concludes that 'it is not persuasive to argue that a Sacharov-type programme is economically infeasible (if longish period of ten to fifteen years is allowed to build up to these high levels), even if we confine ourselves to the constraint that aid has to be economically productive and not just income-redistributive at the international level'.[4]

Looking at the continuing exploitative and niggardly attitudes of the rich nations, it appears that aid flows of 20 per cent of the GNP proposed by Sacharov for both productive and income-redistributive purposes or even of 5 to 10 per cent for productive purposes only as suggested by Bhagwati are day dreams of well meaning intellectuals and visionaries. The rich nations seem to have no intention whatsoever of making 'special efforts to relieve the poverty . . . of the poorest countries where about one billion people live'[5] as the World Bank President, Mr Robert McNamara urged them to do in his speech at the Joint Session of the World Bank and the IMF in Washington. As a matter of fact, aid even from the richest country of the world, the United States of America, declined

---

[3]The quote is by Bhagwati in Economics and World Order, from a translation from the Russian original in the hands of Professor Zacharias of M.I.T.
[4]Ibid.
[5]Robert McNamara. September 1977. Editorial, Times of India, New Delhi.

from 0.57 per cent of its GNP in 1967 to less than half that value (0.25 per cent) in 1972. Its terms also worsened and both the amount of grants as well as commitments with maturity of over 25 years dropped significantly.

According to McNamara, the real income of the rich countries rose by 40 per cent during the 1967-77 decade but the level of official development assistance, if anything fell. The W.B. had stipulated that every advanced state should contribute at least 0.7 per cent of its GNP as aid to poor countries but not even half this amount has been collectively given although the Scandanavian countries contributed their share and kept their word. What is worse, the developed countries have been busy erecting higher and higher protective tariff and quota barriers against the import of various third world manufactures. A glaring example of this protectionism which has hit this country hard is the restriction imposed by E.E.C. Countries on the import of handloom garments. Paradoxical, though it may seem, poor nations are exhorted to diversify and modernise their economies, and the moment they succeed in doing so, they are prevented from selling their produce. If rich countries 'with basically strong economies panic at the slightest discomfiture and hit out at those nations which are most vulnerable, what hope there can be of the rich states accepting the substantial reduction of their present power that the establishment of the new international economic order—the declared goal of the temporarily interrupted North-South dialogue—implies'?[6] The answer is, none whatsoever. Ever since the price hike by the oil producing and exporting countries (OPEC), the rich countries have been doing their level best to prevent a similar get together of other producers of primary goods. As an example after 18 months of North-South dialogue which ended for the time being in Paris in June 1977, the rich countries conceded only one demand—the creation of a common fund to guarantee stable prices for primary commodities—out of the several, made by the poor countries. Even this commitment of setting up the fund was made grudgingly and only in "principle". The prosperity of Western Europe and America, as has been explained elsewhere in this book,[7] has been built on massive capital flows from poor countries like India and China in the nineteenth

[6]Ibid.
[7]See Chapter on the Choice of A Paradigm.

century. And although some poor nations have won their liberation from the colonial powers during the past 30 years, the capital flow from the poor countries to the rich, continue unabated. To expect, therefore, that present type of aid will help reverse capital flows in favour of poor countries, is to live in a fool's paradise. The under-developed countries, if they are at all concerned about the poverty of their people, must cease to depend for aid on the rich countries. For such a driblet or trickle of aid,—juxtaposed to 'a capitalist buccaneering and exploitation of the resources of the helpless and the needy, on terms laid down by the rich industrial nations'—is sheer chicanery. It is double-dealing, imposture, fraud.

II

The word aid is a misnomer and its letters stand for Agency for International Development. It is cunningly devised and used deli-berately to mislead the common people who understand it to mean free help or grant, which it definitely is not. The aid as a matter of fact is a loan and has to be repaid with interest which is often quite high. It is usually tied to exports from the creditor country.

Approximately one-fifth of all US exports are at present financed by the US Government loans and military expenditure abroad. A tied aid implies that the recipient country is not free to buy its requirements at competitive prices in the open market, and the prices it has to pay are usually inflated and exorbitant. A typical example is that of Peru when that country was asked to buy US planes, subsonic and more expensive instead of cheaper supersonic mirages. Millions worth of obsolete plant which would be scrap in the United States, has been sold to underdeveloped countries at extravagant prices.

Aid is used for encouraging capitalist development and neo-imperialism, to distort economies and to subvert and control the political machinery of the recipient countries. It is used to throttle and curtail investment in the public sector and to encourage the growth of the private sector. It is used to open up the most profitable areas of the economy which governments would wish to reserve for public enterprise to private firms both national and international. It is used to soften social and economic tensions in the society which are absolutely necessary for social change and economic growth. It destroys self-reliance and encourages dependence on foreign help. Its denial during periods of crisis, turns it into an instrument for punishment in the hands of the mighty donor. The United States has used this method time and again, to hamper land reform, to cut down helpful expenditure on education, health, housing and other social programmes, to enforce wage freezes, devaluations, taxation cuts for corporations, removal of restrictions on imports, control of credits and other measures calculated to further its own interests.

Aid in the amount and the manner in which it has been given, has benefited the donor countries like the United States, and not so much the recipient countries which have quite often become poorer than they were before the receipt of aid. In any case, due to the dual nature of the economies which prevail in these countries, the benefit if any of aid has accrued only to certain privileged classes or groups within the unprivileged part of the international community. In India, both aid and foreign private capital has helped in increasing manifold the assets of the kulaks and the barons of industry, and has stood in the path of national socio-economic integration which seems to be a crucial problem of the underdeveloped countries for the coming decades. In the words of Paul Sweezy, 'aid perpetuates the conditions for which it is initially given'. The veracity of the statement is brought home by the phenomenal growth of China, Cuba and North Korea which received little or no aid and the continued poverty of India, Pakistan and Latin American countries which received relatively more aid.

III

Thomas E. Weisskopf[9] traces the dependent relationship of the contemporary poor countries to their colonial legacy and the dual character of their economies. A large part of the economic activity in the modern industrial enclaves in these countries depends either directly on foreign ownership and control, or indirectly on foreign aid and technical collaboration. This places a considerable part of the domestic capital class in a position of subordination and

[8]M.V. Kamath. 6 October 1977. Times of India, New Delhi.
[9]Thomas E. Weisskopf. 1972. In Economics And World Order, Ed. Jagdish N. Bhagwati, London.

dependence on the foreign capitalist class. For the same reasons the governments of the underdeveloped countries are also dependent upon advanced capitalist powers for economic, political and military support. Weisskopf concludes 'that capitalism in the poor countries today is not the relatively independent capitalism of old, which stimulated the economic growth of England, the United States, Japan and other rich capitalist countries. Rather, the capitalism which is spreading in today's poor countries is far better described as a dependent form of capitalism embedded within the world capitalist system as a whole'.[10] He then lists a number of factors—the demonstration effect, the monopoly effect, the brain-drain effect and the factor-bias effect--among the factors at work within the capitalist system, which reinforce the subordination of the poor or aid-receiving countries to the rich and developed countries of the world. First, the increasingly close ties between the poor and the rich countries associated with the integration of the world capitalist system, give rise to a demonstration effect whereby the consumption patterns of the affluent countries are imitated by the elites and even the middle classes in the poor countries. And to the extent that this happens, their consumption of similar goods tends to rise. This raises the foreign exchange requirements of the poor countries as these must be either directly imported or even if they are indigenously manufactured in the country, require import of machinery, components and technology. Prohibition or restriction of import of such consumer articles, leads to their large-scale smuggling as happened in India during the Congress rule and continues today. Secondly, the distinct advantages in finance, markets, technology and know-how which foreign companies have over domestic enterprise, confer on them an almost monopolistic control over much of the economic activity of the poor countries, perpetuate the economic dependence of the poor countries on the rich and account for the interest the rich countries have in investing in the underdeveloped countries. Even where foreign investments are not direct, domestic firms must often rely on foreign collaborations and some kind of indirect affiliation with foreign firms and this involves an unavoidable relationship or dependence. It is in the interest of the foreign private enterprise to maintain the conditions in which its activities or aid are essential, and not to impart

[10]Ibid.

to a domestic firm the knowledge or the skills or the advantages upon which its commercial success is based. In these circumstances the interest of a part of the indigenous capitalist class becomes identified with that of their foreign collaborators or benefactors and the impetus as well as the means for them to develop into an autonomous national bourgeoisie is dulled.[11] Thirdly, the technical and managerial dependence of the third world countries is augmented by the brain drain of engineers, doctors, scientists, business managers or other highly educated persons from the underdeveloped to the developed countries where they get better emoluments and a more stimulating work environment. The last factor that reinforces the economic dependence of the poor countries on the rich is the choice of technology used by both foreign and domestic firms in the modern sectors of the economy. It is typically influenced by production techniques that are used in the rich countries and are suitable for countries in which labour is scarce and capital relatively abundant. They are more capital-intensive and labour-saving than is desirable in poor countries. These techniques are also foreign-exchange intensive. This effect is most pronounced when a foreign firm directly establishes itself in a poor country but it also results indirectly from the collaboration of domestic with foreign firms; or even if they simply use technology bought or borrowed from the developed countries.

Continued economic dependence in the form of short and long-term economic aid from developed capitalist countries or international agencies (the World Bank and the IMF) funded by them, results in political subordination and restricts the political autonomy of poor countries. Furthermore, due to the nature of the relationship between the domestic and foreign private enterprise, 'a significant part of the domestic capitalist class is likely to be relatively uninterested in national automony in so far as it conflicts with the interests of its foreign capitalist partners or benefactors. Thus the state is likely to be under considerable domestic pressure to curtail whatever nationalistic interests it might otherwise have'.[12] From economic dependence and political subordination to cultural penetration of the poor countries is but a short way.

[11]Ibid.
[12]Ibid.

IV

For India's First Five Year Plan (1951-56) which was financed mainly from her own resources combined with her sterling balances, the required external assistance was of the order of Rs 178 crore or 9.1 per cent of the Plan outlay. For the Second Plan (1956-61), due to her vastly increased need of capital goods, her need for foreign assistance shot up to Rs 1,090 crore or 23.7 per cent of the Plan outlay. She applied for aid to the United States but the US Congress annoyed over Nehru's foreign policy refused to come to India's help but when in 1955 the Soviet Union initiated its economic assistance programme to India, stressing major capital goods investment, the effect on the US Government was soon perceptible in increased sympathy for the Indian development. There was a shift in the US attitude towards India's non-alignment which was becoming respectable in official circles. Nehru's second visit to the US was planned for late 1956. It coincided fortuitously with "condemnation" by America of the British—French—Israeli invasion of Egypt. Nehru was impressed by the American stand and in a speech on 20 December 1956 to the American Association for United Nations said, 'I imagine that all the riches and power have not increased the reputation of the United States so much as a certain attitude that it has taken up in recent weeks, a certain attitude in regard, let us say, to Egypt . . .' The Nehru-Eisenhover meeting at the Presidential farm came as a successful contrast to the Nehru-Truman meeting of 1949 and heralded the beginning of an American aid programme for India.

The figure for external assistance during the Third Five Year Plan was further stepped up to Rs 2,423 crore or 28.3 per cent of the total outlay. On account of the heavy imports of defence equipment and foodgrains during the period of the Annual Plans (1966-69), the external assistance rose to 35.9 per cent of the outlay during this period. The table on p. 227 gives the inflow of the gross and net foreign assistance from 1969 onwards.

A perusal of the table shows that Rs 4,144 crore was received as external assistance during the Fourth Plan period. In formulating the Fourth Plan the Government had estimated that it would be possible to bring the net transfer of aid to zero by the early 1970s. This pious hope was expressed once more at the time of formulation of the draft for the Fifth Plan but the goal of self-reliance (net zero

TABLE

Inflow of Foreign Assistance (Rs Crore)

	1969-70	1970-71	1971-72	1972-73	1973-74	1974-75	1975-76
I Gross Foreign Assistance	856	791	834	666	999	1337	1639
	(100.0)	(100.0)	(100.0)	(100.0)	(100.0)	(100.0)	(100.0)
II Total Food Aid	147	93	112	4	150	162	156
	(17.2)	(11.8)	(13.4)	(0.6)	(15.0)	(12.1)	(9.5)
III Gross Aid excluding Food Aid (I minus II)	709	698	722	662	849	1175	1483
	(82.8)	(88.2)	(86.2)	(99.4)	(85.0)	(87.9)	(90.5)
IV Total Debt Servicing	412	450	479	507	595	626	700
	(48.1)	(56.8)	(57.4)	(76.1)	(60.1)	(46.8)	(42.7)
(a) Amortization payment	268	290	299	327	399	411	470
(b) Interest payment	144	160	180	180	196	215	230
V Net Flow of Assistance	297	248	243	155	254	549	783
	(34.7)	(31.4)	(29.1)	(23.3)	(30.0)	(41.1)	(47.8)

Source : Economic Survey, 1975-76.

aid) by the end of the Plan in 1979, was again given the go-by in October 1976 when the Fifth Plan which had been collecting dust for over two years, was finalized. Actually the amount of external assistance for the four years of the Fifth Plan which came to an end in March 1978, was roughly Rs 6,620 crore (Rs 1,337 crore for 1974-75; Rs 1,639 crore for 1975-76, Rs 1,747 crore for 1976-77, and Rs 1,900 crore for 1977-78), a figure which exceeds the foreign assistance received in the Fourth Plan period by nearly Rs 2,675 crore. If the Fifth Plan were to run its full course of five years, another Rs 2,000 crore of external assistance would probably have been needed bringing the total assistance for the entire plan period to Rs 8,620 crore—a figure which is more than double the amount of assistance required for the Fourth Plan. What better example of self-reliance or net zero aid can anyone cite or seek? Even a casual look at the table brings out two other important facts: 1 the debt servicing including amortization and interest payments has been rising (it was Rs 412 crore in 1969-70 and increased to Rs 700 crore in 1975-76) and 2 the net inflow of assistance in financial terms diminished from Rs 297 crore in 1969-70 to Rs 155 crore in 1972-73, increased again to Rs 783 crore in 1975-76. But when the price rise during the period is taken into account the net flow has continuously been shrinking.

V

Foreign aid may be bilateral or multilateral, tied or untied. During recent years it has come to be more and more tied. It can be tied to specific projects which means it must be spent on the project. Again it may be tied to the country of origin which means all purchases—machinery, components, food etc.—must be made in the aid-giving country. Project tied aid has several advantages for the donor country. First, it is easily identifiable. Many educated Indians know that the Durgapur Steel Plant was built with British aid and the Bhillai Steel Plant with the Russian aid. If the aid is spread over several small projects and especially over import of raw materials, components and spares, it would not give the donor the same measure of political credit in the recipient country. Secondly, project-tied aid has the advantage of ensuring that the aid is usefully spent and not frittered away on import of luxury items. But in practice this does not always happen. The story is related of the Austrian authorities who were planning to build a power house out of their own funds and wished to use the Marshall Plan aid to rebuild the Opera House. When the American Government refused to approve the plan of rebuilding the Opera House out of the Marshall Plan funds, the Austrian Government diverted the Marshall Aid to build the power plant and built the Opera House out of their own funds.

When aid is tied to the country of origin, the primary reason perhaps is political and originates from pressure groups interested in export markets. But the economic argument is equally strong. Like project-tied aid, country-tied aid can also be switched away from the donor country provided there are adequate previous imports from the aid-giving country and provided further that they are not tied to specific projects. If switches are not possible, country-tied aid frequently imposes heavy economic cost upon the recipient country, partly because prices in the donor country may be higher due to increased cost of production and partly because prices are marked up, the moment it is known that the purchases have to be made in the country. An additional economic burden frequently results from the country-tied aid when the technology used by the advanced donor country is not appropriate for the developmental needs of the underdeveloped country.

Both project-tied aid and country-tied aid, restrict the usefulness of the developmental assistance to the underdeveloped countries. This is highlighted by the Indian experience between 1956 and 1965. Enough foreign exchange was available during this period to set up additional capacity but none of this was available to utilize even the existing industrial capacity. Impediments of this kind can be avoided if aid is hitched not to projects but to programmes.

Country-tied aid is characteristic of bilateral aid and most of the aid to this country before 1966, was bilateral. Bilateral aid is also preferred by the donor countries and this is easy to understand. The United States will not, for instance give aid to North Korea or Vietnam, nor will the Soviet Union assist South Korea or Taiwan. Multilateral aid is preferred by the recipient and is administered by international agencies like the World Bank and the International Monetary Fund or the Aid Consortium. Bilateral aid suffers from a number of disadvantages: 1 It is linked with politics and with political pressures from the donor country,[13] 2 it prevents

---

[13]Not that political pressures can be altogether avoided when aid is multi-

the growth of progressive burden-sharing among the donor countries, and 3 the distribution of aid among the recipient countries follows a political and not a need-based economic or ethical pattern.

VI

A few words in the end about aid statistics and aid to India. Gunnar Myrdal[14] has shown beyond the shadow of a doubt how statistics are juggled by the developed countries and the Development Assistance Committee (DAC) to magnify the quantum of aid to recipient countries. All the inflow loans, investments, reinvested profits, export credits and private flows become development assistance or plainly "development aid". The outflows or the backflows account for only amortization payments on outstanding loans and repatriated capital. Profits, interest payments, payments for licenses, flight capital etc., are not included in the backflows.

The twist of statistics in the field of aid by the Development Assistance Committee of the Organization for Economic Cooperation and Development (OECD), with headquarters in Paris, results from the figures supplied by the officials of the member governments. These figures are taken as authoritative practically everywhere and 'uncritically relied upon by economists and other professional students of development problems, officials, politicians, authors of popular books and articles, journalists etc., by the secretariat of other inter-governmental agencies and by special expert groups set up from time to time'. Myrdal shows surprise that spokesmen and experts coming from underdeveloped countries themselves uncritically accept the DAC Secretariat's conception of total public and private financial outflows. To show how "reliable" the DAC flows are, Myrdal quotes from the criticism offered against these figures by Krister Wickman.[15]

---

lateral. India was forced to devalue the rupee in 1966 under pressure from the World Bank and had to agree to have her economy "overhauled" as Jeremiah Novak has shown (See Chapter on industries) before World Bank—IMF loans were approved in 1974.

[14] Gunnar Myrdal. 1968, 1972. Asian Drama, Challenge of World Poverty, London.

[15] He was Minister of Industry in the Swedish Government.

' . . . It is very clear, that the net concept used does not come in the neighbourhood of net figures. In 1967 the DAC figures for "net" flow of resources (official and private) from the DAC members was 11.4 billion. This could be compared with that the UN Secretary General has presented for the total net inflow of resources to the developing countries. This latter figure which is based on IMF statistics is 3 billion. . . . Due regard being taken to errors and omissions, time lags and so on, the chief explanation of this difference is that the DAC figure represents a very incomplete coverage of the financial transactions with regard to the return flows to the DAC members from the less developed countries. Some DAC members may even find after a close look that their balance of payments with the third world shows a surplus'.[16]

As for aid to India, seven-eights is interest bearing loan and India has been meticulously honouring its debt and paying it back with interest. The largest share of the aid allocations pertains to shipment of surplus commodities, chiefly wheat and PL 480 and PL 660 loans. Wheat is purchased from American markets at exorbitant prices. Is it not a subsidy to the American farmer? The Development Loan Fund (DLF) established in 1957 for manufacturing industries is tied to purchases in the United States. So is the loan from the Export-Import Bank. Gunnar Myrdal says 'tying aid to exports implies a curtailment of the aid-receiving country's freedom to buy the most suitable commodity and at the most favourable price'. He adds, 'In polite form this practice has been pointed to on the side of the underdeveloped countries as implying a subsidy proffered to the American economy'.[17]

Whom does this aid help? The question has been asked by Galo Plaza of the Organization of American Studies (OAS). 'A semantic cloud hangs over the US aid programmes and makes it difficult to see them as they really are. Most US aid under the Alliance for Progress is not a gift (but) is in the form of loans that are being repaid. . . . It is not all unrealistic to turn the picture, and think about the benefits accruing to the United States as a result of what we call aid. . . . Nearly all of this (the loans) is being spent in the United States on the United States goods. In this way they help

[16]Crister Wickman. 1972. Quoted by Gunnar Myrdal in Challenge of World Poverty.
[17]Gunnar Myrdal. 1972. Challenge of World Poverty, London.

create jobs for US workers. They generate earnings for US manufacturing enterprises and their stockholders, and taxable income for the US Government. They give the US a surplus in its payments with Latin America'.[18]

With regard to India the effect of aid both on agriculture and industry has been adverse. It has made both the rulers and the people complacent and taken away from them the stimulus they needed for an initiative and a drive to grow more food and to produce more wage goods in the country itself. Foreign aid to India has not made a significant contribution to India's economic development. But it has helped a section of its people. It has helped the rich farmer who has successfully appropriated most of the benefits that accrued from aid programmes on irrigation and power projects. It has also helped the industrialist who by entering into collaboration with multinational giants has also swallowed the major part of the aid. And finally, it has helped the corrupt minister and bureancrat who by negotiating collaboration agreements on terms advantageous to the foreign partners, has secured sizable financial benefits for himself and his family and relations. Aid has softened social tensions which hasten social change and has perpetuated archaic social structures which come in the way of growth and development. The PL 480 funds have been reportedly used in the country in the past for subversive ends. The US Government runs an expensive and well-planned system of espionage and subversion all over the world and particularly in Asia, Africa and Latin America. It operates its programmes through the CIA, the US embassies, the USIS Centres, the American Foundations, the Peace Corps, the international giants like the ITT, the United Fruit and the Union Carbide, Banks, Aid agencies, American experts, and university professors and scholars. It spends huge amounts of funds on scholarships, fellowships and travel grants for postgraduates; university and technical institute-teachers, operating in host countries; members of the Houses of Legislatures; political, trade union and student leaders; journalists; civil and military government officials—to send them to the United States for the purpose of teaching them the "American Way of Life" and the value of "free enterprise". The services of some select people in these groups are then utilized to change the course of elections, foment student and labour unrest,

[18]Ibid.

provoke communal conflicts, buy tax and other exemptions for American trade and industries, and promote coups and overthrow unfriendly governments.

VII

Gandhiji had desired India to remain economically self-reliant. If the Congress Governments under Jawaharlal and Indira Gandhi had listened to him and accepted his advice, the country would not be in the economic mess in which it is today. China discarded industrialization and the Russian model in the late 1950s and refused further offers of aid. She became self-reliant and decentralized her economy much on the Gandhian lines. In less than two decades, she has not only succeeded in providing the basic necessities of life for all its people. She has also eliminated illiteracy and made giant strides in the fields of science and technology. China is today no longer an underdeveloped country. She is a developing country and in the remaining years of the century, hopes to catch up with the advanced countries of the West.

China's economic development may be traced in three stages. The first stage viz. of industrialization on the Russian pattern, was a failure. The second stage built on the Gandhian model of self-reliance and decentralization has secured the minimum needs of all its citizens and has also made it militarily invulnerable to all enemy attacks. She has now entered her third stage of development and plans to modernize and raise the standard of living of those for whom it ensured the minimum standards earlier during the second stage of her economic development.

This is as it should be. Gandhiji had said that he was not for ascetic standards of living for the Indian people for all time. After a minimum standard was secured for everybody, there was no objection to achieving higher standards. This is precisely what the Chinese are now proposing to do.

Thirty years of deprivation and disillusionment has brought India to the realization of the fact that she is at a stage in which the Chinese found themselves within less than a decade of their independence. There is also a growing realization of the fact both in India and abroad that development is no longer possible on the paradigm of industrialization on which the rich countries of the West developed in the nineteenth century[19] which Nehru chose for this country after the achievement of independence by India. The Nehru Paradigm has not solved the problems of economic growth, distributive justice and unemployment. There is urgent need, therefore, today to fall back on the Gandhian model of self-reliance and decentralization—a model which may not build an affluent society but which is certain to satisfy the basic minimum needs of its people within a period of five to ten years, as it has done for China.

For this we do not need any foreign aid. We have at present a well-developed infrastructure, a fairly advanced technology for our needs, an ample skilled manpower force and no balance of payments problems; and aid even if it were needed at some previous stage, is no longer necessary. The accent today is on development of agriculture, irrigation and village industries which do not need any foreign exchange.

The implications of aid for India today are 1 that rupee resources have to be found to execute projects to which it makes no contribution, 2 that it goes to further swell the foreign exchange resources for which proper use has not yet been found,[20] 3 that it will obscure the real foreign trade and payments position, 4 that it will encourage laxity in foreign exchange spending,[21] 5 that it will help pre-emption of domestic resources under conditions of overall stringency for a line of development which is sponsored by aid-giving countries and not related to the order of priorities, 6 that it does not make any addition to available supplies, 7 that it is bound to accentuate inflationary pressures, 8 that it is likely to impede the effort to increase domestic savings and raise domestic resources, and finally distort the direction and content of the entire process of planning and development.

Aid has increased India's debt burden, increased her dependence on and subordination to developed countries, pushed her into the capitalist trap and impeded both her growth and employment opportunities. Paltry aid in thimblefuls is a camouflage and a cover for future exploitation by capitalist buccaneers and thieves. Let my countrymen know.

---

[19] A.K. Bagchi. August 1972. Economic and Political Weekly, Bombay.
[20] Indian Express. 25 October 1977.
[21] Restrictions on foreign travel have already been relaxed.

FOURTEEN

Foreign Investment

On 30 June 1948, according to the Reserve Bank of India figures, the value of total foreign business investment in India in manufacturing, mining, utilities, transport, trading, financial, plantation, and other industries, was Rs 3,024 million, of which Rs 2,301 million or 71.9 per cent were British investment alone, followed by the United States of America with Rs 179.7 million or 5.7 per cent. Between 1948 and 1955 the British investment rose to Rs 4,000 million and of this one-third was invested in plantation industries and manufacturing. The chief manufacturing industries included cigarettes, tobacco, food products, jute, coir goods, electrical goods, cosmetics, detergents and pharmaceuticals.

By the end 1972-73, there were 740 foreign companies operating in India. Of these 536 operated as branches and 202 as subsidiaries of the multinationals. Great Britain had 320 branches and 140 subsidiaries, the United States had 88 branches and 28 subsidiaries and Switzerland, Japan, West Germany and Sweden had respectively 21, 18, 17 and 14 affiliates—both branches and subsidiaries. The total assets of these branches and subsidiaries amounted to Rs 29,220 million, out of which the assets of the British companies accounted for Rs 18,180 million and those of the US Companies for Rs 5,420 million. The total assets of multinationals rose to Rs 23,900 million in 1977-78 and the profit before tax was Rs 523 million. As far subsidiaries their assets in 1977-78 were Rs 17,400 million and the profit Rs 1,406 million. The remittances made by the multinationals and their subsidiaries were Rs 807 million in 1971-72 and rose to Rs 1,153 million by 1977-78.

A perusal of the above figures shows that though the American subsidiaries are making a steady headway, the dominant position is still held by the British capital. The gain in the total assets of the British subsidiaries during the period 1967-68 to 1972-73 was approximately Rs 200 million whereas for the United States the corresponding figure was Rs 150 million. If the increase in the two cases is reckoned as a percentage of the total assets, the increase in the US assets is significant and if the assets of both the countries continue to increase at the same rate, the United States may soon overtake the British capital. The total number of branches of the two countries dropped from 350 in 1969-70 to 320 in 1972-73 but their assets improved from Rs 8,230 million to Rs 10,840 million during the same period. For the United States the number of branches increased from 84 to 88 and the assets from Rs 2,370 million to Rs 3,500 million, the US lead again remaining significant.

As regards the composition of the investment, the maximum (Rs 13,480 million) is still in the processing and manufacturing industries in which cigarettes, tobacco, food processing, detergents, cosmetics, medical and pharmaceutical preparations take the lead. Next come trade and finance which together account for Rs 11,850 million. It is clear that foreign investment is chiefly confined to the sector in which capital requirement is small and exploitation of labour and skills and raw meterials is easy.

Before World War II, the US investment in India was hardly Rs 40 million. After the war it rapidly increased, at first in the traditional import-export operations, the most important of which were petroleum products by Stanvac and Caltex. Later on American capital to India came via automobile companies, chiefly the Ford and the General Motors. Investments were also made in jute, tyre manufacture and office equipment. Firestone set up a factory in Bombay and Remington established a typewriter factory in West Bengal. The US Mellon-controlled Aluminium Company of Canada, invested in aluminium and owned half of the capital of Indian Aluminium Company. After 1951, when the new policy inviting foreign capital was announced, American investments in India were stepped up. An agreement was signed with the Standard Vacuum on 30 November 1951 for setting up an oil refinery in Bombay. A similar agreement was made with Caltex for a refinery in Vishakhapatnam. The Cyanamid and Parke Davis set up their drug factories in Bombay.

A new form of penetration of Indian economy by foreign companies was through technical collaborations. Upto the end of June 1976, there have been 4,687 collaborations in Indian industry. Of these, 636 have been in the field of drugs and chemicals, 638 in electrical equipment and components, 685 in industrial machinery other than textiles and 364 in transport equipment. A countrywise distribution has been: United Kingdom 30 per cent, the United States 20 per cent, West Germany 15 per cent and Japan 7 per cent. In many cases, collaboration agreements have been signed by foreign companies with their own Indian subsidiaries; this arrangement has obvious advantages for the foreign investor. Out of a total of 50 of the largest multinationals operating in the world about 20 operate in this country directly through branch or subsidiary, or indirectly through foreign collaboration. Their names are: Exxon, General Motors, Benz, British Petroleum, Gulf Oil, General Electric, Westinghouse, I.T.T., Philips, Siemens, I.C.I. Hoechst, Bayers, British American Tobacco, Nestle, Union Carbide, Good Year, Hitachi and Mitsubishi.

If one takes into consideration the fact that the total sales of each one of these multinationals are more than the annual budget of the Indian Government, and that the sales of the multinationals originating from the same country exceed the GNP of this country, one can gauge to some extent the power that these companies wield in their relations with the Government. The impact of the multinationals on the economic and the cultural life of the people is even more pervasive and more profound.

The collaboration agreements suffer from a large number of harmful features. Among these are:

1. Agreements have been made for manufacture of nonessential products or for those which could be produced with the help of technology already available in the country or which could be easily developed. Such items include toothpastes, lipsticks, cosmetics, brassiers, biscuits, gin, beer, ready made garments etc. Collaborations are entered in case of most such products owing to the advantage the foreign brand names possess in sale promotion.

2. Technology is not imported on a national basis and this leads to a repetitive import of the same or similar technology; if technology is imported by a Central Government agency and passed on to the public sector or private firm or firms according to the country's need, much expense could be saved.

3. If technology for the same or similar products is imported from different countries, it makes the situation further comp-

licated owing to differences in raw materials, designs, specifications and spare parts. This hinders standardization, leads to uneconomic inventory accumulation and locking up of working capital.

4. The terms of the collaboration are invariably weighted in favour of the foreign companies.

5. The foreign collaborator prepares the project report and the lists of the machinery and components etc. to be imported. He prepares the blue prints, supervises the erection of plant, prepares designs and lays down the specifications. He also makes the supplies. Due to his dual role of both the judge and the beneficiary, there is little wonder that the prices are marked up and there is also over-import of equipment.

6. Quite often the technology imported is inefficient and obsolete.

7. The terms of payment of know-how fee and the royalties are often extortionist.

8. Restrictions are placed on the diffusion of the technology and the Indian partners are compelled to keep the know-how secret even after the expiry of the agreement. This policy leads to a multiplicity of collaborations.

9. Restriction has been placed against the introduction of local changes by stipulating that manufacture will be carried out strictly according to stipulation. Paradoxically other agreements have insisted on the Indian enterpreneur to continuously incorporate changes introduced by the foreign collaborator. Such conditions impede local adaptation and absorption of imported technology and lead to continued dependence on the foreign companies.

10. Control over purchases from abroad has been exercised through the conditions that these should be made directly or indirectly through the foreign collaborators.

11. Restrictions have also been placed on exports and extra royalty demanded on export sales.

Two reasons why poor countries invite foreign capital are 1 because they need net addition to investible resources, and 2 because it is desired to bring in new technology, better management, superior marketing skill, higher export earning and a favourable balance of payments position. So far as India is concerned the multinationals have not made any significant contribution to any of the two objectives.

The direct foreign investment of the multinational corporations in the form of paid-up capital, loans, etc., is around Rs 1,800 crore or about 3 per cent of the total investment in the corporate sector and a part of this is made up by retained local earnings. If both total inflows and outflows are taken into consideration, it would be seen that during the period between 1964-65, and 1969-70, there was a net outflow of foreign exchange of Rs 684 crore. The import figures for subsidiaries alone amount to Rs 749 crore against their export of Rs 284 crore with a net outflow of Rs 501 crore. In the case of imports and exports resulting from technical and financial collaborations, the imports amounted to Rs 2,342 crore whereas the exports were only Rs 901 crore. The net outflow amounted to Rs 1,441 crore. Examination of 53 companies by Streeton and Lal revealed that 48 foreign companies operating in India had a negative impact on the foreign exchange balance. In respect of two US companies—IBM and the Coca Cola,—it was said in the Indian Parliament, that there had been a net foreign exchange outflow.

As regards the second objective of inviting foreign companies— the gain in technology and training in managerial skills,—the Indian experience has once again not been happy. Not only has a very high price been extracted for the transfer of technology but the technology transfered has not always been the one suited to the needs of the country. Adoption of borrowed technology has more-over created a dependence on the foreign collaborator both for maintenance or modifications.

In spite of the foregoing negative features, owing first, to uncertainly of official capital transfers, and secondly, to a pro-longed stagnation industry, the government of India has in the past and still is, in favour of inviting foreign capital. Numerous inducements and incentives have been offered to the private sector including foreign companies to step up investment in technolo-gically challenging and risky ventures. Since early 1973 inducements for expansion and diversification are being offered, and new and priority areas thrown open to foreign companies and their subsidiaries. Even the policy of equity dilution which was originally proposed as a device for curbing foreign control, due to its linkage with expansion, diversification and increased profitability, has not only failed to shake off the control of foreign capital but has actually backfired. The foreign companies without any or much import of capital or technology, have been able to raise local capital to dilute the equity and put their resources and assets, enlarged over the years, into new business investments for higher profits. According to Balraj Mehta, 'the policy of dilution resolves their problem fully and wholly falls in line with their interests'.[1] Foreign companies and multinationals like Hindustan Lever, Union Carbide, Indian Tobacco Co., Indian Oxygen etc., have put forward specific proposals for expansion and diversification but they are all in the high profitability areas like hotels,[2] fisheries, food processing, garments etc., intended primarily for elitist consumption. No incentives and no allurements have succeeded in tempting them to invest in high priority and technologically challenging fields for which the government has been trying to attract foreign capital and know-how.

[1]Balraj Mehta. 1974. Failures of Indian Economy, New Delhi.
[2]The recent collaboration deals between B.H.E.L. and Seimens and, I.T.C. and Sheraton for building a chain of 5-star hotels in the country have drawn lot of criticism in the press and in the Parliament. In respect of the 5-star hotels at least, the criticism appears to be fully justified. India can surely do without more 5-star hotels.

FIFTEEN

Epilogue

In its election manifesto, the Janata Party promised much to all people. After success at the hustings, it pledged at Gandhiji's Samadhi to restore civil liberties and carry out the Gandhian socio-economic programme. Among other things it promised: a decentralized economy; intensive development of agriculture and cottage and village industries; production by masses; eradication of illiteracy, unemployment, under-employment and poverty with provision of basic necessaries of life for everybody within a period of ten years; abridgement of the three gulfs—between the rich and the poor, the educated and the uneducated, and the country and city dwellers; and amelioration of the condition of the scheduled castes and the scheduled tribes.

It is tragic that during the two years that have elapsed since these promises were made, the Party leaders and the constituents of the Party, have been engaged in internecine feuds, and not a step has been taken towards the fulfilment of the promises. According to the latest appraisal of the economy by the National Council of Applied Economic Research, the overall economic growth rate in 1978-79 would be nearly 3 per cent which is much lower than the 6 per cent in 1977-78 and the targeted 4.7 per cent for the current year. During the earlier Five Year Plans the growth rates were 3.8, 3.7, 3.2, 3.5 and 3.3 per cent respectively. The change-over to Janata, therefore, shows only a worsening of the economy. The reasons given for the deterioration include power shortages, transport bottle-necks, shortages of raw materials such as coal and cement, and labour trouble. In the rural sector foodgrain production is placed at 126 million tons as against 125.6 million tons last year but the pace of land reform has shown no advance. Even where the land is known to be surplus, it has not been distributed to the landless agricultural labour. The performance of the industrial sector has been poor. According to the figures provided by the Reserve Bank of India, the 'Index of Industrial Production with base 100 in 1970, increased gradually from 1.6 per cent in 1973 to 4.7 per cent in 1975 and 10.6 per cent in 1976. Thereafter, there was a slackening in the tempo and the growth rate receded to 5.3 in 1977. The trend continued in the first quarter of 1978 and the increase in industrial production during the quarter over the first quarter of 1977 was only 1.9 per cent'.[1] The performances of the Public sector with a colossal investment of Rs 12,803 crore, is not very heartening. Coal India, The Shipping Corporation of India and plants that come under the Steel Authority of India (SAIL), all show losses. The widest gap between promise and performance of the Janata Government is in the field of employment and unemployment and underemployment have increased during the past two years. On the labour front, the number of industrial disputes and the total number of man-days lost, has increased and the Industrial Relation Bill 1978 with its "undemocratic character, bureaucratic dominance and unnecessary restrictions placed on the unions", has alienated the workers and has been uniformly condemned and opposed by all trade unions. In respect of education Mr Chunder and his Ministry have not even after two year, taken a decision on the policy framework for educational transformation. The Family Planning programme after the setback it received following the enforced sterilizations during the emergency, is in abeyance. The atrocities on the Schedule Castes have increased. The law and order situation has worsened.

The failures of the Janata Government as of the Congress Government before it, must be attributed to its class composition. Despite the socialist professions of Jawaharlal Nehru and Indira Gandhi, a tripartite alliance was forged as has been stated earlier in the book, between the ruling elites, the barons of industry and the rich farmers. It helped to keep the Congress in power for nearly three decades. The Government tilted during the Congress era in favour of the industrialists who contributed liberally to the Congress election funds. They were, quid per quo, permitted to amass large assets and build industrial empires. The rich farmers were also not ignored. They acted as the vote banks of the Congress and were in return permitted to block legislation of land re-

[1]Reserve Bank of India Bulletin, March, 1978,

form and stall its implementation even after legislation. They were further rewarded by exclusion from the tax net by the refusal of the Congress Government to tax agricultural produce against the repeated advice of the economists and the Planning Commission.

The tripartite alliance has not been abrogated. In continues. During the Janata regime, the Party and the grovernment tilt is, at any rate now, in favour of the rural sector—the rich farmer. The two previous budgets introduced by H.M. Patel, were not very different from the earlier Congress budgets. They gave numerous subsidies and tax exemptions to the corporate sector which seems to have a pull both with Morarji Desai and H.M. Patel. The third Janata budget, introduced by the new Finance Minister, has a rich-farmer bias. This is understandably so. Every politician is indebted—for the power he acquires and wields—to those who have financed him. Charan Singh has received financial support from the rich farmer whose cause he has espoused, for many long years. His massive Kissan rally which restored his cabinet post to him, was organized with the funds provided by the rich farmer. It was the rich farmer who provided the thousands of trucks and tractors which brought the Kissans to New Delhi. It was with these funds that he paid for his aerial travels in planes belonging to the Haryana State Government. It is with the help of these funds again that a campaign is being mounted by his friends and followers for his ascension to the Prime Minister's berth. No wonder when it comes to gifts to the super-rich farmers, Charan Singh does not stop at giving more. He gives still more.[2]

If the super-rich farmer who has so far escaped the tax net on his produce, has been rewarded even beyond his expectation and is jubilant, the private industrial sector—almost untouched by the budget —is not unduly worried. The cotton and the artificial-fibre industry has been lightly let off, and is pleased. The labour—displacing power-tiller manufacturer is receiving encourgement and is gladsome. The manufactuers of fertilizer, PVC—pipes for irrigation and subsidized pumpsets, are overjoyed. The share market is buoyant.

With the largest dose ever of indirect taxes, the budget will hit the rest of the population in the belly. The middle class, the fixed income salaried class, the poorer sections and the workers in the urban areas, and the poor and marginal farmer and the landless

[2]Editorial, 8-21 March 1979, *Fortnight*, New Delhi.

labourer in the rural areas will all be badly hurt. In the urban areas with the general rise in prices due to higher costs of petroleum products and the transport charges, and the rise in price of commodities on which levies have been imposed, the buying power of the people will be affected adversely. This will in its turn, result in a decrease of demand and a fall in employment and production. In the rural sector, as C.N. Hanumantha Rao, Director of the Institute of Economic Growth, points out, the disparaties will increase.[3] It happened in the mid-sixties when the Union Food and Agriculture Minister, C. Subramaniam, introduced the Intensive Area Agricultural Programme (IAAP). An entire package of inputs—high yielding variety of seeds, fertilizer, pesticides, irrigation, cheap credit, incentive prices and trained manpower—were pressed into the service of the rich farmer. His marketable surpluses and high procurement prices brought him immense financial gains but caused intense hardship for the marginal farmer and the landless labourer who had to pay higher prices for the foodgrains he needed. The requirements of the small farmer and those outside the selected areas were ignored. The result for the country as a whole was unmitigated disaster. Tenants, and sharecroppers were thrown out and ejected, and small farmers were compelled to sell their small patches and were reduced to the state of paupers and landless labourers.

At the N.D.C. meeting in New Delhi in the autumn of 1976, Indira Gandhi admitted that the New Strategy was a mistake. But she justified it by saying that it was necessitated by a period of serious food shortage. Its reintroduction with higher subsidies and exemptions, by Charan Singh, at a time when the country's food stores are bursting at the seams, is a blunder of the highest magnitude and its consequences for the rural poor and for the country's economy would be nothing short of calamitous.

It is a matter of great surprise and also of deep concern that the erstwhile socialists in the Janata Government and the Party have fallen in line with the reactionary thinking and programme of the casteist, Kulak-King who wears a Gandhian mask. It should be clear to anyone that the ageing Jat leader is interested only in himself and his clansmen and friends. He will not help build a

---

[3]C.N. Hanumantha Rao. 10 March 1970. Mainstream, New Delhi.

Gandhian economy—egalitarian, casteless and socialist. For this to come about, the younger Janata men should get together, drop the dead wood both from the government and the Party, and forthwith select dynamic honest men to lead the country and fulfil their promises to the electorate.[4] If they fail, nemesis is sure to overtake them.

[4]Unfortunately this did not happen. On the contrary the thoroughly unprincipled and selfish struggle for power by top politicians kept on gathering momentum. An explosive situation arose due to a notice by leader of the opposition, of a motion of no confidence against the Morarji Government. More than 80 members of the Parliament representing the B.L.D., the C.F.D. and the Socialist groups defected and joined hands with the Congress S and the Congress I. The Janata Government was reduced to a minority and fell on 15 July 1979. A coalition government with Charan Singh as Prime Minister was sworn but lasted only 24 days.

The crisis of character which has overtaken the Indian politician during the past two decades and the mind which has come to stick to his name, he will not be able to shake off as along as he lives. A mid-term poll has been announced for December 1979, but as the political system remains unchanged and the same old candidates who destroyed the couutry earlier, are likely to get tickets and get elected to the Parliament and the state legislatures, the outlook for the Country's political, social and economic future cannot be anything but dismal.

Index

Advani, L.K., 62

Agency for International Development, 222

Agrarian non-tax campaign, 42

Agriculture, and industry, relationship between, 165; inequality in, 12; during the First Plan, 51; during the Second Plan, 55; impact of education on, 115; influence of malnutrition and ill-health of, 157-158; Janata Party on, 215; lack of incentives to, 146-147; level of productivity of the worker, 153-157; low priority for, 142-147; Michael Lipton strategy for, 144-145; neglect causes of, 133; new agricultural strategy, 147-153, 214; reasons for adequate level of, 131-133; shortfalls in, 54; targets of, 145

Agricultural credit Corporation, role of, 150

Agricultural District Programme (IADP), 147

Agricultural Economic Research Centre, University of Delhi, study by, 116

Agriculture education, emphasis on, 115; faults and failures of, 156-157

Agricultural labour force, under-utilization of, 153-157

Agriculture Price Commission, recommendation of, 151-152

Ahmed, Fakhruddin Ali, 165

Ali, Yusuf Meher, 43

Allahabad High Court verdict, 64-65, 183

American Association for United Nations, Nehru's speech at, 226

Amin, Samir, views of, 25-26

Appropriate Technology, need of, 217-218

Appropriate technology cell, 215; concept of, 210; formation and implementation of, 210-211; setting up of, 210

Bagchi, A.K., on capital growth, 195

Balance of payment crisis, 52, 54-55

Basic education, Gandhi's concept of, 96-97

Bhakra-Nangal dam, 51

Bihar turmoil in, 62-63

Birla, G.D., on unemployment problem, 205

Birth rate, 79-80

Blaug, M., on primary education, 114, 156

Bloc Production Plan, pillars of, 163

Bombay High, finding of, 20-21

Bonuses, restrictions on issue of, 63

Bose, Subhash Chandra, 40

Bowles, Chester, 37

Brown, Harrison, on technology, 207

Brain drain, Estimates Committee comment on, 122-123; see also Education

Budgets, of 1977 and 1978, 72-73; Congress and Janata compared, 243

Calcutta, *bustee* people's life and conditions of, 17; population of, 16-17

Capital formation, components of,